Two Cheers
for Capitalism

TWO CHEERS
FOR
CAPITALISM

Irving Kristol

Basic Books, Inc., Publishers   New York

Chapters 1, 7, 25, and 26 originally appeared in *The Public Interest* in 1972, 1973, 1974, and 1975.
Chapters 2, 3, 4, 5, 6, 8, 9, 10, 11, 12, 13, 14, 15, 16, 17, 18, 19, 20, 21, 24, 27, 28, 29, 30, and the epilogue originally appeared in the *Wall Street Journal* in 1970, 1973, 1974, 1975, 1976, and 1977.
Chapter 22 originally appeared in *Imprimus,* vol. 2 (Hillsdale, Michigan: Hillsdale College, April 1973). Copyright © 1973 by Hillsdale College. Reprinted with permission.
Chapter 23 originally appeared in *Commentary* in November, 1972.

Library of Congress Cataloging in Publication Data

Kristol, Irving.
    Two cheers for capitalism.

    Includes index.
    1. Corporations—United States. 2. United States—
Economic conditions. 3. Capitalism. 4. Social
justice. I. Title.
HD2791.K68   330.12′2′0973   77-20408
ISBN: 0-465-08803-1

For Bea

CONTENTS

PART THREE
What Is "Social Justice"?

PREFACE

WHY NOT THREE CHEERS? Or, on the other hand, why any cheers at all? The purpose of this preface is to answer both questions as best I can—and thereby, I hope, to define the point of view ("neo-conservative," it is now called) that has shaped the matter of this book.

E. M. Forster, one may recall, as a literary man who basically despised politics, gave only "two cheers for democracy" because he felt that the full trinity should be reserved for "love, the beloved republic." I think he was saying that, whatever the absolute or relative merits of democracy, the satisfactions of private life are inherently superior to those provided by any political order. What he did not say, perhaps because he was not aware of it, is that this is a specifically bourgeois-capitalist notion of the good life, and of the relationship of that good life to politics. A capitalist society does not want more than two cheers for itself. Indeed, it regards the impulse to give three cheers for any social, economic, or political system as expressing a dangerous—because it is misplaced—enthusiasm.

Obviously, this view of things does not strike a responsive chord among many of our contemporaries, who indict bourgeois capitalism not only for failing to create a utopia for humanity to dwell in, but for failing even to try. As against this, I would assert that the habit, so ingrained in the modern political imagination, of judging an actual social-economic-political order by some utopian standard is quite pernicious. It encourages a moral self-righteousness about one's "ideals" combined with a moral affectlessness about the means by which these ideals are to be "realized," and this combination is as explosive as it is self-destructive. A capitalist order, in contrast, begins with the assumption that the world is full of other people, moved by their own interests and their own passions, and that the best we can reasonably hope for is a society of civil concord, not a community of mutual love.

But the fact that a capitalist order has so keen a sense of its own limitations—limitations inseparable from its virtues—does not make these limitations any the less real. The main such limitation involves the prosaic quality of life, the bourgeois mode of existence, that is most appropriate to it.

Capitalism is the least romantic conception of a public order that the human mind has ever conceived. It does not celebrate extraordinary heroism in combat, extraordinary sanctity in one's religious life, extraordinary talent in the arts; in short, there is no "transcendental" dimension that is given official recognition and sanction. It does not necessarily denigrate such things either, but, in contrast to previous societies organized around an axis of aristocratic or religious values, it relegates them to the area of personal concern, whether of the isolated individual or of voluntary associations of individuals. Only there may we find "love, the beloved republic." What previous cultures would have called "the domestic virtues" are what capitalism most prizes in its citizens: prudence, diligence, trustworthiness, and an ambition largely channeled toward "bettering one's condition." As for the rest, well, that is one's private affair, to be freely coped with as best one can.

Now, the first thing to be said about this extraordinary (in historical terms) conception of a social order is that it works. It works in a quite simple, material sense: people who, individually or collectively, subscribe to the social philosophy of a capitalist order, and to those bourgeois virtues associated with it, do indeed better their condition. The history of the past two centuries affirms this truth unequivocally. It is also the case—as some critics will quickly point out—that this prosperity is not equally shared. But over the longer term everyone does benefit, visibly and substantially.

The second thing to be said about a capitalist order is that it is peculiarly congenial to a large measure of personal liberty. One should not exaggerate, as some defenders of "free enterprise" or "a free society" are wont to do. Capitalism itself is not identical with civil or political liberty. We have seen regimes that permit considerable freedom of action in the economic sphere while being quite illiberal politically and culturally. On the other hand, though capitalism may not be a sufficient condition for a liberal society, it does seem to be a necessary condition of it. History does not provide us with any instance of a society that repressed the economic liberties of the individual while being solicitous of his other liberties. It is the diffusion of wealth and power and status in a market economy that creates the "social space" within which civil and political liberty can flower, or at least be preserved to some degree.

Paradoxically, however, such success breeds its own kind of frustration. The better the system works, the more affluent and freer the society, the more marked is the tendency to impose an ever greater psychic burden upon the individual. He has to cope with his "existential" human needs—with the life of the mind, the psyche, and the spirit—on his own. At the same time, precisely because the bourgeois-capitalist order is so "boring" from this "existential" point of view—what poet has ever sung its praises? what novelist was ever truly inspired by the career of a businessman?—the psychic needs are more acute. A dangerous dialectic is thereby created. Young people, no longer hard pressed to "better their condition," are all the more free to experience the limitations of their social world, to rebel against them, to participate in what Lionel Trilling called "the adversary culture." In retrospect, one is led to question the validity of the original liberal idea that it is possible for the individual, alone or in purely voluntary association with others, to cope with the eternal dilemmas of the human condition. The moral authority of tradition, and some public support for this authority, seems to be needed. This is, beyond all doubt, an authentically "conservative" thought, a pre-capitalist thought, and how it can be assimilated into a liberal-capitalist society is perhaps the major intellectual question of our age.

In addition to this spiritual malaise, capitalism, as it de-
velops, also gives rise to certain institutional problems. The
capitalist economy and capitalist society have, in the course
of their growth, been transformed into something very different from what Adam Smith had in mind. To put it simply, it
is to an ever-increasing degree dominated by large, bureaucratic institutions of all kinds (economic, political, educational, etc.). The degree of this dominance is frequently
exaggerated for polemical purposes: the majority of the
American people still work for small or medium-sized enterprises (or for themselves). Nevertheless, the transformation is
real and troublesome, raising all sorts of questions about the
future structure of liberal-capitalist society. We have not
made much progress in answering these questions, in part because the critics of capitalism are uninterested in answering
them, in part because the business community is reluctant to
confront them. They are nevertheless real questions which
anyone concerned for the preservation of a liberal-capitalist
order must grapple with.

But is it worth preserving? I believe it is, at least in its essentials. It is worth preserving because (and one cannot repeat it too often) it really does work; it does deliver on its
promises, limited as these promises are by certain criteria. It
does improve people's material standard of living, and it does
give each person the opportunity to exercise a more meaningful freedom of choice in the shaping of his life. The fact that
a relatively affluent society produces a substantial number of
young people who then choose to despise bourgeois comfort
and convenience, preferring various political fantasies of their
own contrivance, is no final judgment on it. Most of the people on this planet, even most in the United States, do not
react in this way. They may wish to mitigate some of the
rigors of this freedom through measures of collective security
—what we call the welfare state—but that need be no threat,
in principle, to capitalism. An affluent society in which people
choose to purchase (through taxes) certain goods collectively
rather than individually (insurance against adversity, basic
scientific research, and the like) represents no rebellion

against the liberal-capitalist order. On the contrary: it tends to make that order more firmly established.

What is true, however, is that a great many people who in the United States are called "liberal"—but in Europe are more accurately designated as socialists or social-democrats—fail to see the connection between economic liberty and all our other liberties. They wish, covertly or mindlessly, to extend the reach of the welfare state so as to transform liberal society into something essentially different. They may, if they are ideologically fervent, call this new order socialism, but this is a childish self-deception. There is no such thing as socialism—understood as a *voluntary* cooperative community—in the real world of the 20th century. There are only versions of more or less coercive, more or less bureaucratic collectivism. There is precious little evidence that the citizens of such countries are now either more prosperous or more content as a result of the anti-capitalist "reforms" that have been effected, and there is a fair amount of evidence that they are not. Indeed, no one is even candidly proposing these polities as models to be emulated. The models that are proposed share the distinctive feature of never having achieved an earthly incarnation. Obviously, such models may easily display a perfection that the real world is lacking.

And this, perhaps, is the most persuasive argument for capitalism. The alternatives being proposed to us range from the hideous to the merely squalid. They do not promote superior economic growth or a greater degree of individual freedom, though they can make us all share more equally in the diminution of both. The political creativity of the 20th century has exhausted itself in the pursuit of chimeras, whether of the Right or the Left. Those peoples who have had the misfortune to be subjected to the collectivist imperatives of these impossible dreams are far more disillusioned by their system than are those who live under liberal capitalism. All that the various "socialist" regimes have to show for the sacrifices they have demanded of their citizens is tyranny and scarcity, or bureaucracy and bankruptcy. Surely freedom and affluence are preferable, whatever the problems generated by this freedom and this affluence. And surely it is more reasonable to think that capitalism can yet cope with these problems in a more efficient and humane way than can the alternatives being offered us.

The contents of this book, written over the past seven years, explore both the criticism directed against liberal-capitalism and the tensions inherent in such a society as ours. I have made no effort to erase all ambiguities, or even an occasional wavering of intellectual purpose—for these represent a candid response to real complexities. In a way, it is a kind of intellectual autobiography, explaining how and why someone who was once simply content to regard himself as a "liberal" has come to be a "neo-conservative," has come to think that liberal-capitalism is worthy of its two cheers, no more but also no less.

New York
October, 1977

PART ONE

The Enemy of Being
Is Having

1

CORPORATE CAPITALISM

IN AMERICA

THE UNITED STATES is the capitalist nation par excellence. That is to say, it is not merely the case that capitalism has flourished here more vigorously than, for instance, in the nations of Western Europe. The point is, rather, that the Founding Fathers *intended* this nation to be capitalist and regarded it as the *only* set of economic arrangements consistent with the liberal democracy they had established. They did not use the term "capitalism," of course; but, then, neither did Adam Smith, whose *Wealth of Nations* was also published in 1776, and who spoke of "the system of natural liberty." That invidious word, "capitalism," was invented by European socialists about a half-century later—just as our other common expression, "free enterprise," was invented still later by anti-socialists who saw no good reason for permitting their enemies to appropriate the vocabulary of public discourse. But words aside, it is a fact that capitalism in this country has a historical legitimacy that it does not possess elsewhere. In other lands, the nation and its fundamental institutions antedate the capitalist era; in the United States, where liberal democracy is not merely a form of government but also a "way of life," capitalism and democracy have been organically linked.

This fact, quite simply accepted until the 1930s—accepted by both radical critics and staunch defenders of the American regime—has been obscured in recent decades by the efforts of liberal scholars to create a respectable pedigree for the emerging "welfare state." The impetus behind this scholarship was justified, to a degree. It is true that the Founding Fathers were not dogmatic laissez-fairists, in a later neo-Darwinian or "libertarian" sense of the term. They were intensely suspicious of governmental power, but they never could have subscribed to the doctrine of "our enemy, the State." They believed there was room for some governmental intervention in economic affairs; and—what is less frequently remarked— they believed most firmly in the propriety of governmental intervention and regulation in the areas of public taste and public morality. But, when one has said this, one must add emphatically that there really is little doubt that the Founders were convinced that economics was the sphere of human activity where government intervention was, as a general rule, least likely to be productive, and that "the system of natural liberty" in economic affairs was the complement to our system of constitutional liberty in political and civil affairs. They surely would have agreed with Hayek that the paternalistic government favored by modern liberalism led down the "road to serfdom."

But one must also concede that both the Founding Fathers and Adam Smith would have been perplexed by the kind of capitalism we have in 1978. They could not have interpreted the domination of economic activity by large corporate bureaucracies as representing, in any sense, the working of a "system of natural liberty." Entrepreneurial capitalism, as they understood it, was mainly an individual—or at most, a family—affair. Such large organizations as might exist—joint stock companies, for example—were limited in

purpose (e.g., building a canal or a railroad) and usually in
duration as well. The large, publicly owned corporation of
today which strives for immortality, which is committed to
no line of business but rather (like an investment banker)
seeks the best return on investment, which is governed by an
anonymous oligarchy, would have troubled and puzzled them,
just as it troubles and puzzles us. And they would have asked
themselves the same questions we have been asking ourselves
for almost a century now: Who "owns" this new leviathan?
Who governs it, and by what right, and according to what
principles?

THE UNPOPULAR REVOLUTION

To understand the history of corporate capitalism in America, it is important to realize in what sense it may be fairly
described as an "accidental institution." Not in the economic
sense, of course. In the latter part of the last century, in all
industrialized nations, the large corporation was born out of
both economic necessity and economic opportunity: the
necessity of large pools of capital and of a variety of tech-
nical expertise to exploit the emerging technologies, and the
opportunity for economies of scale in production, marketing,
and service in a rapidly urbanizing society. It all happened
so quickly that the term "corporate revolution" is not inappropriate. In 1870, the United States was a land of small
family-owned business. By 1905, the large, publicly owned
corporation dominated the economic scene.

But the corporate revolution was always, during that period, an unpopular revolution. It was seen by most Americans
as an accident of economic circumstance—something that
happened to them rather than something they had created.
They had not foreseen it; they did not understand it; in no
way did it seem to "fit" into the accepted ideology of the
American democracy. No other institution in American history—not even slavery—has ever been so consistently unpopular as has the large corporation with the American public.
It was controversial from the outset, and it has remained
controversial to this day.

This is something the current crop of corporate executives find very difficult to appreciate. Most of them reached maturity during the postwar period, 1945–1960. As it happens, this was—with the possible exception of the 1920s—just about the only period when public opinion was, on the whole, well-disposed to the large corporation. After 15 years of depression and war, the American people wanted houses, consumer goods, and relative security of employment—all the things that the modern corporation is so good at supplying. The typical corporate executive of today, in his fifties or sixties, was led to think that such popular acceptance was "normal," and is therefore inclined to believe that there are novel and specific forces behind the upsurge of anti-corporate sentiment in the past decade. As a matter of fact, he is partly right: there *is* something significantly new about the hostility to the large corporation in our day. But there is also something very old, something coeval with the very existence of the large corporation itself. And it is the interaction of the old hostility with the new which has put the modern corporation in the critical condition that we find it in today.

The old hostility is based on what we familiarly call "populism." This is a sentiment basic to any democracy—indispensable to its establishment but also, ironically, inimical to its survival. Populism is the constant fear and suspicion that power and/or authority, whether in government or out, is being used to frustrate "the will of the people." It is a spirit that intimidates authority and provides the popular energy to curb and resist it. The very possibility of a democratic society—as distinct from the forms of representative government, which are its political expression—is derived from, and is constantly renewed by, the populist temper. The Constitution endows the United States with a republican form of government, in which the free and explicit consent of the people must ultimately ratify the actions of those in authority. But the populist spirit, which both antedated and survived the Constitutional Convention, made the United States a democratic nation as well as a republican one, committed to "the democratic way of life" as well as to the proprieties of constitutional government. It is precisely the strength of that commitment which has always made the American democracy somehow different from the democracies of Western Europe—a difference which every European observer has been quick to remark.

But populism is, at the same time, an eternal problem for the American democratic republic. It incarnates an antinomian impulse, a Jacobin contempt for the "mere" forms of law and order and civility. It also engenders an impulse toward a rather infantile political utopianism, on the premise that nothing is too good for "the people." Above all, it is a temper and state of mind which too easily degenerates into political paranoia, with "enemies of the people" being constantly discovered and exorcised and convulsively purged. Populist paranoia is always busy subverting the very institutions and authorities that the democratic republic laboriously creates for the purpose of orderly self-government.

In the case of the large corporation, we see a healthy populism and a feverish paranoia simultaneously being provoked by its sudden and dramatic appearance. The paranoia takes the form of an instinctive readiness to believe anything reprehensible, no matter how incredible, about the machinations of "big business." That species of journalism and scholarship which we call "muckraking" has made this kind of populist paranoia a permanent feature of American intellectual and public life. Though the businessman per se has never been a fictional hero of bourgeois society (as Stendhal observed, a merchant may be honorable but there is nothing heroic about him), it is only after the rise of "big business" that the businessman becomes the natural and predestined villain of the novel, the drama, the cinema, and, more recently, television. By now most Americans are utterly convinced that all "big business" owes its existence to the original depredations of "robber barons"—a myth which never really was plausible, which more recent scholarship by economic historians has thoroughly discredited, but which probably forever will have a secure hold on the American political imagination. Similarly, most Americans are now quick to believe that "big business" conspires secretly but most effectively to manipulate the economic and political system—an enterprise which, in prosaic fact, corporate executives are too distracted and too unimaginative even to contemplate.

Along with this kind of paranoia, however, populist hostility toward the large corporation derives from an authentic bewilderment and concern about the place of this new institution in American life. In its concentration of assets and power—power to make economic decisions affecting the lives of tens of thousands of citizens—it seemed to create a dangerous disharmony between the economic system and the political. In the America of the 1890s, even government did not have, and did not claim, such power (except in wartime). *No one* was supposed to have such power; it was, indeed, a radical diffusion of power that was thought to be an essential characteristic of democratic capitalism. The rebellion of Jacksonian democracy against the Bank of the United States had been directed precisely against such an "improper" concentration of power. A comparable rebellion now took place against "big business."

"BIG BUSINESS" OR CAPITALISM?

It was not, however, a rebellion against capitalism as such. On the contrary, popular hostility to the large corporation reflected the fear that this new institution was subverting capitalism as Americans then understood (and, for the most part, still understand) it. This understanding was phrased in individualistic terms. The entrepreneur was conceived of as a real person, not as a legal fiction. The "firm" was identified with such a real person (or a family of real persons) who took personal risks, reaped personal rewards, and assumed personal responsibility for his actions. One of the consequences of the victorious revolt against the Bank of the United States had been to make the chartering of corporations—legal "persons" with limited liability—under state law a routine and easy thing, the assumption being that this would lead to a proliferation of small corporations, still easily identifiable with the flesh-and-blood entrepreneurs who founded them. The rise of "big business" frustrated such expectations.

Moreover, the large corporation not only seemed to be but actually was a significant deviation from traditional capitalism. One of the features of the large corporation—though more a consequence of its existence than its cause—was its need for, and its ability to create, "orderly markets." What businessmen disparagingly call "cutthroat competition," with its wild swings in price, its large fluctuations in employment, its unpredictable effects upon profits—all this violates the very *raison d'être* of a large corporation, with its need for relative stability so that its long-range investment decisions can be rationally calculated. The modern corporation always looks to the largest and most powerful firm in the industry to establish "market leadership" in price, after which competition will concentrate on quality, service, and the introduction of new products. One should not exaggerate the degree to which the large corporation is successful in these efforts. John Kenneth Galbraith's notion that the large corporation simply manipulates its market through the power of advertising and fixes the price level with sovereign authority is a wild exaggeration. This is what all corporations *try* to do; it is what a few corporations, in some industries, sometimes succeed in doing. Still, there is little doubt that the idea of a "free market," in the era of large corporations, is not quite the original capitalist idea.

The populist response to the transformation of capitalism by the large corporation was, and is: "Break it up!" Antitrust and anti-monopoly legislation was the consequence. Such legislation is still enacted and reenacted, and antitrust prosecutions still make headlines. But the effort is by now routine, random, and largely pointless. There may be a few lawyers left in the Justice Department or the Federal Trade Commission who sincerely believe that such laws, if stringently enforced, could restore capitalism to something like its pristine individualist form. But it is much more probable that the lawyers who staff such government agencies launch these intermittent crusades against "monopoly" and "oligopoly"— terms that are distressingly vague and inadequate when ap-

plied to the real world—because they prefer such activity
to mere idleness, and because they anticipate that a successful prosecution will enhance their professional reputations.
No one expects them to be effectual, whether the government
wins or loses. Just how much difference, after all, would it
make if AT&T were forced to spin off its Western Electric
manufacturing subsidiary, or if IBM were divided into three
different computer companies? All that would be accomplished is a slight increase in the number of large corporations, with very little consequence for the shape of the economy or the society as a whole.

True, one could imagine, in the abstract, a much more
radical effort to break up "big business." But there are good
reasons why, though many talk solemnly about this possibility, no one does anything about it. The costs would simply be too high. The economic costs, most obviously: an adverse effect on productivity, on capital investment, on our
balance of payments, etc. But the social and political costs
would be even more intolerable. Our major trade unions,
having after many years succeeded in establishing collective
bargaining on a national level with the large corporation, are
not about to sit back and watch their power disintegrate for
the sake of an ideal such as "decentralization." And the nation's pension funds are not about to permit the assets of the
corporations in which they have invested to be dispersed,
and the security of their pension payments correspondingly
threatened.

One suspects that even popular opinion, receptive in principle to the diminution of "big business," would in actuality
find the process too painful to tolerate. For the plain fact is
that, despite much academic agitation about the horrors of
being an "organization man," a large proportion of those who
now work for a living, of whatever class, have learned to prefer
the security, the finely calibrated opportunities for advance-
ment, the fringe benefits, and the paternalism of a large corporation to the presumed advantages of employment in
smaller firms. It is not only corporate executives who are
fearful of "cutthroat competition"; most of us, however
firmly we declare our faith in capitalism and "free enter-

prise," are sufficiently conservative in our instincts to wish to avoid all such capitalist rigors. Even radical professors, who in their books find large bureaucratic corporations "dehumanizing," are notoriously reluctant to give up tenured appointments in large bureaucratic universities for riskier opportunities elsewhere.

So the populist temper and the large corporation coexist uneasily in America today, in what can only be called a marriage of convenience. There is little affection, much nagging and backbiting and whining on all sides, but it endures "for the sake of the children," as it were. Not too long ago, there was reason to hope that, out of the habit of coexistence, there would emerge something like a philosophy of coexistence: a mutual adaptation of the democratic-individualist-capitalist ideal and the bureaucratic-corporate reality, sanctioned by a new revised version of the theory of democracy and capitalism—a new political and social philosophy, in short, which extended the reach of traditional views without repudiating them. But that possibility, if it was ever more than a fancy, has been effectively canceled by the rise, over the past decade, of an anti-capitalist ethos which has completely transformed the very definition of the problem.

THE ANTI-LIBERAL LEFT

This ethos, in its American form, is not *explicitly* anti-capitalistic, and this obscures our perception and understanding of it. It has its roots in the tradition of "progressive reform," a tradition which slightly antedated the corporate revolution but which was immensely stimulated by it. In contrast to populism, this was (and is) an upper middle-class tradition—an "elitist" tradition, as one would now say. Though it absorbed a great many socialist and neo-socialist and quasi-socialist ideas, it was too American—too habituated to the rhetoric of individualism, and even in some measure to its reality—to embrace easily a synoptic, collectivist vision of the future as enunciated in socialist dogmas. It was willing to contemplate "public ownership" (i.e., ownership by the political authorities) of *some* of the "means of production," but on the whole it preferred to think in terms of *regulating* the large corporation rather than nationalizing it or breaking it up. It is fair to call it an indigenous and peculiarly American counterpart to European socialism: addressing itself to the same problems defined in much the same way, motivated by the same ideological impulse, but assuming an adversary posture toward "big business" specifically rather than toward capitalism in general.

At least, that is what "progressive reform" used to be. In the past decade, however, it has experienced a transmutation of ideological substance while preserving most of the traditional rhetorical wrappings. That is because it embraced, during these years, a couple of other political traditions, European in origin, so that what we still call "liberalism" in the United States is now something quite different from the liberalism of the older "progressive reform" impulse. It is so different, indeed, as to have created a cleavage between those who think of themselves as "old liberals"—some of whom are now redesignated as "neo-conservatives"—and the new liberals who are in truth men and women of "the Left," in the European sense of that term. This is an important point, worthy of some elaboration and clarification, especially since the new liberalism is not usually very candid about the matter.*

The Left in Europe, whether "totalitarian" or "democratic," has consistently been anti-liberal. That is to say, it vigorously repudiates the intellectual traditions of liberalism —as expressed, say, by Locke, Montesquieu, Adam Smith, and Tocqueville—and with equal vigor rejects the key institution of liberalism: the (relatively) free market (which necessarily implies limited government). The Left emerges

---

* It must be said, however, that even when it is candid, no one seems to pay attention. John Kenneth Galbraith has recently publicly defined himself as a "socialist," and asserts that he has been one—whether wittingly or unwittingly, it is not clear—for many years. But the media still consistently identify him as a "liberal," and he is so generally regarded. Whether this is mere habit or instinctive protective coloration—for the media are a crucial wing of the "new liberalism"—it is hard to say.

out of a rebellion against the "anarchy" and "vulgarity" of a civilization that is shaped by individuals engaged in market transactions. The "anarchy" to which it refers is the absence of any transcending goal or purpose which society is constrained to pursue and which socialists, with their superior understanding of History, feel obligated to prescribe. Such a prescription, when fulfilled, will supposedly reestablish a humane "order." The "vulgarity" to which it refers is the fact that a free market responds, or tries to respond, to the appetites and preferences of common men and women, whose use of their purchasing power determines the shape of the civilization. Since common men and women are likely to have "common" preferences, tastes, and aspirations, the society they create—the "consumption society," as it is now called—will be regarded by some critics as shortsightedly "materialistic." People will seek to acquire what they want (e.g., automobiles), not what they "need" (e.g., mass transit). Socialists are persuaded that they have a superior understanding of people's true needs, and that the people will be more truly happy in a society where socialists have the authority to define those needs, officially and unequivocally.

Obviously, socialism is an "elitist" movement, and in its beginnings—with Saint-Simon and Auguste Comte—was frankly conceived of as such. Its appeal has always been to "intellectuals" (who feel dispossessed by and alienated from a society in which they are merely one species of common man) and members of the upper-middle class who, having reaped the benefits of capitalism, are now in a position to see its costs. (It must be said that these costs are not imaginary: socialism would not have such widespread appeal if its critique of liberal capitalism were entirely without substance.) But all social movements in the modern world must define themselves as "democratic," since democratic legitimacy is the only kind of legitimacy we recognize. So "totalitarian" socialism insists that it is a "people's democracy," in which the "will of the people" is mystically incarnated in the ruling party. "Democratic socialism," on the other hand, would like to think that it can "socialize" the economic sec-

tor while leaving the rest of society "liberal." As Robert
Nozick puts it, democratic socialists want to proscribe only
"*capitalist* transactions between consenting adults."

The trouble with the latter approach is that democratic
socialists, when elected to office, discover that to collectivize
economic life you have to coerce all sorts of other institutions
(e.g., the trade unions, the media, the educational system)
and limit individual freedom in all sorts of ways (e.g., freedom to travel, freedom to "drop out" from the world of work,
freedom to choose the kind of education one prefers) if a
"planned society" is to function efficiently. When "democratic
socialist" governments show reluctance to take such actions,
they are pushed into doing so by the "left wings" of their
"movements," who feel betrayed by the distance that still
exists between the reality they experience and the socialist
ideal which enchants them. Something like this is now happening in all the European social-democratic parties and in a
country like India.

THE "NEW CLASS"

The United States never really had any such movement of the
Left, at least not to any significant degree. It was regarded as
an "un-American" thing, as indeed it was. True, the movement of "progressive reform" was "elitist" both in its social
composition and its social aims: it, too, was distressed by
the "anarchy" and "vulgarity" of capitalist civilization. But
in the main it accepted as a fact the proposition that capitalism and liberalism were organically connected, and it proposed to itself the goal of "mitigating the evils of capitalism,"
rather than abolishing liberal capitalism and replacing it
with "a new social order" in which a whole new set of human relationships would be established. It was an authentic
reformist movement. It wanted to regulate the large corporations so that this concentration of private power could not develop into an oligarchical threat to democratic-liberal capitalism. It was ready to interfere with the free market so that
the instabilities generated by capitalism—above all, instabil-

ity of employment—would be less costly in human terms. It
was even willing to tamper occasionally with the consumer's
freedom of choice where there was a clear consensus that
the micro-decisions of the marketplace added up to macro-
consequences that were felt to be unacceptable. And it hoped
to correct the "vulgarity" of capitalist civilization by educat-
ing the people so that their "preference schedules" (as economists would say) would be, in traditional terms, more ele-
vated, more appreciative of "the finer things in life."

Ironically, it was the extraordinary increase in mass higher
education after World War II that, perhaps more than anything else, infused the traditional movement for "progressive
reform" with various impulses derived from the European
Left. The earlier movement had been "elitist" in fact as well
as in intention, i.e., it was sufficiently small so that, even while
influential, it could hardly contemplate the possibility of
actually exercising "power." Mass higher education has converted this movement into something like a mass movement
proper, capable of driving a President from office (1968) and
nominating its own candidate (1972). The intentions remain
"elitist," of course; but the movement now encompasses some
millions of people. These are the people whom liberal capitalism had sent to college in order to help manage its affluent,
highly technological, mildly paternalistic, "post-industrial"
society.

This "new class" consists of scientists, lawyers, city planners, social workers, educators, criminologists, sociologists,
public health doctors, etc.—a substantial number of whom
find their careers in the expanding public sector rather than
the private. The public sector, indeed, is where they prefer
to be. They are, as one says, "idealistic," i.e., far less interested in individual financial rewards than in the corporate
power of their class. Though they continue to speak the language of "progressive reform," in actuality they are acting
upon a hidden agenda: to propel the nation from that modified version of capitalism we call "the welfare state" toward
an economic system so stringently regulated in detail as to
fulfill many of the traditional anti-capitalist aspirations of
the Left.

The exact nature of what has been happening is obscured
by the fact that this "new class" is not merely liberal but truly
"libertarian" in its approach to all areas of life—except economics. It celebrates individual liberty of speech and expression and action to an unprecedented degree, so that at times
it seems almost anarchistic in its conception of the good life.
But this joyful individualism always stops short of the border
where economics—i.e., capitalism—begins. The "new class"
is surely sincere in such a contradictory commitment to a
maximum of individual freedom in a society where economic
life becomes less free with every passing year. But it is instructive to note that these same people, who are irked and
inflamed by the slightest noneconomic restriction in the
United States, can be admiring of Maoist China and not in
the least appalled by the total collectivization of life—and
the total destruction of liberty—there. They see this regime
as "progressive," not "reactionary." And, in this perception,
they unwittingly tell us much about their deepest fantasies
and the natural bias of their political imagination.

Meanwhile, the transformation of American capitalism
proceeds apace. Under the guise of coping with nasty "externalities"—air pollution, water pollution, noise pollution,
traffic pollution, health pollution, or what have you—more
and more of the basic economic decisions are being removed
from the marketplace and transferred to the "public"—i.e.,
political—sector, where the "new class," by virtue of its expertise and skills, is so well represented. This movement is
naturally applauded by the media, which are also for the
most part populated by members of this "new class" who believe—as the Left has always believed—it is government's
responsibility to cure all the ills of the human condition, and
who ridicule those politicians who deny the possibility (and
therefore the propriety) of government doing any such ambitious thing. And, inevitably, more explicitly socialist and
neo-socialist themes are beginning boldly to emerge from the
protective shell of reformist-liberal rhetoric. The need for
some kind of "national economic plan" is now being dis-
cussed seriously in Congressional circles; the desirability of

"public"—i.e., political—appointees to the boards of directors of the largest corporations is becoming more apparent
to more politicians and journalists with every passing day;
the utter "reasonableness," in principle, of price and wage
controls is no longer even a matter for argument, but is subject only to circumstantial and prudential considerations.
Gradually, the traditions of the Left are being absorbed
into the agenda of "progressive reform," and the structure of
American society is being radically, if discreetly, altered.

"THE ENEMY OF BEING IS HAVING"

One of the reasons this process is so powerful, and meets
only relatively feeble resistance, is that it has a continuing
source of energy within the capitalist system itself. That
source is not the "inequalities" or "injustices" of capitalism,
as various ideologies of the Left insist. These may represent
foci around which dissent is occasionally and skillfully mo-
bilized. But the most striking fact about anti-capitalism is
the degree to which it is *not* a spontaneous working-class phenomenon. Capitalism, like all economic and social systems,
breeds its own peculiar discontents, but the discontents of
the working class are, in and of themselves, not one of its
major problems. Yes, there is class conflict in capitalism;
there is always class conflict, and the very notion of a possible society without class conflict is one of socialism's most
bizarre fantasies. (Indeed, it is this fantasy that is socialism's original contribution to modern political theory; the
importance of class conflict itself was expounded by Aristotle
and was never doubted by anyone who ever bothered to look
at the real world.) But there is no case, in any country that
can reasonably be called "capitalist," of such class conflict
leading to a proletarian revolution. Capitalism, precisely because its aim is the satisfaction of "common" appetites
and aspirations, can adequately cope with its own class con-
flicts, through economic growth primarily and some version
of the welfare state secondarily. It can do so, however, only

if it is permitted to—a permission which the anti-capitalist spirit is loath to concede. This spirit *wants* to see capitalism falter and fail.

The essence of this spirit is to be found, not in *The Communist Manifesto*, but rather in the young Marx who wrote: *"The enemy of being is having."* This sums up neatly the animus which intellectuals from the beginning, and "the new class" in our own day, have felt toward the system of liberal capitalism. This system is in truth "an acquisitive society," by traditional standards. Not that men and women under capitalism are "greedier" than under feudalism or socialism or whatever. Almost all people, almost all of the time, want more than they have. But capitalism is unique among social and economic systems in being organized for the overriding purpose of giving them more than they have. And here is where it runs into trouble: Those who benefit most from capitalism—and their children, especially—experience a withering away of the acquisitive impulse. Or, to put it more accurately: they cease to think of acquiring money and begin to think of acquiring power so as to improve the "quality of life," and to give *being* priority over *having*. That is the meaning of the well-known statement by a student radical of the 1960s: "You don't know what hell is like unless you were raised in Scarsdale." Since it is the ambition of capitalism to enable everyone to live in Scarsdale or its equivalent, this challenge is far more fundamental than the orthodox Marxist one, which says—against all the evidence—that capitalism will fail because it *cannot* get everyone to live in Scarsdale.

Against this new kind of attack, any version of capitalism would be vulnerable. But the version of corporate capitalism under which we live is not merely vulnerable; it is practically defenseless. It is not really hard to make a decent case, on a pragmatic level, for liberal capitalism today—especially since the anti-capitalist societies the 20th century has given birth to are, even by their own standards, monstrous abortions and "betrayals" of their originating ideals. And corporate capitalism does have the great merit of being willing to provide a milieu of comfortable liberty—in uni-

versities, for example—for those who prefer *being* to *having*.
But the trouble with the large corporation today is that it
does not possess a clear theoretical—i.e., ideological—legitimacy within the framework of liberal capitalism itself. Consequently the gradual usurpation of managerial authority by
the "new class"—mainly through the transfer of this authority to the new breed of regulatory officials (who are the very
prototype of the class)—is almost irresistible.

BUREAUCRATIC ENTERPRISE

So long as business was an activity carried on by real individuals who "owned" the property they managed, the politicians, the courts, and public opinion were all reasonably
respectful of the capitalist proprieties. Not only was the businessman no threat to liberal democracy; he was, on the contrary, the very epitome of the bourgeois liberal-democratic
ethos—the man who succeeded by diligence, enterprise,
sobriety, and all those other virtues that Benjamin Franklin
catalogued for us, and which we loosely call "the Protestant ethic." *

On the whole, even today, politicians and public opinion
are inclined to look with some benevolence on "small business," and no one seems to be interested in leading a crusade
against it. But the professionally managed large corporation
is another matter entirely. The top executives of these enormous bureaucratic institutions are utterly sincere when they
claim fealty to "free enterprise," and they even have a
point: managing a business corporation, as distinct from
a government agency, does require a substantial degree of
entrepreneurial risk-taking and entrepreneurial skill. But it
is also the case that they are as much functionaries as entrepreneurs, and rather anonymous functionaries at that. Not
only don't we know who the chairman of General Motors is;
we know so little about the kind of person who holds such a

---

* I say "loosely call" because, as a Jew, I was raised to think that this
was an ancient "Hebrew ethic," and some Chinese scholars I have spoken
to feel that it could appropriately be called "The Confucian ethic."

position that we haven't the faintest idea as to whether or not we want our children to grow up like him. Horatio Alger, writing in the era of pre-corporate capitalism, had no such problems. And there is something decidedly odd about a society in which a whole class of Very Important People is not automatically held up as one possible model of emulation for the young, and cannot be so held up because they are, as persons, close to invisible.

Nor is it at all clear whose interests these entrepreneur-functionaries are serving. In theory, they are elected representatives of the stockholder-"owners." But stockholder elections are almost invariably routine affirmations of management's will, because management will have previously secured the support of the largest stockholders; and for a long while now stockholders have essentially regarded themselves, and are regarded by management, as little more than possessors of a variable-income security. A stock certificate has become a lien against the company's earnings and assets—a subordinated lien, in both law and fact—rather than a charter of "citizenship" within a corporate community. And though management will talk piously, when it serves its purposes, about its obligations to the stockholders, the truth is that it prefers to have as little to do with them as possible, since their immediate demands are only too likely to conflict with management's long-term corporate plans.

It is interesting to note that when such an organization of business executives as the Committee on Economic Development drew up a kind of official declaration of the responsibilities of management a few years ago, it conceived of the professional manager as "a trustee balancing the interests of many diverse participants and constituents in the enterprise," and then enumerated these participants and constituents: employees, customers, suppliers, stockholders, government—practically everyone. Such a declaration serves only to ratify an accomplished fact: the large corporation has ceased being a species of private property, and is now a "quasi-public" institution. But if it is a "quasi-public" institution, some novel questions may be properly addressed to it: By what right does the self-perpetuating oligarchy that consti-

tutes "management" exercise its powers? On what principles
does it do so? To these essentially political questions management can only respond with the weak economic answer that
its legitimacy derives from the superior efficiency with which
it responds to signals from the free market. But such an argument from efficiency is not compelling when offered by a
"quasi-public" institution. In a democratic republic such as
ours, public and quasi-public institutions are not supposed
simply to be efficient at responding to people's transient desires, are not supposed to be simply *pandering* institutions,
but are rather supposed to help shape the people's wishes,
and ultimately, the people's character, according to some version, accepted by the people itself, of the "public good" and
"public interest." This latter task the "new class" feels itself
supremely qualified to perform, leaving corporate management in the position of arguing that it is improper for this
"quasi-public" institution to do more than give the people
what they want: a debased version of the democratic idea
which has some temporary demagogic appeal but no permanent force.

THE CORPORATION AND LIBERAL DEMOCRACY

Whether for good or evil—and one can leave this for future
historians to debate—the large corporation has gone
"quasi-public," i.e., it now straddles, uncomfortably and un-
certainly, both the private and public sectors of our "mixed
economy." In a sense one can say that the modern large corporation stands to the bourgeois-individualist capitalism of
yesteryear as the "imperial" American polity stands to the
isolated republic from which it emerged. Such a development may or may not represent "progress," but there is no
turning back.

The danger which this situation poses for American democracy is not the tantalizing ambiguities inherent in such a
condition; it is the genius of a pluralist democracy to convert such ambiguities into possible sources of institutional
creativity and to avoid "solving" them, as a Jacobin democ-

racy would, with one swift stroke of the sword. The danger is rather that the large corporation will be thoroughly integrated into the public sector, and lose its private character altogether. The transformation of American capitalism that *this* would represent—a radical departure from the quasi-bourgeois "mixed economy" to a system that could be fairly described as kind of "state capitalism"—does constitute a huge potential threat to the individual liberties Americans have traditionally enjoyed.

One need not, therefore, be an admirer of the large corporation to be concerned about its future. One might even regard its "bureaucratic-acquisitive" ethos, in contrast to the older "bourgeois-moralistic" ethos, as a sign of cultural decadence and still be concerned about its future. In our pluralistic society we frequently find ourselves defending specific concentrations of power, about which we might otherwise have the most mixed feelings, on the grounds that they contribute to a general diffusion of power, a diffusion which creates the "space" in which individual liberty can survive and prosper. This is certainly our experience vis-à-vis certain religious organizations—e.g., the Catholic Church or the Mormons—whose structure and values are, in some respects at least, at variance with our common democratic beliefs, and yet whose existence serves to preserve our democracy as a free and liberal society. The general principle of checks and balances, and of decentralized authority too, is as crucial to the social and economic structures of a liberal democracy as to its political structure.

Nevertheless, it seems clear that the large corporation is not going to be able to withstand those forces pulling and pushing it into the political sector unless it confronts the reality of its predicament and adapts itself to this reality in a self-preserving way. There is bound to be disagreement as to the forms such adaptation should take, some favoring institutional changes that emphasize and clarify the corporation's "public" nature, others insisting that its "private" character must be stressed anew. Probably a mixture of both strategies would be most effective. If large corporations are to avoid having government-appointed directors on their boards, they will have to take the initiative and try to preempt that possibility by themselves appointing distinguished "outside" directors, directors from outside the business community. At the same time, if corporations are going to be able to resist the total usurpation of their decision-making powers by government, they must create a constituency—of their stockholders, above all—which will candidly intervene in the "political game" of interest-group politics, an intervention fully in accord with the principles of our democratic system.

In both cases, the first step will have to be to persuade corporate management that some such change is necessary. This will be difficult: corporate managers are (and enjoy being) essentially economic-decision-making animals, and they are profoundly resentful of the "distractions" which "outside interference" of any kind will impose on them. After all, most chief executives have a tenure of about six years, and they all wish to establish the best possible track record, in terms of "bottom line" results, during that period. Very few are in a position to, and even fewer have an inclination to, take a long and larger view of the corporation and its institutional problems.

At the same time, the crusade against the corporations continues, with the "new class" successfully appealing to populist anxieties, seeking to run the country in the "right" way, and to reshape our civilization along lines superior to those established by the marketplace. Like all crusades, it engenders an enthusiastic paranoia about the nature of the Enemy and the deviousness of His operations. Thus, the *New Yorker*, which has become the liberal-chic organ of the "new class," has discovered the maleficent potential of the multinational corporation at exactly the time when the multinational corporation is in full retreat before the forces of nationalism everywhere. And the fact that American corporations sometimes have to bribe foreign politicians—for whom bribery is a way of life—is inflated into a rabid indictment of the personal morals of corporate executives. (That such bribery is also inherent in government-aid programs to the underdeveloped countries is, on the other hand, *never* taken to reflect on those who institute and run such programs, and is thought to be irrelevant to the desirability or success of the programs themselves.) So far, this crusade has been immensely effective. It will continue to be effective until the corporation has decided what kind of institution it is in today's world, and what kinds of reforms are a necessary precondition to a vigorous defense—not of its every action but of its very survival as a quasi-public institution as distinct from a completely politicized institution.

It is no exaggeration to say that the future of liberal democracy in America is intimately involved with these prospects for survival: the survival of an institution which liberal democracy never envisaged, whose birth and existence have been exceedingly troublesome to it, and whose legitimacy it has always found dubious. One can, if one wishes, call this a paradox. Or one can simply say that everything, including liberal democracy, is what it naturally becomes—is what it naturally evolves into—and our problem derives from a reluctance to revise yesteryear's beliefs in the light of today's realities.

2

BUSINESS AND
THE "NEW CLASS"

EVERYONE wants to be loved, and it always comes as a shock to discover that there are people who dislike you for what you really are rather than for what they mistakenly think you are. Indeed, most of us desperately resist such a conclusion. We keep insisting, to ourselves and others, that those people out there who are saying nasty things about us are merely ill-informed, or misguided, or have been seduced by mischievous propaganda on the part of a handful of irredeemably perverse spirits. And we remain confident, in our heart of hearts, that if they only understood us better, they would certainly dislike us less.

In this respect businessmen are as human—and are as capable of self-deception—as anyone else. On any single day, all over the country, there are gatherings of corporate executives in which bewilderment and vexation are expressed at the climate of hostility toward business to be found in Washington, or in the media, or in academia—or even, incredibly, among their own children. And, quickly enough, the idea is born that something ought to be done to create a better understanding (and, of course, appreciation) of "the free enterprise system." A television series on economics and business for the high schools? Space advertising in the print media? Face-to-face encounters between businessmen and college students? Long and serious luncheons with the editors of major newspapers and newsmagazines? In the end, many of these ideas come to fruition, at substantial costs in money and time—but with depressingly small effect.

Now, I do not wish to seem to be underestimating the degree of ignorance about business and economics which does in fact exist in the United States today. It is indeed amazing that, in a society in which business plays so crucial a role, so many people come to understand so little about it—and, at the same time, to know so much about it which isn't so. We have, for instance, managed to produce a generation of young people who, for all the education lavished on them, know less about the world of work—even the world of their fathers' work—than any previous generation in American history. They fantasize easily, disregard common observation, and appear to be radically deficient in that faculty we call common sense.

Nor, it must be said, are their teachers in a much better condition. The average college professor of history, sociology, literature, political science, sometimes even economics, is just as inclined to prefer fantasy over reality. On every college campus one can hear it said casually by faculty members that the drug companies are busy suppressing cures for cancer or arthritis or whatever; or that multinational corporations "really" make or unmake American foreign policy; or that "big business" actually welcomes a depression because it creates a "reserve army of the unemployed" from which it can recruit more docile workers.

So there is certainly room for all kinds of educational endeavors on the part of the business community, and I do not wish to be interpreted as in any way discouraging them. The fact that they seem so relatively ineffectual is not necessarily an argument against them. Education is at best a slow

and tedious process, and that kind of education which tries
to counteract a massive, original miseducation is even slower
and more tedious. Too many businessmen confuse education
with advertising, and almost unconsciously impose the short
time horizon of the latter on the former. The unit of time
appropriate to the process of education is not a year but a
generation.

Having said this, however, I should like to pursue the
truly interesting question of *why* so many intelligent people
manage to entertain so many absurd ideas about economics in
general and business in particular. In truth, one can properly
put that question in a much stronger form: Why do so many
intelligent people seem *determined* to hold those ideas and to
resist any correction of them? Such determination there
must be, because mere error and ignorance are not of themselves so obdurate. When they are, it is usually because they
also are an integral part of an ideology which serves some
deeper passion or interest.

And the more attentively one studies the problem, the
clearer it becomes that what is commonly called a "bias" or
an "animus" against business is really a by-product of a
larger purposiveness. There are people "out there" who find
it convenient to believe the worst about business because
they have certain adverse intentions toward the business
community to begin with. They dislike business for what it is,
not for what they mistakenly think it is. In other words,
they are members of what we have called "the new class."

This "new class" is not easily defined but may be vaguely
described. It consists of a goodly proportion of those college-
educated people whose skills and vocations proliferate in a
"post-industrial society" (to use Daniel Bell's convenient
term). We are talking about scientists, teachers and educational administrators, journalists and others in the communication industries, psychologists, social workers, those lawyers and doctors who make their careers in the expanding
public sector, city planners, the staffs of the larger foundations, the upper levels of the government bureaucracy, and
so on. It is, by now, a quite numerous class; it is an indispensable class for our kind of society; it is a disproportion-

ately powerful class; it is also an ambitious and frustrated class.

Kevin Phillips calls this class "the mediacracy," in a book of that title. Though the book has many shrewd observations, the term he chooses seems to me to be unfortunate. It helps prolong what might be called the "Agnew illusion," i.e., that many of our troubles derive from the fact that a small and self-selected group, whose opinions are unrepresentative of the American people, have usurped control of our media and use their strategic positions to launch an assault on our traditions and institutions. Such a populist perspective is misleading and ultimately self-defeating. Members of the new class do not "control" the media, they *are* the media—just as they *are* our educational system, our public health and welfare system, and much else. Even if the president of CBS or the publisher of *Time* were to decide tomorrow that George Wallace would be the ideal President, it would have practically no effect on what is broadcast or published. These executives have as much control over "their" bureaucracies as the Secretary of HEW has over his, or as the average college president has over his faculty.

What does this "new class" want and why should it be so hostile to the business community? Well, one should understand that the members of this class are "idealistic," in the 1960s sense of that term, i.e., they are not much interested in money but are keenly interested in power. Power for what? Well, the power to shape our civilization—a power which, in a capitalist system, is supposed to reside in the free market. The "new class" wants to see much of this power redistributed to government, where *they* will then have a major say in how it is exercised.

From the very beginnings of capitalism there has always existed a small group of men and women who disapproved of the pervasive influence of the free market on the civilization in which we live. One used to call this group "the intellectuals," and they are the ancestors of our own "new class," very few of whom are intellectuals but all of whom inherit the attitudes toward capitalism that have flourished among intellectuals for more than a century-and-a-half. This attitude may accurately be called "elitist," though people who are convinced they incarnate "the public interest," as distinct from all the private interests of a free society, are not likely to think of themselves in such a way. The elitist attitude is basically suspicious of, and hostile to, the market precisely because the market is so vulgarly democratic—one dollar, one vote. A civilization shaped by market transactions is a civilization responsive to the common appetites, preferences, and aspirations of common people. The "new class"—intelligent, educated, and energetic—has little respect for such a commonplace civilization. It wishes to see its "ideals" more effectual than the market is likely to permit them to be. And so it tries always to supersede economics by politics—an activity in which *it* is most competent—since it has the talents and the implicit authority to shape public opinion on all larger issues.

ITS OWN GRAVEDIGGER?

So there is a sense in which capitalism may yet turn out to be its own gravedigger, since it is capitalism that creates this "new class"—through economic growth, affluence, mass higher education, the proliferation of new technologies of communication, and in a hundred other ways. Moreover, it must be said that the "idealism" of this "new class," though in all respects self-serving, is not for that reason insincere. It really is true that a civilization shaped predominantly by a free market—by the preferences and appetites of ordinary men and women—has a "quality of life" that is likely to be regarded as less than wholly admirable by the better-educated classes. To be sure, these classes could try to improve things by elevating and refining the preferences of all those ordinary people; that, supposedly, is the liberal and democratic way. But it is so much easier to mobilize the active layers of public opinion behind such issues as environmentalism, ecology, consumer protection, and economic planning, to give the governmental bureaucracy the power to regulate and coerce, and eventually to "politicize" the economic decision-making process. And this is, of course, exactly what has been happening.

There can be little doubt that if these new imperialistic impulses on the part of "the public sector" (i.e., the political sector) are unrestrained, we shall move toward some version of state capitalism in which the citizen's individual liberty would be rendered ever more insecure. But it is important not to have any illusions about how much can be done to cope with this situation. The "new class" is here, it is firmly established in its own societal sectors, and it is not going to go away. It is idle, therefore, to talk about returning to a "free enterprise" system in which government will play the modest role it used to. The idea of such a counter-reformation is utopian. Ronald Reagan was a two-term governor of California, and whatever his accomplishments, the restoration of "free enterprise" was not one of them. Had he become a two-term President, he (and we) would have found that, after the ideological smoke had cleared, not all that much had changed.

Not that the situation is hopeless—it's just that one has to recognize the limited range of the possible. It *is* possible, I think, at least to preserve a substantial and vigorous private sector—not only a business sector, but also a nongovernmental, not-for-profit sector—in the United States. This can happen, not because of the self-evident virtues of business, but because of the profound appeal of individual liberty to all Americans, and because of the equally profound distrust of big government by all Americans. In this appeal and this distrust even members of the "new class" share, to one degree or another. It is our good fortune that they are not doctrinaire socialists, as in Britain, even if they sometimes look and sound like it. They have long wanted their "place in the sun"—they are in the process of seizing and consolidating it —and now they have to be assimilated into the system (even as the system will have to change to assimilate them). It will be a slow and painful business but need not end in calamity.

A good part of this process of assimilation will be the education of this "new class" in the actualities of business and

economics—*not* their conversion to "free enterprise"—so
that they can exercise their power responsibly. It will be an
immense educational task, in which the business community
certainly can play an important role. But before it can play
this role, business has first to understand the new sociological
and political reality within which it is now operating.
That, too, is an educational task of no small proportion.

3

THE FRUSTRATIONS

OF AFFLUENCE

WHY, as our industrialized nations get richer and richer, and as the real per capita income moves ever upwards, do so many of our citizens seem to get more querulous about their economic condition? The fact of affluence is indisputable: if you look at the radical economic tracts of the 1930s (by Stuart Chase, Lewis Corey, Norman Thomas, and others), with their glowing statistics on how marvelously well off we would all be under a planned economy, you discover that the economic reality today far surpasses their heady visions. Nevertheless, not many of us *feel* that well off. The instinct for contentment seems to have withered even as our economic condition has radically improved. Why is that?

The most familiar answer is that human beings are insatiably greedy creatures, and that if you give them more, it will only quicken their appetites for still more. We even have fancy sociological terms in which to express this thesis: "relative deprivation," "the revolution of rising expectations," and so on. Now, there is certainly some truth in this explanation, but I cannot accept it as the whole truth, or even the better part of the truth. Indeed, as a general proposition it strikes me as a slander against human nature. We all have our lusts, but not many of us are mere creatures of lust.

For example, there is one of my acquaintances, a distinguished professor of the liberal persuasion who is in favor of radical tax reform and a significant redistribution of wealth and income. Five years ago, he was saying that "the rich," with incomes over $30,000 a year, ought to pay a larger share of our taxes. Recently, he mentioned casually that "the rich" getting more than $50,000 a year ought to pay higher taxes. It is likely that, in a few more years, he will see as "rich" those who earn more than $75,000 a year. A cynic would simply assume that his income has moved sharply upwards during these past five years—which it certainly has, and which it will continue to do. But that cynical assumption is not necessarily an adequate explanation of his changing perspective on what it means to be "rich." It could be that he has made some interesting and objectively valid discoveries about the nature of "affluence" in our affluent society. In other words, the change could be an intelligent response to true information, rather than the result of a flawed character. Indeed, since I believe him to be a man of fine character, if erroneous opinions, I think the latter hypothesis is more likely. It is at the very least worth exploring.

It was, I believe, the French social theorist, Bertrand de Jouvenel, who first pointed out the ways in which a dynamic, growing economy may frustrate the *reasonable* expectations which people have of it. This frustration is linked to the two crucial aspects of the affluent society: (1) its dependence on technological innovation, and (2) the effects of mass affluence upon the individual consumer.

Technological innovation is a highly capricious force. It makes many things cheaper and makes some things much, much cheaper. But it also has the unintended consequence of making other things much more expensive. The degree of satisfaction that technological innovation offers you will ultimately depend not on the amount but the *kinds* of things you want.

We can easily discern those commodities and services which technology has made cheaper. Refrigerators, washing machines, freezers, air conditioners, telephones, the automobile, air travel, television, and radio—these are all tangible contributions to our higher standard of living. And they are *real* contributions—despite the existence of so much fashionable anti-technological snobbery, especially among young people who have never lived without these conveniences. One may sneer all one likes at television, but it is an unqualified blessing for old people and has marvelously enriched their daily lives. Similarly, one may think jet airplanes make too much noise, but this is as nothing compared to the way cheap and fast air travel has permitted members of a family to see one another more frequently.

Obviously, the benefits of such technological innovation are most appreciated by those who have had to do without them. That is why the least discontented people in our affluent society are those members of the working class who have moved up from poverty or near-poverty to the kind of "affluence" represented by an ability to enjoy these fruits of modern technology. That explains the so-called "hard-hat" phenomenon of the late 60s, which has so distressed all those who think the working class has some kind of revolutionary mission.

But what if you are not all that interested in having your standard of living raised in this way? Or what if you have already experienced those benefits of an affluent society? You are then in trouble, because the other kinds of benefits you looked forward to, as a result of rising income, turn out to be scarcer and more expensive than they used to be— and sometimes are not available at all. If you thought that, at $25,000 a year, you could go to the theater or opera once a week, you soon learn otherwise. If you really don't care for air travel but have always wanted a sleep-in maid, you are just out of luck. If you had hoped to have your cocktail or dinner parties catered, you find out that, though this was once commonplace at your level of real income, it is now out of the question.

In other words, technological innovation increases one's standard of living in certain, often unpredicted, ways but actually lowers it in other ways. Any images of "gracious living" you may have formed in your childhood or youth turn out to be largely irrelevant. Technology does not necessarily provide you with what you wanted; it offers you what it can, on a like-it-or-lump-it basis. If you are poor, you are certainly delighted to like it. If you are middle class, or have a vision of the good life based on traditional middle-class experience, you are puzzled and vexed that your affluence, in real income, somehow doesn't translate itself into "affluence" as you always conceived it.

What this comes down to is the fact that human values are inevitably shaped by human memories, whereas the "values" offered by technological innovation are shaped by emerging technological possibilities. There is no fault or blame here—humanity cannot obtain its values, nor can technology achieve its ends, in any other way. But there is enough incompatibility in this partnership to make for a persistent, gnawing frustration.

COMPETING FOR THE "GOOD THINGS"

In addition to this incompatibility there is another: mass affluence. In and by itself it constantly frustrates the perfectly normal and traditional desires of those with above-average incomes. It does so by making marginal benefits extraordinarily expensive. A hundred years ago, it took a relatively small amount of money to make a person much better off. Today, it takes substantial amounts of money to make a person (above the working-class level) only a little better off. The reason is that middle-class people now have to compete with working-class and lower-middle-class people for those "good things in life" they had always aspired to.

When you were twenty-one, and looked forward to making, say, $30,000 a year, you certainly assumed that you would be able to afford more living space. Now that you are fifty-one, and have reached the $30,000 level, you find every extra square foot to be exorbitant in price; the spacious apartment or home of your dreams—and yesteryear's reality —is now beyond your means. The reason, of course, is that the laborer who built your apartment or house used to occupy perhaps one-half the space of a well-to-do citizen, whereas now he can afford to occupy two-thirds the space. The available space being limited, its price at the margin increases fantastically.

The same holds true in other areas of life. You thought that, as you joined those in the top 15 percent of the income continuum—making $20,000 a year or more—you could eat occasionally in fine restaurants. You now find that fine restaurants these days can only be afforded by those with twice your income. You looked forward to a summer cottage in East Hampton or Martha's Vineyard but you now find these desirable places far beyond your means. You thought of taxiing to work, instead of crowding into the subway, but that, too, is beyond your economic reach. Item after item which used to be available to those who were *relatively* rich (top 15 percent bracket) are now available only to those who are *very* rich (top 5 percent bracket). The increased affluence of your fellow citizens has sent these amenities skyrocketing in price.

It is this state of affairs which accounts for an extraordinary phenomenon of American society today: so many people who are statistically "rich" (in the top 15 percent or 10 percent income segment) but who don't feel "rich," cannot believe they are "rich," and do not have the political or cultural attitudes one associates with "well-to-do" people. Many of these people, indeed, are all in favor of "taxing the rich" rather than themselves, and it comes as a great shock to them to learn that "taxing the rich" means taxing themselves. At this point, they become the avant-garde of a taxpayer's revolt. The legislator who takes their complaints literally will soon, as Senator McGovern discovered, be caught in a cross fire.

Now, in view of the very real economic problems which

non-rich Americans face, it is easy to be supercilious about the kind of discontent I have been describing. These people do not go hungry, they live comfortably enough, and their "deprivations" are not exactly calamitous. True, they definitely need not be objects of our compassion. But I do think they are worthy of our attention. A society which fails to breed contentment among its more successful citizens would seem to have a rather serious problem on its hands. Besides, the numbers in this class are increasing every year. Even now they are not a negligible political quantity and their votes have gradually been shifting away from the traditional conservatism that was associated with high income. If one cannot count on these people to provide political, social, and moral stability—if they do not have a good opinion of our society—how long, one wonders, can that stability and good opinion survive?

4

IDEOLOGY AND FOOD

LATELY Americans have seemed to be peculiarly fascinated with the themes and images of catastrophe. Our movie critics have been pointing out with some puzzlement that the most popular films of the moment deal with terrible earthquakes, burning skyscrapers, sinking ocean liners, and various end-of-the-world spectacles. The press, for its part, seems suddenly to be fascinated with leaking oil tankers off the coast of Singapore or blown oil wells in the North Sea; it appears that the demon of Ecological Disaster is creeping upon us. Any economist who will declare positively that any imminent sign of recession is but a prelude to economic collapse and social chaos is certain of getting a respectful hearing.

But surely the most interesting and significant of the prophets of calamity are those thinkers—physical scientists and social scientists for the most part, but itinerant moralists of all kinds as well—who are informing us that we have already entered upon a period of world famine, that hundreds of millions of people will shortly be starving to death, and

that this situation presents us with intolerable moral
dilemmas, requiring a completely new way of thinking about
the world's problems and a radical revision of American ways
of life. The word "triage"—the system of sorting out the
wounded in wartime, saving the savable, and letting the hopeless cases go—has abruptly entered the English language, and
few discussions of the world's food problem fail to make
use of it. Agronomists who never before gave a thought to
moral philosophy now speak glibly of "lifeboat ethics," of
saving a limited number of lives while deliberately letting
others die. One distinguished biologist has demanded compulsory sterilization of the populations of India and other countries, suggesting, once again, how easy it is for the unthinking
politics of compassion to shade into the politics of tyranny.

Now, all this is of the greatest importance, for the food
problem—unlike the threat of earthquakes or the actuality of
occasional oil spills—is unquestionably a grave one. People in
this world really are starving to death, and large-scale famine
is only too possible. The matter demands authentic concern
and serious thought. Unfortunately, while the concern evidently exists, serious thought is in scarce supply. Instead, there
almost seems to be a kind of puritanical yearning for disaster
as somehow an appropriate judgment on this wicked world, a
divine remonstrance which will cleanse our sullied souls. It is
fairly certain that, so long as we approach the problem with
this attitude, disaster is what we shall get.

Yet it is not at all clear that worldwide famine is our
ineluctable destiny. Nor is it at all clear that our human condition today is so radically novel that traditional moral beliefs offer us no guide through our perplexities. Before we
resign ourselves to political despair, or abandon ourselves
to a jejune moral Machiavellianism overlaid with a self-
satisfying pathos, we ought to stop, and look, and above all
reflect.

Why is there a food shortage in the world today? The
usual answer one will hear is that it is the result of population growth outstripping the growth of food supply. Now,
that is a terribly interesting answer. It is interesting to begin

with, because it is patently and demonstrably false: over the past quarter-century, the world food supply has been growing almost twice as fast as population. It is perhaps an even more interesting answer in what it reveals about the state of mind of those who offer it, i.e., a deep ideological reluctance to make certain kinds of elementary judgments in the realms of economics and politics.

There are three main reasons for the current food shortage and the threat of world famine which it evokes. These three reasons are: (1) Russia, (2) China, and (3) India. More specifically, the condition of agriculture and of agricultural productivity in these nations is at the root of the matter—a condition that has only a little to do with geography or demography, much to do with economics, and everything to do with politics.

Ever since the Russian Revolution, but especially since the forced collectivization of the early 1930s, agriculture in the Soviet Union has been a Communist disaster area. The literature on this subject is voluminous in extent and unanimous in its conclusion: the application of Communist dogmas has been ruinous to agricultural productivity. Peter Drucker, in his *Age of Discontinuity*, has pointed out that an economist in 1912, simply by projecting ahead the rate of economic development in Russia for the previous decades, could have accurately predicted that Russian industry would be pretty much at today's levels. (In that respect, the Russian Revolution can be deemed to have been superfluous.) But the same economist would also have predicted a far higher level of agricultural productivity than now exists in the Soviet Union. The only—repeat: the *only*—reason the Soviet Union is importing large quantities of food rather than being a food exporter is that its political regime, for ideological reasons, has made it necessary.

And the same is almost surely true for China. One has to use the qualifying "almost" because one knows so relatively little about conditions inside China. But we do know some things. We know that China is importing some four million tons of wheat this year from Canada, the United States, and

other sources. We also know that, if agricultural productivity
in mainland China approached the level that now prevails on
Taiwan, such imports would be unnecessary, and that an export surplus might even exist. So it is reasonable to conclude
that Chinese agriculture is experiencing the Russian fate,
and for identical reasons. Such a conclusion is all the more
reasonable in that *every* country—e.g., Chile, Peru, Mexico—
which has launched experiments in collectivized agriculture
has quickly witnessed a decline in agricultural productivity.

If the Soviet Union and China were not importing food,
and if the Soviet Union were instead exporting food (which
it is inherently and easily capable of doing), a significant
portion of today's world food shortage would simply not
exist. Which leaves us with India—a special case in some
ways, though not nearly so special as is popularly thought.

Americans have always had marked feelings of concern and
friendship for India. The movement for Indian independence
from Britain naturally evoked a sympathetic response in
this nation; postwar India was and is a democracy, and we
like to think well of other democracies, especially newborn
ones; and the idea that a prosperous United States has
some kind of moral obligation to the poor masses of India
has long been taken for granted. It is not surprising, then,
that during the 1960s we gave $10 billion of aid to India,
almost as a matter of course.

The problem with India today is that it has reached a
point where (a) ever greater aid is needed, and (b) it is
clear that the effect of this aid will only be to ensure an
interminable need for still greater quantities of aid in the
future. Why is this so? Again, we are told that it has to do
with the "population explosion" in that subcontinent. But
the proportion of arable land to population in India is not
much different from what it is in France. And other lands
with even fewer natural resources than India and an equally
rapid rate of population growth—South Korea, notably—
are faring much better.

Moreover, only a few years ago India was close to self-sup-
porting in food; indeed, official Indian economists were pre-

dicting a gradually improving condition in the years ahead, even taking population growth into account. True, Indians would continue to be poor, but there was no foreseeable reason why they should be on the verge of starvation. And it was further assumed that economic growth and eventual industrialization in India would gradually reduce the birth rate, as it has practically everywhere else. The outlook for India, in short, was not exactly bleak, though it would be an abuse of language to call it optimistic. India would be very poor for decades to come, but it would, with each passing decade, become somewhat less poor.

What happened to these forecasts and expectations? Well, the Indian government mucked them up by a stubborn and doctrinaire insistence that the nation's economy be subordinated to a vague set of "socialist principles." Agricultural prices at all levels were fixed so as to provide "cheap food for the masses." As a result, the farmers lost any incentive to grow more food and distributors lost any incentive to market food. Added to this has been an elaborate system of controls over business generally, so that all forms of economic enterprise are being smothered to death by a huge and vastly inefficient bureaucracy, and a xenophobic hostility to foreign capital that prevents other enterprises such as fertilizer plants, oil refineries, and manufacturing of agricultural equipment from ever being born.

In The Washington *Post* for Jan. 11, 1975, India's food minister pointed out in an interview that, even now, the quantity of food that India can produce is sufficient to avoid famine. His explanation as to why famine is nevertheless a real threat is that the wealthy Indians are eating too much, leaving too little for the poor. In view of the relatively small proportion of Indians who are wealthy, and of the universal limitations of the human stomach, this interpretation is clearly preposterous. But that is the way Indian officialdom thinks. And, it must be said, their silliness is matched only by their arrogance. Even at this moment, negotiations for American aid are being held up because India will not agree to a "no export" clause apparently because it wishes to send

much of the American aid to Russia, to whom it "owes" two
million tons of wheat!

SHORTAGES AND INCENTIVES

I do not wish to suggest that all those nations now suffering
a food shortage have brought this fate upon themselves.
Some are simply victims of what lawyers curiously call "acts
of God"—droughts, floods, blight, and war. To such nations,
whatever their ideological complexion, we have a clear moral
obligation, a simple human obligation, to provide all necessary assistance. But the sum total of these instances do not
add up to a world food crisis.

Nor do I wish to suggest that you have to be some kind of
socialist to ruin your agriculture. It helps, as the case of
Burma proves beyond all doubt; once a major rice exporter,
it now can barely feed itself. But, in truth, any kind of detailed government intervention and regulation will do. Ar-
gentina, for instance, which should in all logic be the Canada
of South America, was set on its way to poverty and perhaps
even famine because of a political philosophy which is closer
to fascism than to socialism. But the basic truths remain:
(1) Whatever the situation with regard to industry, agriculture is most productive when individual incentives prevail
and the free market for agricultural produce predominates.
(2) The existing threat of famine in various parts of the
world is largely the derivative of a political ideology that
thinks otherwise.

The intriguing question is why our scholars and scientists
and journalists so resolutely shy away from these truths, and
why they prefer to think and talk about an apocalyptic crisis
in world history rather than a quite mundane and vulgar
crisis in a particular ideology. I think the answer is not so
hard to guess at. There really are a lot of intellectuals in this
world for whom the prospect of saying—or even seeming to
say—a few kind words for capitalism is a fate worse than
death.

5

THE ENVIRONMENTALIST

CRUSADE

THERE IS in the United States a tradition of evangelical reform that has no exact counterpart in any other nation. It emerges, one assumes, from our Protestant origin, with its conception of this new nation as being "a city upon a hill," "a light unto the nations"—in short, as properly striving for and being able to achieve a degree of perfection that is beyond the reach of less blessed peoples elsewhere. All of us, for the most part without even realizing it, subscribe to this American dogma, which is why we constantly find ourselves being enlisted into movements of enthusiastic reformation.

In some respects, this reform impulse is one of our glories. It gives American politics a permanent moral dimension and moral thrust that is entirely proper to a democratic republic, one of whose major functions must be to ennoble the common men and women we all most certainly are. But it has its dangers, too. It is so easy to move from the moral to the moralistic, from a concern for what is right to a passionate self-righteousness, from a desire to improve our social reality to a blind and mindless assault against the real world which so stubbornly fails to conform to our ideological preconceptions. In short, the great temptation which all American reform movements experience is to become a crusade. It is a temptation, alas, that the reform impulse frequently succumbs to, with all the disagreeable results that have always attended upon crusades.

The antislavery movement before the Civil War and the temperance movement before World War I are two examples of reform movements which degenerated into crusades. Both addressed themselves, with commendable fervor, to very real evils: slavery (about which nothing need be said) and working-class alcoholism (whose ravages, we forget, were far more devastating than those of drugs today). Both, in time, permitted their moralistic enthusiasm to overwhelm all prudential judgment, so that both the abolitionist crusade and the prohibitionist crusade ended up by alienating public opinion, despite all sorts of legalistic victories they could proudly point to. And it can be said that their "final solutions"—the Civil War perhaps, the 18th Amendment most certainly—created at least as many problems as they solved. Barry Goldwater to the contrary notwithstanding, extremism in defense of liberty—or virtue, or whatever—is *always* a vice because extremism is but another name for fanaticism which is a vice by definition.

A SERIOUS DANGER

Is the environmentalist movement now in danger of being transformed into such an immoderate and ultimately self-defeating crusade? It certainly is beginning to look that way. This movement began with a massive reservoir of public sympathy. There is no doubt that a competitive economic system does create noxious "externalities"—general effects on our lives that are beyond the purview or control of any single enterprise. But an effort by any single enterprise to take such "externalities" into account would put it at an

immense competitive disadvantage. The only way to cope
with them is by legislation and regulation, and there can be
little question that the public has been, and to a good extent
still is, supportive of such efforts. But there is now considerable evidence that the environmentalist movement has lost its
self-control, or, to put it bluntly, has become an exercise in
ideological fanaticism. It is mindlessly trying to impose its
will—sometimes in utterly absurd and self-contradictory ways,
and very often in unreasonable ways—on a reality that is always recalcitrant to any such imposition, by anyone. And it
is not too hard to predict that, as this becomes more widely
perceived, public opinion will become rapidly less amiable.

Nothing, I think, illustrates so nicely the kind of historical blind alley that environmental extremism seems headed
for than the way in which the Environmental Protection
Agency has involved itself in urban planning. Because urban
sprawl involves extensive use of the automobile, and because
air pollution can then become a serious problem (as in Southern California), the EPA is trying to discourage extensive,
low-density suburban and exurban development. Well,
that's reasonable enough, though even here there are
difficulties.

The difficulties arise because the EPA does not concern itself merely with those areas of the nation where the air is
polluted, or on the verge of being polluted, or in striking
distance of being polluted, but also with those areas where
air pollution in the judgment of the average citizen, or even
of EPA's own scientists, is simply not a real problem. In
these other areas, the EPA proceeds as if its mission were not
to protect Americans from dirty air, but to protect clean air
from Americans. Most of us, not being air-worshippers, are
bound to regard this order of priorities as more than a little
odd. We all like the air to be cleaner rather than dirtier, but
very few of us really want to define our individual lives or
our national purpose in terms of achieving the greatest possible air purity, regardless of cost or consequence. Such an
idea does seem to verge on the fanatical.

Still, in view of the air-pollution problems that do exist, and
of our hitherto neglectful attitude toward them, one might

put a benign interpretation on the EPA's single-minded enthusiasm. After all, sometimes one does initially need such enthusiasm to get things moving at all. But any such benign interpretation is soon put to the test by the fact that the EPA seems not only to be opposed to urban sprawl but to urban concentration as well! For urban concentration, though it may minimize the individual's use of his particular automobile, does produce a large concentration of automobiles and trucks, which do create some degree of air pollution. So the EPA is now insisting that it have the right to approve and disapprove the construction of inner-city convention centers, cultural centers, shopping centers, department stores, parking lots, amusement parks, housing projects, industrial parks, etc. And it is being very grudging in its approvals, highly peremptory in its disapprovals.

Now, this is really bizarre. To begin with, Congress, when it established the EPA, and public opinion, when it supported this reform, certainly never intended to give a handful of bureaucrats such immense powers. If the EPA's conception of its mission is permitted to stand, it will be the single most powerful branch of government, having far greater direct control over our individual lives than Congress, or the Executive, or state and local government. No one ever contemplated such a situation, nor are the American people likely to permit it to endure. Clean air is a good thing —but so is liberty, and so is democracy, and so are many other things.

What makes the situation even more bizarre is that this bureaucratic usurpation of power is wedded to an utterly irresponsible use of such power. For example, in New York City a low-income housing project was delayed for months and finally had to be expensively redesigned because the EPA perceived a threat of "noise pollution." Noise pollution in a New York slum! People are being mugged right and left, children are being bitten by rats, junkies are ripping out the plumbing of decaying tenements—and the EPA is worried about noise pollution! These same EPA officials, of course, go home at night and tranquilly observe their children doing their homework to the accompaniment of thumping, blaring, rock-and-roll music. And if the neighbors should complain, they get very testy.

A MAJOR OBSTACLE

The EPA has now become a major obstacle to the redevelopment of the inner city. It has also become a major obstacle to the development of new suburban communities. Indeed, it seems to be spending much of its time and energy figuring out how to be an obstacle to practically anything that Americans want to do. What began as a movement for environmental temperance has become a crusade for environmental prohibition. It could take some time before Congress and the American people decide to call an end to this crusade, just as it took some time to repeal the 18th Amendment. Nevertheless, it is only a matter of time.

But the area of urban and suburban planning is only one instance of environmentalist crusaders rushing in where more reasonable men would tread more warily. In just about every aspect of American life, the environmentalists are imposing their regulations with all the indiscriminate enthusiasm of Carrie Nation swinging a baseball bat in a saloon. Common sense seems to have gone by the board, as has any notion that it is the responsibility of regulators and reformers to estimate the costs and benefits of their actions.

We all agree that the United States needs desperately to increase its domestic oil production—indeed, dealing with the "energy crisis" threatens to become the very centerpiece of domestic policy. Geologists tell us that offshore drilling along the Atlantic seaboard offers us the best—perhaps the only—opportunity to achieve this aim. The environmentalists promptly declare themselves as adamantly opposed to any such enterprise. Why? Well, there is always the possibility that one of these offshore wells will malfunction, the oil will mix with the waters of the Atlantic Ocean, and many fish will then come to an untimely end. With all due respect to the natural rights of our fellow creatures of the deep, this verges on madness. After all, the high cost of oil is resulting in millions of Americans losing their jobs. Is such "unem-

ployment pollution"—already a fact, not a mere prospect—
really more tolerable than the risk of increasing the mortal-
ity rate among the fish of the Atlantic Ocean? It is interesting to note that such nations as Britain and Norway, which
do not have our tradition of evangelical reform, have no
compunctions about offshore drilling. Precautions against
environmental dangers are taken, but the drilling gets done.
Do we really think that Britain and Norway are more bar-
barous than we are? Or are they merely being more sensible?

Or take the case of the strip-mining of coal. We have enormous reserves of coal which can substitute for oil, and which
can be strip-mined easily, cheaply, and safely. That last feature of strip-mining—the fact that far fewer miners get in-
jured or killed in the process—might seem to be a mighty
argument in its favor. We are so concerned about miners'
safety that we have just enacted complicated (and expensive) rules and regulations governing deep-pit mining. Good
—so strip-mining should be the preferred alternative. But
no: our environmentalists want to prohibit strip-mining altogether. Why? Because it defaces the landscape, at least
temporarily. The question then naturally arises: What price
do we wish to pay to avoid a temporary disfigurement of
the landscape? But it is forbidden to raise this question and
the environmentalists will not even discuss it. Indeed, anyone
who does raise it will quickly find himself being excoriated
and slandered as an unprincipled enemy of the true, the
good, the beautiful.

RECALLING AUDEN

In one of his last poems, the late W. H. Auden wrote:

> Nothing can be loved too much,
> but all things can be loved
> in the wrong way.

One wishes our more rabid environmentalists would take
these lines to heart. They might then reconsider their crusade, which has by now gone beyond the limits of even the
purest reason. Making the world safe for the environment is
not the same thing as making the environment safe for our
world.

tunately, there are no* comprehensive, precise estimates available. But one can get a sense of the magnitude of such costs from the following bits and pieces of information.

• In 1977 U.S. Steel signed a seven-year agreement with federal, state, and local environmental agencies that will require it to spend $600 million over that period to eliminate air pollution from its Clairton Coke Works in Pittsburgh.

• The steel industry as a whole will be spending well over $1 billion annually on pollution controls—and that is a conservative estimate. This expenditure amounts to over one quarter of the industry's total annual capital investment.

• Meeting EPA's 1983 waste pollution standards will cost all of American industry, over the next seven years, about $60 billion for capital equipment and another $12 billion annually in operating and maintenance costs.

• Meeting noise pollution standards, as mandated by Congress and enforced by the Occupational Safety and Health Administration (OSHA), will involve expenditures of over $15 billion in capital costs and $2 billion to $3 billion in operating costs in the years immediately ahead. If these noise standards are raised to the level recommended by the U.S. National Institute for Occupational Safety and Health— a recommendation endorsed by the EPA—the capital costs will climb over $30 billion.

• According to the *Wall Street Journal*, new health regulations in the cotton industry will, in the period from 1977 through 1983, cost some $3 billion. It has been estimated by Professor Murray Weidenbaum that American industry's cost to meet OSHA safety standards in 1977 alone were over $4 billion.

• The EPA is on record—for what that is worth—as calculating that industry's total capital investment requirements for all kinds of pollution control equipment will, in the decade 1972–81, add up to $112 billion.

None of the above figures is particularly reliable, and they may not even be entirely consistent with one another. But they do suffice to give a pretty fair indication of what is going on. Even so, important costs are omitted—those, for example, which involve product redesign or the design of the work place. Thus, the increased cost of housing over these past years results, to a significant degree, from various environmental regulations. And Ewan Clague, former U.S. Commissioner of Labor Statistics, points out that productivity in bituminous mining has decreased 30 percent since 1970, largely as a result of the passage in that year of the Coal Mine Health and Safety Act. These indirect costs are not capitalized, of course, and technically are not "hidden." On the other hand, who would claim that the public appreciates their dimensions?

As one contemplates those numbers, various inferences suggest themselves. One is that a clear distinction ought to be made between "capital spending" and "capital investment." We were told, for instance, that capital investment in 1976 amounted to $121 billion, and economists were somewhat disappointed that this represented only a 7.5 percent increase over 1975. But if, as seems likely, as much as 10 percent of that figure should not have been counted as "capital investment" at all—since it consisted of economically unproductive *expenditures*—where does that leave us? It leaves us, I would suggest, with a net reduction in true capital investment in 1976, the economic effects of which will be with us for years ahead. One such probable effect, a decline in the rate of growth of the American worker's productivity, has already been noticed, though never accounted for.

It may be argued that these economically unproductive expenditures do, after all, create jobs (temporarily) and do contribute to the Gross National Product. But so would the corporate construction of beautiful pyramids, at governmental behest. That would create jobs (temporarily), inflate the GNP, and provide us with a "social good" (a great spectacle). But it would be a cost to the economy, and if our conventional statistics are incapable of showing it as such, then those statistics need revision.

COSTS PASSED ALONG

It is also true that, in many cases, corporations are able to maintain their profit margins by passing on their increased

costs directly to the consumer and indirectly to their stockholders (by holding down dividends) or to their employees
(by granting lower wages than they otherwise might). But
that is what usually happens to corporate taxes; they get
passed on to *someone* since the corporation itself is only an
economic mechanism, not an economic person (except, fic-
titiously, in law). In the world market of today, however,
not all corporations can pass on those costs. In those instances, we get declining businesses, declining industries, and
a sagging economy. In any case, those costs—passed on or not
—should be visible, instead of hidden as they now are. The
Federal Reserve's index of plant capacity, for example, apparently makes no effort to distinguish between capital expenditures and capital investments, and to that degree is
misleading.

It is true, too, that firms can depreciate their uneconomic,
mandated capital expenditures. But that equipment will
have to be replaced as it depreciates with age; we are not
talking about a one-time expense.

The situation we have gotten ourselves into would be ridiculous if it were not so serious. We have been much exercised—and quite rightly—by the fact that the OPEC monopoly has cost this country well over $30 billion in increased
oil prices since 1972. But in that time we have inflicted upon
ourselves much larger economic costs through environmental and other regulations and will continue to do so, perhaps
at an increasing rate.

Yes, these economic costs do buy real "social goods." But
may the price not be too high? Is the resulting inflation of
prices, constriction of productive capacity, and increase in
unemployment worth it? Would it not be appropriate for us
to ask ourselves this question openly, instead of going along
with the environmentalists' pretense—so pleasing to our politicians—that our "social goods" cost us nothing at all? Isn't
it time that business stopped bleating in a general way about
those costs and showed us what they really mean, all the way
down to the bottom line?

7

CAPITALISM, SOCIALISM,

AND NIHILISM

WHENEVER and wherever defenders of "free enterprise," "individual liberty," and "a free society" assemble these days, one senses a peculiar kind of nostalgia in the air. It is a nostalgia for that time when they were busily engaged in confronting their old and familiar enemies, the avowed proponents of a full-blown "collectivist" economic and social order. In the debate with these traditional enemies, advocates of "a free society" have, indeed, done extraordinarily well. It is therefore a source of considerable puzzlement to them that, though the other side seems to have lost the argument, their side seems somehow not to have won it.

Now, I am aware that within this group itself there are different ideological and philosophical tendencies. Friedrich Hayek is not Milton Friedman, for instance, nor vice versa, and there are interesting differences between the 19th-century liberal individualism of the one and the 19th-century radical individualism of the other. Still, these twain do meet—and not only in Switzerland. There can be little doubt, for instance, that their thinking has converged into a powerful attack on the traditional socialist notions of central economic planning and a centrally administered economy. And there is absolutely no doubt, in my own mind, that this attack has been enormously successful—far more successful than one would have dreamed possible 25 years ago.

This attack, like so many successful attacks, has taken the form of a pincer movement. On the one hand, Professor Hayek has explored, in *The Counterrevolution of Science*, the ideological origins in the 19th century of the notion of large-scale "social engineering," and his critical history of what he calls—and of what we now call, after him—"scientism" is a major contribution to the history of ideas. It is in good part because of Professor Hayek's work in this area, and also because of his profound insights—most notably in *The Constitution of Liberty*—into the connection between a free market, the rule of law, and individual liberty, that you don't hear professors saying today, as they used so glibly to say, that "we are all socialists now." They are far more likely to say that the question of socialism is irrelevant and they would prefer not to discuss it.

Milton Friedman, on the other hand, has launched his main attack on "the planned society" through the jungles of social and economic policy, as distinct from the highlands of theory. No other thinker of our time has so brilliantly exposed and publicized the perversities that can be engendered by governmental intervention in the economic life of a nation. Whereas Hayek demonstrated why large-scale, centralized planning does not have the wonderful results it is supposed to, Friedman shows us how governmental rules and regulations so frequently get results that are the opposite of those intended. In addition, Friedman has instructed us all —including most socialists and neo-socialists—in the unsuspected, creative powers of the market as a mechanism for solving social problems. Indeed, we have now reached the stage where planners will solemnly assemble and contemplate ways of using the powers of government *to create markets* in order to reach their goals.

As a result of the efforts of Hayek, Friedman, and the
many others who share their general outlook, the idea of a
centrally planned and centrally administered economy, so
popular in the 1930s and early 1940s, has been discredited.
Even in the socialist nations, economists are more interested
in reviving the market than in permanently burying it.
Whether they can have a market economy without private
property is, of course, an issue they will shortly have to face
up to.

The question then naturally arises: If the traditional economics of socialism has been discredited, why has not the
traditional economics of capitalism been vindicated? I should
say that the reasons behind this state of affairs are quite
obvious and easily comprehensible—only they are terribly
difficult to explain to economists.

ON "THINKING ECONOMICALLY"

The original appeal of the idea of central economic planning—like the traditional appeal of socialism itself—was cast
primarily in economic terms. It was felt that such planning
was necessary to (a) overcome the recurrent crises—i.e.,
depressions—of a market economy, and (b) provide for
steady economic growth and greater material prosperity for
all. This importance which traditional socialism—the Old
Left, as we would call it today—ascribed to economics was
derived from Marxism, which in turn based itself on the
later writings of Marx. But the socialist impulse always had
other ideological strands in it, especially a yearning for "fraternity" and "community," and a revulsion against the "alienation" of the individual in liberal-bourgeois society. These
ideological strands were prominent among the "utopian socialists," as Engels was to label them, and in the early thought
of Karl Marx himself, in which economics received much
less attention than religion and political philosophy. They
are prominent again today, in the thinking of what is called
the "New Left."

The Old Left has been intellectually defeated on its chosen

battleground, i.e., economics. But the New Left is now launching an assault on liberal society from quite other directions. One of the most astonishing features of the New Left—astonishing, at least, to a middle-aged observer—is how little interest it really has in economics. I would put it even more strongly: the identifying marks of the New Left are its refusal *to think economically* and its contempt for bourgeois society precisely because this is a society that does think economically.

What do I mean by "thinking economically"? I have found that it is very hard to convey this meaning to economists, who take it for granted that this is the only possible way for a sensible man to think—that, indeed, thinking economically is the same thing as thinking rationally. Economics is the social science *par excellence* of modernity, and economists as a class find it close to impossible to detach themselves from the philosophical presuppositions of modernity. This would not be particularly significant—until recently has not been particularly significant—were it not for the fact that the New Left is in rebellion against these philosophical presuppositions themselves.

Let me give you a simple illustration. One of the keystones of modern economic thought is that it is impossible to have an *a priori* knowledge of what constitutes happiness for other people; that such knowledge is incorporated in an individual's "utility schedules"; and this knowledge, in turn, is revealed by the choices the individual makes in a free market. This is not merely the keystone of modern economic thought; it is also the keystone of modern, liberal, secular society itself. This belief is so deeply ingrained in us that we are inclined to explain any deviation from it as perverse and pathological. Yet it is a fact that for several millennia, until the advent of modernity, people did not believe any such thing and would, indeed, have found such a belief to be itself shockingly pathological and perverse. For all pre-modern thinkers, *a priori* knowledge of what constituted other people's happiness was not only possible, it was a fact. True, such knowledge was the property of a small elite—religious, philosophical, or political. But this was deemed to be altogether proper: such uncommon knowledge could not be expected to be found among common men. So you did not need a free market or a free society to maximize individual happiness; on the contrary, a free market, not being guided by the wisdom of the elite, was bound to be ultimately frustrating, since the common people could not possibly know what they *really* wanted or what would really yield them "true" happiness.

Now, we know from our experience of central economic planning that this pre-modern approach is fallacious—but if, and only if, you define "happiness'" and "satisfaction" in terms of the material production and material consumption of commodities. If you do not define "happiness" or "satisfaction" in this way, if you refuse to "think economically," then the pre-modern view is more plausible than not. It is, after all, one thing to say that there is no authentically superior wisdom about people's tastes and preferences in commodities; it is quite another thing to deny that there is a superior wisdom about the spiritual dimensions of a good life. Even today, that last proposition does not sound entirely ridiculous to us. And if you believe that man's spiritual life is infinitely more important than his trivial and transient adventures in the marketplace, then you may tolerate a free market for practical reasons, within narrow limits, but you certainly will have no compunctions about overriding it if you think the free market is interfering with more important things.

THE SHAMEFACED COUNTERREVOLUTION

Modern economists are for the most part unaware that their habit of "thinking economically" only makes sense within a certain kind of world, based on certain peculiarly modern presuppositions. They insist that economics is a science, which is certainly true, but only if you accept the premises of modern economics. Thus, one of our most distinguished economists, Ludwig Von Mises, wrote:

Economics is a theoretical science and as such abstains from any

judgment of value. It is not its task to tell people what ends they
should aim at. It is a science of the means to be applied for the
attainment of ends chosen, not . . . a science of the choosing of ends.

That statement sounds terribly modest and uncontroversial and platitudinous. But is it? Is it really so easy to
separate means from ends? What, for example, if we are
members of a monastic community and our end is holy
poverty—not just poverty but holy poverty, a poverty suffused
with a spiritual intention? Can economics help us attain
this end? Or, to take a somewhat less extreme instance:
What if we are loyal members of the kind of Orthodox
Jewish community that even today is to be found in sections of New York City? In such a community, where most
people are engaged in business, there unquestionably is some
role for an economist—but only within narrow limits. In the
end, the superior purpose of such a community is obedience
to sacred Law and meditation on the meaning of this Law.
For the maximization of such an end, economics is of little
use.

Modern, liberal, secular society is based on the revolutionary premise that there is no superior, authoritative information available about the good life or the true nature
of human happiness, that this information is implicit only
in individual preferences, and that therefore the individual
has to be free to develop and express these preferences. What
we are witnessing in Western society today are the beginnings
of a counterrevolution against this conception of man and society. It is a shamefaced counterrevolution, full of bad faith
and paltry sophistry, because it feels compelled to define itself as some kind of progressive extension of modernity instead of, what it so clearly is, a reactionary revulsion
against modernity. It is this failure in self-definition that
gives rise to so much irrelevant controversy.

The debate provoked by the writings of John Kenneth
Galbraith is, it seems to me, a case in point. Galbraith thinks
he is an economist and, if one takes him at his word, it is
easy to demonstrate that he is a bad one. But the truth is
that Galbraith is not really an economist at all; he can be
more accurately described as a reluctant rabbi. His essential

thesis is one familiar to pre-modern moralists and theologians: consumption *ought not to be* a constant function of relative income. Implicit in this thesis are the corollaries that (1) Galbraith knows better than any common man what "utility schedule" will provide all common men with enduring and meaningful satisfaction, and (2) if common men were uncorrupted by capitalist propaganda, they would permit Galbraith to prescribe "utility schedules" for them. Some of Galbraith's critics think they have refuted him when they make all this explicit. What they have done, I should say, is to enlighten him as to his own true purpose. That he so stubbornly resists such enlightenment is to be explained by his naive conviction that, because he is attacking bourgeois society, he must be a "progressive" thinker.

THE NEW LEFT VS. "ECONOMIC MAN"

A similar confusion, I should say, arises in connection with what we call the "environmentalist" movement. Economists and politicians both—the one with naivety, the other with cunning—have decided to give a literal interpretation to the statements of this movement. And, given this literal interpretation, the thrust of environmentalism is not particularly subversive. If people today are especially concerned about clean air and clean water, then economic analysis can show them different ways—with different costs and benefits—of getting varying degrees of clean air and clean water. But it turns out that your zealous environmentalists do not want to be shown anything of the sort. They are not really interested in clean air or clean water at all. What *does* interest them is modern industrial society and modern technological civilization, toward which they have profoundly hostile sentiments. When they protest against "the quality of life" in this society and this civilization, they are protesting against nothing so trivial as air or water pollution. Rather they are at bottom rejecting a liberal civilization which is given shape through the interaction of a countless sum of individual preferences. Since they do not like the shape of that civilization, they are moved to challenge—however indirectly or slyly—the process that produces this shape. What environmentalists really want is very simple: they want the authority, the power to create an "environment" which pleases them; and this "environment" will be a society where the rulers will not want to "think economically" and the ruled will not be permitted to do so.

Something similar is going on with the "consumers' protection movement," whose true aim is not to "protect" the consumer but rather to circumscribe—and ultimately abolish —his "sovereignty." The objection to such sovereignty is that common people *do* "think economically" when they are liberated from traditional constraints and are encouraged to do whatever they think best for themselves. The "consumers' protection movement," like the "environmentalist" movement, is a revulsion against the kind of civilization that common men create when they are given the power, which a market economy does uniquely give them, to shape the world in which they wish to live.

I think we can summarize our situation as follows: the Old Left accepted the idea of the common good proposed by bourgeois-liberal society. The essential ingredients of this idea were material prosperity and technological progress. Bourgeois liberalism insisted that individual liberty was a precondition of this common good; the Old Left insisted that centralized planning was a precondition but that individual liberty would be an eventual consequence. The experience of the post-World War II decades has revealed that the Old Left simply could not compete with bourgeois liberalism in this ideological debate. The result has been the emergence of a New Left which implicitly rejects both the bourgeois-liberal and the Old Left idea of the common good, and which therefore rejects (again implicitly, for the most part) the ideological presuppositions of modernity itself. This movement, which seeks to end the sovereignty over our civilization of the common man, must begin by seeking the death of "economic man," because it is in the marketplace that this sovereignty is most firmly established. It thinks of itself as a "progressive" movement, whereas its import is regressive. This is one of the reasons why the New Left, every day and in every way, comes more and more to resemble the Old Right, which never did accept the liberal-bourgeois revolutions of the 18th and 19th centuries.

THE INADEQUACIES OF LIBERALISM

One is bound to wonder at the inadequacies of bourgeois liberalism that have made it so vulnerable, first to the Old Left and now to the New. These inadequacies do not, in themselves, represent a final judgment upon it; every civilization has its necessary costs and benefits. But it does seem to be the case that, in certain periods, a civilization will have greater difficulty striking an acceptable balance than in others, and that sometimes it arrives at a state of permanent and precarious "tilt" for reasons it cannot quite comprehend. What it is important to realize, and what contemporary social science finds it so hard to perceive, is that such reasons are not necessarily new events or new conditions; they may merely be older inadequacies—long since recognized by some critics—that have achieved so cumulative an effect as to become, suddenly, and seemingly inexplicably, intolerable.

Certainly, one of the key problematic aspects of bourgeois-liberal society has long been known and announced. This is the fact that liberal society is of necessity a secular society, one in which religion is mainly a private affair. Such a disestablishment of religion, it was predicted by Catholic thinkers and others, would gradually lead to a diminution of religious faith and a growing skepticism about the traditional consolations of religion—especially the consolations offered by a life after death. That has unquestionably happened, and with significant consequences. One such consequence is that the demands placed upon liberal society, in the name of temporal "happiness," have become ever more urgent and ever more unreasonable. In every society, the overwhelming majority of the people lead lives of considerable frustration, and if society is to endure, it needs to be able to rely on a goodly measure of stoical resignation. In theory, this could be philosophical rather than religious; in fact, philosophical stoicism has never been found suitable for mass consumption. Philosophical stoicism has always been an aristocratic prerogative; it has never been able to give an acceptable rationale of "one's station and one's duties" to those whose stations are low and whose duties are onerous. So liberal civilization finds itself having spiritually expropriated the masses of its citizenry, whose demands for material compensation gradually become as infinite as the infinity they have lost. All of this was clearly foreseen by many of the anti-modern critics who witnessed the birth of modernity.

Another, and related, consequence of the disestablishment of religion as a publicly sanctioned mythos has been the inability of liberal society ever to come up with a convincing and generally accepted theory of political obligation. Liberal philosophers have proposed many versions of utilitarianism to this end, but these have remained academic exercises and have not had much popular impact. Nor is this surprising: No merely utilitarian definition of civic loyalty is going to convince anyone that it makes sense for him to die for his country. In actual fact, it has been the secular myth of nationalism which, for the past century and a half, has provided this rationale. But this secular myth, though it has evolved hand in hand with bourgeois society, is not intrinsically or necessarily bourgeois. Nationalism ends by establishing "equal sacrifice" as the criterion of justice; and this is no kind of bourgeois criterion. We have seen, in our own day, how the spirit of nationalism can be utterly contemptuous of bourgeois proprieties, and utterly subversive of the bourgeois order itself.

THE DEPLETION OF MORAL CAPITAL

Even the very principles of individual opportunity and social mobility, which originally made the bourgeois-liberal idea so attractive, end up—once the spirit of religion is weakened—by creating an enormous problem for bourgeois society. This is the problem of publicly establishing an acceptable set of rules of distributive justice. The problem does not arise so long as the bourgeois ethos is closely linked to what we call the Puritan or Protestant ethos, which prescribes a connection between personal merit—as represented by such bourgeois virtues as honesty, sobriety, diligence, and thrift—and worldly success. But from the very beginnings of modern capitalism there has been a different and equally influential definition of distributive justice. This definition, propagated by Mandeville and Hume, is purely positive and secular rather than philosophical or religious. It says that, under capitalism, whatever is, is just—that all the inequalities of liberal-bourgeois society must be necessary, or else the free market would not have created them, and therefore they must be justified. This point of view makes no distinction between the speculator and the bourgeois-entrepreneur: both are selfish creatures who, in the exercise of their private vices (greed, selfishness, avarice), end up creating public benefits.

Let us leave aside the intellectual deficiencies of this conception of justice—I myself believe these deficiencies are radical—and ask ourselves the question which several contemporaries of Mandeville and Hume asked before us: Will this positive idea of distributive justice commend itself to the people? Will they accept it? Will they revere it? Will they defend it against its enemies? The answer, I submit, is as obvious as it is negative. Only a philosopher could be satisfied with an *ex post facto* theory of justice. Ordinary people will see it merely as a self-serving ideology; they insist on a more "metaphysical" justification of social and economic inequalities. In the absence of such a justification, they will see more sense in simple-minded egalitarianism than in the discourses of Mandeville or Hume. And so it has been: As the connection between the Protestant ethic and liberal-bourgeois society has withered away, the egalitarian temper has grown ever more powerful.

For well over a hundred and fifty years now, social critics have been warning us that bourgeois society was living off the accumulated moral capital of traditional religion and traditional moral philosophy, and that once this capital was depleted, bourgeois society would find its legitimacy ever more questionable. These critics were never, in their lifetime, either popular or persuasive. The educated classes of liberal-bourgeois society simply could not bring themselves to believe that religion or philosophy was that important to a polity. *They* could live with religion or morality as a purely private affair, and they could not see why everyone else—after a proper secular education, of course—could not do likewise. Well, I think it is becoming clear that religion, and a moral philosophy associated with religion, is far more important politically than the philosophy of liberal individualism admits. Indeed, I would go further and say that it is becoming clearer every day that even those who thought they were content with a religion that was a private affair are themselves discovering that such a religion is existentially unsatisfactory.

LIBERTARIANISM AND LIBERTINISM

But if the grave problems that secularization would inevitably produce for liberal-bourgeois society were foreseen, if only in general terms, not all the problems that our liberal society faces today were foreseen. While many critics predicted a dissolution of this society under certain stresses and strains, none predicted—none could have predicted—the blithe and mindless self-destruction of bourgeois society which we are witnessing today. *The enemy of liberal capitalism today is not so much socialism as nihilism.* Only liberal capitalism doesn't see nihilism as an enemy, but rather as just another splendid business opportunity.

One of the most extraordinary features of our civilization today is the way in which the "counterculture" of the New Left is being received and sanctioned as a "modern" culture appropriate to "modern" bourgeois society. Large corporations today happily publish books and magazines, or press and sell records, or make and distribute movies, or sponsor television shows which celebrate pornography, denounce the

institution of the family, revile the "ethics of acquisitive-
ness," justify civil insurrection, and generally argue in favor
of the expropriation of private industry and the "liquidation" of private industrialists. Some leaders of the New Left
are sincerely persuaded that this is part of a nefarious conspiracy to emasculate them through "cooptation." In this, as
in almost everything else, they are wrong. There is no such
conspiracy—one is almost tempted to add, "alas." Our capitalists promote the ethos of the New Left for only one reason:
they cannot think of any reason why they should not. For
them, it is "business as usual."

And indeed, why shouldn't they seize this business opportunity? The prevailing philosophy of liberal capitalism gives
them no argument against it. Though Milton Friedman's writings on this matter are not entirely clear—itself an odd
and interesting fact, since he is usually the most pellucid of
thinkers—one gathers that he is, in the name of "libertarian-
ism," reluctant to impose any prohibition or inhibition on
the libertine tendencies of modern bourgeois society. He
seems to assume, as I read him, that one must not interfere
with the dynamics of "self-realization" in a free society. He
further seems to assume that these dynamics cannot, in the
nature of things, be self-destructive—that "self-realization"
in a free society can only lead to the creation of a self that
is compatible with such a society. I don't think it has been
sufficiently appreciated that Friedman is the heir, not only to
Hume and Mandeville, but to modern romanticism too. In
the end, you can maintain the belief that private vices, freely
exercised, will lead to public benefits only if you are further
persuaded that human nature can never be utterly corrupted by these vices, but rather will always transcend them.
The idea of bourgeois virtue has been eliminated from Friedman's conception of bourgeois society, and has been replaced by the idea of individual liberty. The assumption is
that, in "the nature of things," the latter will certainly lead
to the former. There is much hidden metaphysics here, and
of a dubious kind.

And Hayek, too, though obviously hostile in temperament
and mood to the new nihilism, has no grounds for opposing

it in principle. When Hayek criticizes "scientism," he does indeed write very much like a Burkean Whig, with a great emphasis on the superior wisdom implicit in tradition, and on the need for reverence toward traditional institutions that incorporate this wisdom. But when he turns to a direct contemplation of present-day society, he too has to fall back on a faith in the ultimate benefits of "self-realization"—a phrase he uses as infrequently as possible, but which he is nevertheless forced to use at crucial instances. And what if the "self" that is "realized" under the conditions of liberal capitalism is a self that despises liberal capitalism, and uses its liberty to subvert and abolish a free society? To this question, Hayek—like Friedman—has no answer.

And yet this is *the* question we now confront, as our society relentlessly breeds more and more such selves, whose private vices in no way provide public benefits to a bourgeois order. Perhaps one can say that the secular, "libertarian" tradition of capitalism—as distinct from the Protestant-bourgeois tradition—simply had too limited an imagination when it came to vice. It never really could believe that vice, when unconstrained by religion, morality, and law, might lead to viciousness. It never really could believe that self-destructive nihilism was an authentic and permanent possibility that any society had to guard against. It could refute Marx effectively, but it never thought it would be called upon to refute the Marquis de Sade and Nietzsche. It could demonstrate that the Marxist vision was utopian; but it could not demonstrate that the utopian vision of Fourier—the true ancestor of our New Left—was wrong. It was, in its own negligent way, very much a bourgeois tradition in that, while ignoring the bourgeois virtues, it could summon up only a bourgeois vision of vice.

THE HUNGER FOR LEGITIMACY

Today, the New Left is rushing in to fill the spiritual vacuum at the center of our free and capitalist society. For the most part, it proclaims itself as "socialist," since that is the only tradition available to it. It unquestionably feeds upon the

old, socialist yearnings for community—for a pre-individual-
ist society—and is therefore, if not collectivist, at least
"communalist" in its economics and politics. But it is also
nihilistic in its insistence that, under capitalism, the individual must be free to create his own morality. The New
Left is best seen as a socialist heresy, in that it refuses to
"think economically" in any serious way. One might say it is
a socialist heresy that corresponds to the liberal heresy it is
confronting: the heresy of a "free society" whose individuals
are liberated from the bourgeois ethos that used to bind
them together in a bourgeois-liberal community. And as the
"free society" produces material affluence, but also moral and
political anarchy, so the New Left—even as it pushes individual liberty beyond anarchy itself—longs for a moral and
political community in which "thinking economically" will
be left to our Helots, the machines. In all their imagined
utopian communities, the free individual who contracts for
"the good life" has to surrender both his individualism and
his freedom.

It is in the nature of heresies to take a part for the whole.
Thus, our version of the "free society" is dedicated to the
proposition that to be free is to be good. The New Left,
though it echoes this proposition when it is convenient for
its purposes, is actually dedicated to the counter-belief—
which is the pre-liberal proposition—that to be good is
to be free. In the first case, the category of goodness is
emptied of any specific meaning; in the second case, it is the
category of freedom which is emptied of any specific meaning. In the war between these two heresies, the idea of a free
society that is in some specific sense virtuous (the older
"bourgeois" ideal) and the idea of a good community that is
in some specific sense free (the older "socialist" ideal as represented, say, by European social democracy) are both emas-
culated; and the very possibility of a society that can be
simultaneously virtuous and free, i.e., that organically weds
order to liberty, becomes ever more remote.

And yet no society that fails to celebrate the union of order and liberty, in some specific and meaningful way, can
ever hope to be accepted as legitimate by its citizenry. The

hunger for such legitimacy is, I should say, the dominant political fact in the world today—in the "free" nations and among the "socialist" countries as well. It is instructive, and rather sad, to observe the enormous popularity of the recent TV serial, *The Forsyte Saga*, in both capitalist and socialist societies. Obviously, it evoked a profound nostalgia for an order—a society where virtue and freedom were reconciled, however imperfectly—which some of these nations had lost, and which others had never even known. I should say that something of the sort also explains the international popularity of *Fiddler on the Roof*, which gives us a picture of a different kind of legitimate order—a picture that has obvious appeal even to people who do not know the difference between the Talmud and the Code Napoleon.

I find even more pathetic the efforts of the governments of the "free world" and of the "socialist" nations to achieve some minimum legitimacy by imitating one another. The "free societies" move haltingly toward collectivism, in the hope that this will calm the turbulence that agitates them and threatens to tear them apart. The "socialist" nations take grudging steps toward "liberalization," for the same purpose. The results, in both cases, are perverse. Each such step, so far from pacifying the populace, further provokes them, since each such step appears as a moral justification of the turbulence that caused it.

What medicine does one prescribe for a social order that is sick because it has lost its soul? Our learned doctors, the social scientists, look askance at this kind of "imaginary" illness, which has dramatic physical symptoms but no apparent physical causes. Some, on what we conventionally call the "right," cannot resist the temptation to conclude that the patient is actually in robust health, and that only his symptoms are sick. Others, on what we conventionally call the "left," declare that the patient is indeed sick unto death and assert that it is his symptoms which are the causes of his malady. Such confusion, of course, is exactly what one would expect when both patient and doctors are suffering from the same mysterious disease.

PART TWO

The Corporation
and the Dinosaur

8

THE CORPORATION
AND THE DINOSAUR

EVERY DAY, in every way, the large corporations look more and more like a species of dinosaur on its lumbering way to extinction. The cultural and political environment becomes ever more hostile; natural adaptation becomes ever more difficult; possible modes of survival seem to be beyond its imaginative capacity.

That the cultural environment is hostile is obvious enough. Today, businessmen, and especially corporate executives, are just about the only class of people which a television drama will feel free to cast as pure villains. Jews and blacks and teachers and journalists and social workers and politicians and trade union leaders and policemen—and just about everyone else—are given protective coloration on the television screen. Where one of them goes bad, there is sure to be a good one nearby, lest the viewers get the impression that it is proper to have a low opinion of the class as a whole. The business executive gets no such dramatic compensation. He is the only unadulterated bad guy. And since these programs are for the most part sponsored by large corporations, which regard them as suitable vehicles for advertising their products, the public is all the more encouraged to believe what it sees.

Among politicians, too, the businessman—and especially the corporate executive—has become the target of opportunity. True, there have always been politicians hostile to business, but they used to constitute a minority. Now, it takes a brave politician not to be hostile to business. If any United States Senator has publicly denounced the scandalous way in which the oil companies have been made the whipping boys for the oil crisis, it has escaped my notice. And every attorney general, in every city and state, knows that his political future will be much enhanced if he announces an investigation into supposed "illegal practices" of large corporations. Most such investigations quietly peter out; but the headlines they engendered endure, and help shape popular opinion.

Just why the climate has turned so hostile to business is a long and complicated story—about as long and complicated as the story of how the dinosaur's environment turned unfavorable to him. It suffices to say that, though it takes time for an institution to experience an environmental crisis, it takes only time. Yesterday it was the university; today it is the large corporation; tomorrow it will doubtless be the mammoth trade union. (In Great Britain, that tomorrow is today.) The question is not how to avoid such crises—they are inevitable—but how to cope with them. And coping means adaptation, *painful* adaptation. If it's not painful, that's a sure sign it's not adaptation.

But, even given an authentic willingness to adapt, one also has to have a sense of the nature of the crisis. Otherwise one doesn't know how to adapt. And it is fairly clear that the American corporation today really doesn't understand what has happened to it in these past decades. It doesn't understand that, whereas the American democratic environment used to perceive it as being a merely economic institution, it now sees it as being to an equal degree a sociological and political institution, and demands that it behave as such. As is usual, in retrospect that change has an air of inevitability about it. A democracy is not likely to permit huge and powerful institutions, with multiple "spillover" effects on large sections of the population, to define their interests in a limited way or to go about pursuing them in a single-minded way. It insists that such institutions show a proper attentiveness to what is conceived to be, at any moment, "the public interest." Nor is it any kind of answer to say that, in the long run, the institution's single-mindedness will be for the good of all. In a democracy, large and powerful institutions, if they seek legitimacy in public opinion, must be visibly and currently attentive to the public interest.

In short, the large corporations used to be a single-purpose institution: an economic institution directed toward economic growth. It was very good at this job, would still be good at this job, but its very size and importance have resulted in its job assignment being changed. Small business can still be single-minded in its pursuit of profitability just as small colleges can still be single-minded in their pursuit of education in the traditional way. But the large corporation, like the large university, impinges on too many people in too drastic a way. And so the executives of the large corporation, like the administrators of the large university, have to learn to govern, not simply to execute or administer. And to govern is to think "politically"—i.e., institutionally—as well as economically or educationally. That is the price of bigness and power.

It will be asked: Won't this have negative consequences for economic growth? Probably, and the corporations should say so. But if a democratic people prefer to sacrifice economic growth in favor of institutions which reassure them as to the reality of popular sovereignty, that is their prerogative. It is a dangerous illusion for the corporation to think that it is predestined by its nature to be an advocate of, and necessarily a propagandist for, economic growth and dynamic change at all costs. True, most corporate executives have an extraordinary aptitude for managing dynamic growth. But in the "natural" environment of today, that aptitude could lead to extinction of the species.

The difference between "thinking economically" and "thinking politically," as I have pointed out, is enormous. Thus one wonders what happened in the boardrooms of the major oil companies in 1973, when those lovely fourth-quarter profits began to roll in. These profits, after all, were directly connected with the hardship, inconvenience, and discomfort then being experienced by the American people. Did the directors and top executives sit around gloomily, muttering: "O Lord, we've got a terrible problem on our hands. What on earth can we do?" This may have been the case with one or two companies, but it obviously did not happen in the main, since nothing was done to cope with the problem. Nothing, that is, except for the preparation of a few press releases containing specious and self-serving arguments.

One such specious argument was to the effect that this new profitability merely brought the return on capital for the oil companies up to the average of all manufacturing companies. This is true, but what kind of argument is it? For all corporations to claim a "right" to an average return on capital is rather like all Americans claiming a "right" to the average family income, or all employees of oil companies claiming a "right" to the average wage for the industry. There is no such "right," and only a fanatical egalitarian would imagine it. Corporate executives are not ordinarily such egalitarians, but apparently they are capable of thinking that way, given sufficient temptation.

Another specious argument was to the effect that most of these swollen profits would be reinvested in the search for oil, the construction of new refineries, and so on. Once again, this argument is true, but what kind of argument is it? One needn't be a left-wing economist to perceive that such a rein-vestment of capital would ultimately result in enriching the company (and its stockholders, and its stock-holding executives) by increasing its assets. And yet, in their publicity, the oil companies point to this intention as evidence of their public spiritedness, pure and simple.

REASSURING THE PUBLIC

Had the oil companies been "thinking politically," there were many things they could have done—some small, some big, all reassuring to the public. For instance, why didn't it occur to one of the companies to announce that, despite these profits, it would declare no increase in dividends or in executives' salaries this year? It might not have helped much, but it could have helped a little. In a bolder vein, why shouldn't the oil companies have simply decided that they couldn't *afford* such large profits in these circumstances? They then could have set the price of oil at a level which would have generated a 15 percent or 20 percent increase in profits, instead of the more spectacular percentages that made the headlines. This would not really have helped the consumer much—not by more than a few pennies, one is told— but it would have helped the oil companies a great deal.

The reason, presumably, that the oil companies did not do this was because they wanted to raise the capital necessary to do "their job." But no large corporation today is free to define its "job" as it sees fit. Had the oil companies been "thinking politically," they would have realized that they had another and more responsible task—securing the trust and confidence and good will of the public. And this second mission, since it is the precondition of survival, must have priority over the first. As it is, the price for "thinking economically" is now being paid. The oil companies will, in the end, surrender a large portion of their profits while shouldering a full portion of public obloquy. Meanwhile *all* American corporations have lost some of their credit with the public.

9

ETHICS AND

THE CORPORATION

AT A TIME when, for all the reasons I have been discussing, the reputation of business in general is low, when the standing in popular opinion of the large, publicly owned corporation is even lower, and when there is a keen post-Watergate concern for probity among officials of all organizations, public or private—at such a time one would expect corporate executives to be especially sensitive even to appearances of conflict of interest, or to the mildest deviations from strict standards of fiduciary behavior. Yet this seems not, on the whole, to be the case.

I do not wish to be misunderstood. The majority of corporate executives are certainly honest and honorable men. This, however, is rather like saying that the majority of New York City's police officers are honest and honorable men. Of course they are. But the statement itself implies that a not altogether insignificant minority are less than that, and the presence of such a minority is fairly taken to constitute a rather serious problem. In the case of the corporation, the situation is worsened by the fact that, whereas honest cops will usually express open indignation at corrupt ones, corporate executives almost never criticize other corporate executives, even when these latter are caught in *flagrante delicto*. No one seems to be "read out" of the corporate community, which inevitably leads the outsider to wonder whether this community has any standards of self-government at all.

But to talk in terms of "corruption" is misleading. Problems of corporate ethics only rarely arise out of illegal actions by corporate executives. Such illegal actions are doubtless more frequent than they ought to be, and the response of the business community certainly is far more lethargic than it ought to be, but in the end such illegalities are quite efficiently disposed of by law enforcement officers. The more common and significant issues in corporate ethics arise from practices which are not illegal, but which seem to reveal a shockingly naive unconcern both for the interests of stockholders and the good opinion of the public. Too many corporate executives seem to be under the illusion that they *are* the corporation. The problem here is rarely one of wicked motives but rather of a bland self-righteousness which does not even perceive an abuse of power for what it is.

ETHICS AND LAW

Take, for instance, a rather extreme and somewhat marginal case: the recent efforts of several smaller corporations which, having gone public during the boom years of the 1960s, now wish to "go private." When such a corporation originally went public, the controlling stockholder sold a portion of his shares at a price substantially higher than the present market price. Now, disillusioned by the contemptuous way the stock market treats "his" firm, he uses his power to have the corporation repurchase, *with corporate funds*, that "public" stock. He ends up, if successful, owning the corporation all over again *and* with a substantial capital gain from the original sale of his stock. However innocent the intentions of the controlling stockholder, the whole operation really amounts to a way for a privately held corporation to use the mechanism of "going public" in order to trade profitably in its own stock.

Apparently, if incomprehensibly, this procedure is perfectly legal. All right: the law will have its loopholes. But is this way of doing business *ethically acceptable* to the financial and corporate communities? There is no doubt that the public which originally purchased this stock is now under the distinct impression that it has been fleeced. That is certainly undesirable, especially since these stockholders usually own stock in other corporations too, and their indignation is all too likely to spill over and touch all corporations. So why does one not observe the Boards of Directors of the New York and American stock exchanges denouncing such a procedure and taking what actions they can to discourage it? Why does one not hear the heads of major Wall Street houses similarly come to the defense of the shareholders? Why don't corporate executives, individually or collectively, put themselves on record? Don't they care?

One supposes they do care; indignant and resentful stockholders are what the financial and business communities least need these days. But apparently they do not regard it as a matter that directly concerns them. Every executive assumes that so long as he personally behaves in a way that is above reproach, he has discharged his moral obligations. This is a fateful error. Precisely because there is never enough individual moral sensitivity to go around, every profession must protect its good name with a measure of collective self-discipline. And it should be clear that if the business community makes so little effort to discipline itself, then the government will step in and do the disciplining for it. That is the least desirable but most predictable outcome.

More directly affecting the large corporations, and therefore with a clear consequence for the good reputation of "big business" generally, is the way in which several firms are fiddling around with stock options for their executives.

The officers of a major corporation, for instance, are voting themselves the right to borrow money from the firm so that they will not have to sell out their positions in the company's stock—positions they acquired through stock options financed in turn by bank loans. Because of the decline in the value of the firm's stock, these executives are faced with margin calls from the banks. They stand to lose a lot of money if they cannot answer these calls. So they are transferring these loans to the company, and are justifying this action by the assertion that they will be able to do their job better if they are not distracted by personal financial worries.

It is all very odd, to put it mildly. To begin with, what kind of relief do these executives obtain by virtue of going into debt to "their" corporation rather than to the banks? A debt is a debt, after all. Why should a corporate executive be less "distracted" if he owes money to his employer instead of to a bank or a brokerage house or a personal loan company? If he does achieve greater peace of spirit, it can only be because there exists in the back of his mind the notion that, at some point, the corporation will be a more indulgent creditor. But this in turn raises even more serious questions about the ethical status of this arrangement.

Besides, many of the forty thousand stockholders of this corporation are in, or have been in, exactly the same situation as these executives, and the corporation certainly never did anything to help *them* cope with margin calls. Is it really the company's view that it is wrong for its executives to lose money in the company's stock but a matter of indifference to it if anyone else does? If a company does badly, and its stock falls, are executives a privileged group to be "made whole" through the use of company funds? The company would surely repudiate both of these propositions. Yet its actions in effect assert them.

Or take the case of another large corporation. Its shares, too, have gone way down, thereby making the stock options of its executives worthless. So the company has simply reduced by 50 percent the price at which these options may be exercised. Again, the assumption seems to be that, even though all stockholders are suffering, corporate executives must not lose money in the company's stock or, in this case, must not fail to make money in the company's stock. But the conventional argument in favor of stock options is that executives are offered an incentive for superior performance. What kind of incentive is it that rewards good and poor performance indifferently?

Now, the case of these two corporations has been amply reported in the *Wall Street Journal* and elsewhere. (Since I am interested in making only a general point, there is little to be gained by naming them accusingly.) What I find most interesting is the reaction within the business community. Or, to be exact, the absence of any discernible reaction. Why, for example, hasn't one of the prestigious organizations of businessmen thought it proper to suggest a code governing the use and abuse of stock options? It seems to have occurred to no one. Instead, the stock exchanges are mute, the major brokerage houses are mute, the corporate community is mute. Is it surprising, therefore, that there are thousands of stockholders out there whose loyalty to the corporation as an institution has been subverted? Is it surprising that these stockholders should infer from their experiences that more rather than less government regulation of corporations is desirable?

One reads with a kind of despair those recurring reports of corporate executives who, having brought their corporations to the brink of ruin, and their stockholders to the brink of desolation, "resign" with huge cash benefits. Thus, an executive of such a corporation recently departed with a $2 million cash payment to console him for the loss of his position. Nor is his case so unusual. It is a fact that the corporate community often more nearly resembles a corporate club, in which the genial spirit of "clubbiness" ensures that everyone is adequately provided for. Nonmembers, of course —stockholders and employees—must learn to cope with the harsh rigors of free enterprise.

It might be said that all this is little more than the froth on the surface of corporate life, of no great significance to the basic economic mission of the corporation, and only remotely relevant to its success in accomplishing that mission.

That is true, but somewhat beside the point. The point is that American corporations do have a critical problem with public opinion, and to cope with this problem spend tens of millions of dollars a year on "public relations." Yet a number of these corporations then proceed to behave in such a way as to offend and outrage the corporation's natural constituency: the stockholders. More important, the business community as a whole remains strangely passive and silent before this spectacle. This disquieting silence speaks far more eloquently to the American people than the most elaborate public relations campaign. And it conveys precisely the wrong message.

10

HORATIO ALGER

AND PROFITS

OVER THESE past few years, I have been attending many conferences of businessmen, and it almost always happens that someone will intervene to inquire plaintively: "What can we do to make the profit motive respectable once again?" Or: "Why, in view of the general prosperity which the free exercise of the profit motive has brought to our society, is it held in such low esteem—indeed, in contempt—by intellectuals, academics, students, the media, politicians, even our very own children?" Or: "Why is the profit-seeking businessman, who creates affluence for everyone, a somewhat less than reputable figure in American society today?"

Whatever the precise wording, it's a fascinating and important question. In some ways, it may be the most important question confronting our liberal-capitalist society. There can be no doubt that, if business as an occupation and businessmen as a class continue to drift in popular opinion from the center of respectability to its margins, then liberal capitalism—and our liberal political system with it—has precious little chance for survival.

But, as phrased, it is also the wrong question in the sense that it reveals how anti-business opinion has shaped the thinking and the language of businessmen themselves. For the idea that the businessman is ruled solely by the "profit motive," that he is simply an acquisitive creature lusting after the greatest possible gain, and that liberal-capitalist society is nothing more than an "acquisitive society," was originally proposed as *an indictment* of our socioeconomic system, and is still taken by many to be exactly that.

Indeed, if the description is true, the indictment is inevitable. Who on earth wants to live in a society in which all—or even a majority—of one's fellow citizens are fully engaged in the hot pursuit of money, the single-minded pursuit of material self-interest? To put it another way: Who wants to live in a society in which selfishness and self-seeking are celebrated as primary virtues? Such a society is unfit for human habitation; thus sayeth the Old Testament, the New Testament, the Koran, the Greek philosophers, the medieval theologians, all of modern moral philosophy. So if capitalism is what this indictment claims it is—if it is what so many businessmen today seem to think it is—then it is doomed, and properly.

But this is not what a liberal-capitalist society is supposed to be like, and it was only in recent decades that anyone thought it was supposed to be like that. As a matter of fact, if this had been the original idea of capitalism, it could never have come into existence—not in a civilization still powerfully permeated by Christian values and Christian beliefs. Certainly capitalism did free the spirit of commercial enterprise from its feudal and mercantilist fetters. It did legitimate the pursuit of self-interest *rightly understood*. And when this capitalist ethic is itself rightly understood *as an ethic*, it turns out to be something quite different from a mere unleashing of "the profit motive."

BUSINESSMEN AS HEROES

If one wants to appreciate the moral dimensions of the liberal-capitalist perspective, there is no better place to look than in the Horatio Alger novels, the only substantial body of American literature where businessmen are heroes rather than villains. These novels, of course, are no longer read today. But prior to World War II, they were still in wide circulation and were being avidly read by adolescent boys. They had by then been enormously popular for half a century, so presumably they corresponded to certain deep American beliefs. And what does one discover when one returns to a reading of Horatio Alger? Well, one discovers nothing like a celebration of "the profit motive," pure and simple. Instead, one finds a moral conception of business as an honorable vocation for honorable men. A profitable vocation, to be sure. *But profitable because honorable,* not vice versa.

The basic assumption of Horatio Alger is that the life of business is a good life because it helps develop certain admirable traits of character: probity, diligence, thrift, self-reliance, self-respect, candor, fair dealing, and so on—all those "bourgeois virtues" which no one quite believes in any more. A young man who enters the vocation of business must have these virtues latent within him, or else he cannot succeed honorably. And if he does succeed honorably, he will represent these virtues in their fullest form. Horatio Alger's success stories are also full-blooded morality tales.

It is also important to notice what Horatio Alger does not say. He does not say you cannot succeed otherwise; "speculators" and "freebooters" (wheeler-dealers) may indeed become wealthy, but such types are not honorable businessmen. Despite their wealth, they are never "success stories," since they have only enriched but not "bettered" themselves; their characters have been in no way improved by their active lives. Nor does he say that success under capitalism is an analogue to the "survival of the fittest" in nature: the law of the jungle is no suitable model for human association in society. He does not state that "private vices" (e.g., selfishness, greed, avarice) are justifiable because they may result in "public benefits" (e.g., economic growth); he insists on a continuity between private ethics and the social ethic of a good society. All of these other apologia for liberal capitalism, which we are familiar with, are curtly

dismissed by him as unacceptable to anyone with a more
than rudimentary moral sensibility.

Now, it is true that Horatio Alger wrote fiction, not fact.
But it will not do to dismiss him as a mere fancifier and myth-
maker. To begin with, he would never have been so popular,
for so long, if his conception of American society had been
utterly fanciful. His readers understood that he was writing
stories, not sociology, but they apparently perceived some
connection between his stories and the reality of their socioeconomic order. There was in fact such a connection, which
even we can still dimly perceive. Some of us are old
enough to remember that there was a time when the only
thing more reprehensible than buying on the installment
plan was selling on the installment plan; it encouraged "feck-
lessness." And we still have some business institutions which
could only have been founded in Horatio Alger's world.
Thus, on the floors of our various stock and commodity exchanges, transactions involving millions of dollars take place
on the basis of nothing more than mutual trust: there, a businessman's word is his bond. Imagine trying to set up such
institutions today! A thousand lawyers, to say nothing of
the SEC, would be quick to tell you that such confidence in
the honor of businessmen is inconsistent with sound business
practices.

What the 20th century has witnessed is the degradation of
the bourgeois-capitalist ethic into a parody of itself—indeed, into something resembling what the critics of liberal
capitalism had always accused it of being. These critics,
intellectuals and men of letters above all, never did like
modern liberal society because it was "vulgar"; it permitted
ordinary men and women, in the marketplace, to determine
the shape of this civilization, a prerogative that intellectuals
and men of letters have always claimed for themselves. (This
is why so many intellectuals and men of letters naturally tend
to favor some form of benevolent despotism, in our time
called a "planned society.") But their criticism was relatively ineffectual so long as liberal capitalism was contained
within a bourgeois way of life and sustained by a bourgeois
ethos, the way of life and the ethos celebrated by Horatio

Alger. The common man has always preferred bourgeois capitalism to its intellectual critics; in the United States, for the most part, he still does.

But the trouble is that capitalism outgrew its bourgeois origins and became a system for the impersonal liberation and satisfaction of appetites—an engine for the creation of affluence. And such a system, governed by purely materialistic conceptions and infused with a purely acquisitive ethos, is defenseless before the critique of its intellectuals. Yes, it does provide more food, better housing, better health, to say nothing of all kinds of pleasant conveniences. Only a saint or a snob would dismiss these achievements lightly. But anyone who naively believes that, in sum, they suffice to legitimize a socioeconomic system knows little of the human heart and soul. People can learn to despise such a system even while enjoying its benefits.

PLACID ACCEPTANCE

Nothing more plainly reveals the moral anarchy that prevails within the business community today than the way in which it can placidly accept—indeed, participate in—the anti-bourgeois culture that is now predominant. How many businessmen walked out indignantly from a movie like *The Graduate*, which displayed them (and their wives) as hollow men and women, worthy of nothing but contempt? Not many, I would think. The capacity for indignation withers along with self-respect. How many businessmen refuse, as a matter of honor and of principle, to advertise in a publication such as *The Rolling Stone* or even *Playboy*, publications which make a mockery of their industry, their integrity, their fidelity, the very quality of their lives? The question answers itself.

If businessmen are nothing but merchants of affluence, then their only claim to their rights and prerogatives is that they can perform this task more efficiently than the government. This assertion is unquestionably true, but it really is irrelevant. Efficiency is not a moral virtue and by itself never legitimizes anything. It is the culture of a society—by which I mean its religion and its moral traditions, as well as its specific arts—which legitimizes or illegitimizes its institutions. For decades now, liberal capitalism has been living off the inherited cultural capital of the bourgeois era and has benefited from a moral sanction it no longer even claims. That legacy is now depleted, and the cultural environment has turned radically hostile.

Today, businessmen desperately try to defend their vocation as honorable because profitable. Without realizing it, they are standing Horatio Alger on his head. It won't work. That inverted moral ethos makes no moral sense, as our culture keeps telling us, from the most popular movie to the most avant-garde novel. This culture is not, as it sometimes pretends, offended by some bad things that some businessmen do; it is offended by what businessmen are or seem to be: exemplars of the naked "profit motive." Businessmen, of course, are unaccustomed to taking culture seriously. They didn't have to, so long as it was mainly a bourgeois culture, with anti-bourgeois sentiments concentrated on the margins. Today, unless they start trying to figure out a way to cope with the new cultural climate, they are likely to catch a deathly chill. It may be a bad time for businessmen to sell stock (or buy stock) but it would seem to be a good time for them to take stock.

11

THE CORPORATION

AS A CITIZEN

A GOOD ECONOMIST has a mind like a razor, which is why he is so useful, and so dangerous. He is useful because he can make sense of a tangled and otherwise bewildering situation. He is dangerous because he can make only economic sense of it, and the world does not move by economic sense alone.

I recently asked a highly successful money manager what was the secret of his success. He thought for a moment and replied: "We never let an economist in the house." And, come to think of it, have you heard of any distinguished economists who recommended the purchase of gold stocks in the early 1970s? On the contrary: they will, with near unanimity, assure you that the increase in the price of gold, over the past several years, makes "no economic sense." I am sure they are right. Only I wish I hadn't listened to them.

As a matter of fact, most of us, most of the time, realize

that economists are not always to be listened to merely because what they say makes sense (of a kind). Thus, economists will inform the politician that the "right" economic way to attack poverty is by giving money and services to poor people. But politicians discover that, in a democracy, the right political way to attack poverty is by giving money and services to *all* the people. This is wasteful, but it is only economically wasteful, not politically wasteful. On the contrary: since it helps the politician survive while strengthening, rather than fragmenting, the bonds of community, it is politically the most productive way to approach the problem of poverty.

Similarly, businessmen usually manage to see the difference between economic sense and business sense, when it is in their interest to do so. The number of businesses which refuse to go bankrupt in order to satisfy the authoritative demands of economic rationality is very large indeed. Rather than obediently ceasing to exist, they begin to "think politically"—in the most vulgar sense of that term—about tariffs, or import quotas, or restricting competition. The oil companies at this moment are quite prepared to approve the arguments in favor of a free market, but these same oil companies have traditionally supported state regulations to limit the output of individual oil fields. Similarly, a *Wall Street Journal* editorial is all in favor of "clearing the market" for gasoline at a higher market price; but the publisher of this same splendid publication is appalled at the prospect of "clearing the market" for second-class mail at a substantially higher price, and insists that a government subsidy of postal rates is necessary to prevent this from happening.

In short, it is always nice to have economists on your side: they argue so powerfully and lucidly. But one would have to be some kind of self-denying fanatic, a monster of dispassion, always to be on the side of the economists, and most of us are just too human to manage it. On the whole, being a humanist rather than an economist, I think this is a good thing.

In some of my writings on the large corporation, which

appear to have created some controversy, I have criticized the major oil companies for being shortsighted, for failing to "think politically" in an enlightened way. Some readers seemed to think that I had in mind what certain high-minded people call "the social responsibility of corporations," i.e., that corporations should stop thinking in businesslike terms and should help shoulder the responsibility for solving the urban crisis, the educational crisis, the religious crisis, and just about every other crisis that the media might discover or invent. I should like to make it clear that I have no such naive belief as to the desirability of the corporation assuming these vast responsibilities, nor do I have any grand illusions as to their competence in coping with such responsibilities. What I had in mind was something much simpler and very practical indeed: I assumed that the large corporation wished to survive as a species of "private enterprise," that it wanted to avoid socialization and burdensome government regulation, that its survival as a business took precedence over its profit-and-loss statement for any single year, and that it wished to retain the good opinion of the American public. I therefore concluded that, as a *business institution*, it had on occasion to think politically rather than economically.

There is nothing particularly radical or even original about this conclusion. After all, is there a single large corporation in the country which, in a crisis, would not accept government assistance rather than go bankrupt? At such a moment, the large corporation behaves like an ordinary citizen in distress, not like some ideal "economic man." Economists might disapprove of such "improper" intercourse between the public and private sectors. But the large corporation affects the lives of so many people, in so many ways, that neither its executives nor government can remain indifferent to its fate. In that sense, the large corporation is willy-nilly invested with the "public interest"—simply because it is so big.

But there is necessarily a *quid pro quo* involved here: namely, when the nation confronts a crisis, the large corporation is expected to be a good citizen and shoulder its share of the burden. In such a crisis, the governing principle in a democracy is always "equality of sacrifice." This is obviously the case in wartime, when no corporation would dare insist on its right to make as much money as the market permits. That would be regarded as "profiteering," i.e., making money out of the trouble that everyone else is in, whereas legitimate profits are supposed to emerge out of economic transactions which make everyone better off. And what is true for wartime is true, if to a lesser degree, of less momentous crises.

The oil crisis, which became established in 1973, is a case in point. What happened, in effect, was that the oil-producing nations suddenly began to levy a tax of tens of billions of dollars on the American people. The major oil companies were put in the position of collecting this levy through higher prices *and of sharing in the proceeds through higher profits.* Can one imagine a more nightmarish position for a large corporation to find itself in? Not only were those new and higher prices extremely painful for the average American; they also resulted in hundreds of thousands of people being thrown out of work, and thousands of small businesses being threatened with insolvency. There was absolutely no way the oil companies could keep their share of this levy without looking like "profiteers." No way.

TAINTED MONEY

Now, I am well aware of the advantages even, or especially, in a crisis situation, of a free market over price controls, government allocations, rationing, or whatever. But the problem the oil companies faced back in 1973–74 was that, in any such free market, they automatically assumed the role of "profiteers," of middlemen making money out of a ransom which we all had suddenly to pay out to foreign powers. It is a prospect they should have shunned like the plague, if only because it represented a political threat to their very survival. Their attitude should have been: let the government be the tax-collector (through an excise tax, probably) for

Saudi Arabia or Iran or Venezuela; let *it* establish a free market or not, as it saw fit, *but we do not want this tainted money*. And there is no doubt that tainted money is precisely what the American people—including, I would say, most American businessmen—perceived it to be.

It has also long been argued that the oil companies "need" these profits so that they can develop more and cheaper sources of energy. To which I can only reply: not *those* profits, created at that time, in that way. And if foregoing those profits, at that time, would only have contributed to the persistence of the energy crisis—well, that again is a problem the political system would have had to cope with. The responsibility of the large oil companies was to get out, as quickly as possible, of an absolutely impossible situation. Instead, they preferred to argue that they didn't create the situation (which is true) and that they would invest the money wisely (which I am prepared to think is true).

Only immensely self-righteous men, who could not see themselves as others saw them, would think for a minute that such arguments might be persuasive. Which is just another way of saying that, at a crucial moment when it was necessary for the oil companies to "think politically," they could not summon up either the will or the intellectual resources to do so.

BUSINESS AND BEHAVIOR

George P. Shultz, an economist with a high regard for the free market, once said: "If efficiency is the cutting edge of economics, then equity—or fairness—is the *sine qua non* of politics. . . . The economic policy-maker must often temper intellectual purity with equitable considerations that are defined in political terms."

Dr. Shultz was referring to public officials, but his remarks also apply to the executives of our very large corporations. They, too, as heads of powerful institutions, are sometimes called upon to play the role of "economic policy-makers." I would emphasize that "sometimes." The public official has always to "think politically"—i.e., in noneconomic terms—while the official of a large corporation has to do so only sometimes. In the normal course of events, the corporate executive can best fulfill his obligations to his firm and to the public by "thinking economically." But when events take an abnormal turn, a persistence in "thinking economically" can alarm public opinion and ultimately threaten the integrity and independence of his firm.

A corporation may be a fictitious person in law, a kind of abstract version of "economic man," but there are moments when it will be expected to behave like a real citizen in fact. Such behavior is both "businesslike" and "responsible" in that it reflects self-interest "rightly understood" (as Tocqueville so grandly put it). That is to say, it takes cognizance of the important truth that, in a liberal democracy, everyone's self-interest is best served if each of us is capable, when required, of temporarily rising above self-interest. *That* is the social responsibility of a corporation: to behave like a citizen when circumstances seem to require it, and regardless of whether or not the law demands it.

12

ON "ECONOMIC EDUCATION"

TODAY there are more programs in "economic education" emerging from the business community than one can keep track of, and they involve the expenditure of many millions of dollars. They all derive from the supposition that corporate executives would have a nice reputation if only people understood the rudiments of business enterprise and the relation between the prosperity of the corporation and the well-being of the citizenry. Some of the programs are quite good, in purely pedagogical terms; many are awful; most fall in between. None of them is likely to have any significant effect.

The worst efforts are those which involve a threefold confusion of the process of education with the procedures of advertising with the purposes of propaganda. These are the kinds of programs that try to respond to the chairman's indignant (or despairing) question: "We are so damned good at selling our products to the public, why can't we sell our ideas?" And so an educational-advertising-propaganda program is born, with "free enterprise" as the commodity.

But advertising is precisely the wrong vehicle for *any* kind of education. Education, properly understood, induces a growing comprehension of abstract ideas and concepts; advertising, properly understood, aims to move people to do something definite and unambiguous. Education is always raising questions; advertising is always giving answers. These are two radically different modes of communication, and their admixture is corrupting to both. It also happens to be ineffectual. People just don't read advertisements in the press, or listen to them on television, in an educational frame of mind, i.e., a mind that is attentive and energetic.

Propaganda has its own unique purpose, which is to shape specific attitudes on specific issues. It can be effectual indeed, but only under special circumstances. One prerequisite for successful propaganda is that it not appear to be propaganda at all, but rather "news" or "facts" or "research." Another is that it concentrate on the vilification of one's enemy, not on the celebration of one's own virtues. Anti-business propaganda of the Ralph Nader variety follows this dual strategy with considerable success. But the business corporation that is concerned for its integrity and self-respect is in no position to engage in this kind of unscrupulous ideological warfare. God forbid that it should try to learn.

I suspect that one of the reasons corporations can so easily confuse education with advertising with propaganda is their long-standing commitment to something called "institutional advertising," which is indeed a mixture of all three. Hard-headed executives really do believe that if they show some dramatic pictures of corporate activity, with the accompanying assurance that "We're involved" or "We're concerned" or "We're working for America" or whatever, that this will somehow persuade people to think well of that particular corporation and of business in general. The notion is absurd. All such institutional advertising collapses into one glossy blur, and has no effect whatsoever on anyone. Well, that's not quite true: it does serve to pacify the anxious chief executive, and to gratify his ego. Perhaps this therapeutic effect is worth the money expended.

Other programs of "economic education" do not involve

the use of advertising media but rather the preparation of
film strips, study guides, etc. for use in the elementary and
high school classroom. Some of these aren't bad at all, and a
teacher of economics could use them in good conscience. Unfortunately, the evidence is overwhelming that such instruction in business economics is rather like instruction in a
foreign language: within months of the end of the term, most
of what was taught has been unlearned. Moreover, favorable
or unfavorable attitudes to business seem to have little or no
correlation with the taking of courses in economics.

This last statement is not surprising, if one stops to think
about it. There are plenty of radical economists, after all,
and even more "liberal" (i.e., anti-business) ones. These people don't have to be told what profits are, or how important
they are for a healthy, growing economy. They have nothing
against profits in a purely accounting sense. They just don't
see why control over these profits should be exercised by
corporate executives rather than by, say, professors of economics or higher civil servants. Their attitude toward
business is a derivative of their political philosophy, not of
anything they know or don't know about economics.

And the same is true for less learned folk. Public opinion
polls reveal that the ordinary man or woman today has far
less favorable attitudes toward business than was the case
twenty or thirty years ago. Did that ordinary man or woman
know more economics then, as compared with now? That is
not only hard to believe; it is impossible to believe. Clearly,
public attitudes toward business are no more a function of
their knowledge of economics than public attitudes toward
government are a function of their knowledge of political science.

These popular attitudes are often provoked, to begin with,
by experience. In recent years, it has been the experience of
inflation that may well have been decisive. Inflation will
always elicit anti-business attitudes from consumers, for obvious reasons. But those attitudes are then given shape and
durability by the general culture, which includes the songs
people—especially young people—sing, the books they read,
the movies and TV programs they see, the paintings they ad-

mire, and the like. It also includes, of course, the kind of
schooling they receive: we do know, for instance, that college seniors are much more anti-business than college fresh-
men, so it is clear that *something* is going on in those class-
rooms, over that four-year period, to achieve this effect.
But that "something" has more to do with their study of
literature, or anthropology, or history, or political theory—
the "value forming" humanities—than with their study or
nonstudy of economics (or physics or engineering). This
process of "value formation" is one in which intellectuals
and academicians and artists are sovereign. For corporations
it is an alien territory where they are not likely to encounter much hospitality, and into which they had best not
intrude.

But this does not mean that the corporation is entirely impotent, or need be impotent, in the struggle to influence public opinion. There are several areas where much can be
done. One such area is the journalistic media, about which
everyone complains without doing anything.

BIAS AND "OBJECTIVITY"

That these media are biased against the business community
is obvious. Indeed, they are so biased they don't even know
they are biased, since their very conception of "objectivity"
incorporates the bias. When they are "objective," which is
occasionally, they are clearly trying to be "fair" to a group
of people whom they don't like and don't trust. The results
of such journalism are utterly predictable and familiar
enough in fact.

But journalists, whatever their media, do like to think of
themselves as professionals, i.e., as observing professional
standards of accuracy and truth-telling. Though most are
biased in a "liberal" direction, only a few are intellectually
dishonest. They may not give a damn what the business community thinks of them, but they care very much what kind
of professional reputation they have among their peers. When
they commit a flagrant error, they are at least mildly dis-

turbed; when they are publicly exposed as having commited such an error, they are embarrassed; and when such public exposure occurs repeatedly, they feel humiliated. So, incredible as it may seem, journalists are vulnerable to the truth. The question is: Who is going to be telling this truth if the journalists themselves do not?

The answer, I would suggest, is the corporation itself. Unfortunately, when a corporation is victimized by distorted reporting, its instinct will be to complain to the publisher or network executive—as if *he* had any more influence over the media than the rest of us! Or the corporation will issue a press release which, since it is assumed to be self-serving, will get no attention. Or the corporation will even call a press conference to which no one will come, since journalists are never eager to collaborate in criticisms of other journalists.

What has to be done, to set the record straight, is a public rebuttal—detailed, polemical, and sharply phrased so as to challenge the reporter's (or newscaster's) professional integrity. And this rebuttal will have to take the form of paid advertising in that media which the reporter and his colleagues read. (In effect, that means the handful of newspapers, newsmagazines, and periodicals with national standing.) The purpose of such advertising is not to affect public opinion directly, but to influence journalistic performance over the longer run. Moreover, if a rebuttal is ignored, then it should be repeated, again and again, so as to constitute a challenge. Journalists are slow learners—since they think they know it all—and have to be hit over the head a few times before they pay attention. When shown to have been in error, they will never issue a retraction; that is asking too much. But they will probably be more scrupulous the next time they find themselves dealing with a comparable problem. And that is gain enough.

THE BEST DEFENSE

I should make it clear that I am not talking about "issue-oriented advertising," which sometimes has its uses but suffers from many of the limitations of "economic educa-tion." I am talking rather about a corporation defending it-self—not the business community, and not "free enterprise," but *itself*—against slander, and acting with the indignation and forcefulness that we expect from an innocent victim of slander. Obviously, to do this a corporation has indeed to be innocent, or, to put it more reasonably, at least not guilty as charged. But where such guiltlessness exists, a mere protestation of it is not enough. As every trial lawyer knows, the best defense for your client is to undermine the credibil-ity of witnesses for the prosecution.

Very few corporations conceive of public relations in this way, or are capable of responding in this way to the chal-lenges which the media are constantly posing. It is a tradi-tional article of faith with corporations that the best strategy is one that does not give offense. Unfortunately, when you are in an adversary situation, the net effect of such a strategy is to persuade the public that, where the media generate so much smoke, there must be fire.

13

INFLATION AND THE
"DISMAL SCIENCE"

JUST ABOUT every thoughtful observer is agreed—indeed, has always agreed—that inflation is essentially a political phenomenon, created by the fiscal irresponsibility of government. Economic circumstances can raise the prices of some commodities (e.g., oil or domestic help), and a major crisis (e.g., war) can temporarily raise the price of all commodities. But a general, enduring, and accelerating rise in the price level will only come about when government itself spends—or permits its citizens to spend—more money than there are resources available for purchase at stable prices.

All this is true enough, but as stated it is somewhat misleading because oversimplified. It encourages us to regard "politics" as a world apart, "politicians" as a breed apart, and allows us to blame *it* and *them* for our problems. This has its convenience, and might even be relatively true for pre-democratic or nondemocratic societies. But in a democratic society such as ours, politics is not really a world apart, nor are politicians really much different from the rest of us. To cite Ernest Hemingway, just as the rich are different from us merely in that they have more money, so politicians differ from us in that they have more power. The uses to which that money and power are put, however, are determined in a democracy by our common culture—by those beliefs about how things are, and those expectations as to how things ought to be, which we jointly share.

It is this culture, as it finds articulate expression in what we call "public opinion," but also as it finds tacit expression in the habits of everyday life, that ultimately governs in a democracy. And if inflation becomes an organic disorder of democracy, it can only be because it has deep cultural roots both in our way of life and our way of thinking about life.

This, I think, is what Albert T. Sommers, an extremely shrewd economist, had in mind when he recently asserted that the explanation for our inflationary condition lay in a "profound historical shift in the social conditions and value systems of democratic capitalism." In the democratic countries, he went on to say, modern economic systems "are living in an explosion of expectations that carry the demands for output far beyond their finite resources. The failure of our political system to contain the growth of social demands within limits tolerable to the free market is the essential first cause of inflation in this society."

Quite right. Only, who incited this "explosion of expectations," and who transformed the "value systems of democratic capitalism" so as to make this explosion so difficult to contain? Well, oddly enough, it is our economists themselves who have to shoulder some of the responsibility. True, it is mainly economists who today are most alarmed by inflation and are most vociferous in demanding that something be done about it. Nevertheless, ever since the end of World War II, economists have been as busy as anyone else in fueling that "revolution of rising expectations" which, *when divorced from the spirit of moderation*, gives birth to the inflationary state and its various disorders.

I have italicized that phrase, "when divorced from the spirit of moderation," because it is so crucial. Capitalism itself emerges historically from dissatisfaction with the stationary society, and is intrinsically allied with *some kind* of revolution of rising expectations. It was such a revolution that brought capitalism into existence, and it is the satisfaction of increased expectations that has legitimated its existence until this day. But this was, from the outset, a moderate revolution that sought to satisfy moderate expectations. And what, above all, imposed a spirit of moderation on this continuing revolution was the science of economics, the "dismal science" as it came to be called, precisely because it set itself so firmly against the utopian extremism which all revolutions stir up, and because it kept insisting that there are no benefits without costs, that reality is so structured as to make hard choices inevitable, that a "free" lunch is pie in the sky. Up until the New Deal, politicians functioned within a climate of opinion shaped by "the dismal science." They didn't understand economics any better than they do today. But they were much more respectful of reality—and of the limits which reality inevitably imposes on our desires—than they are today.

Economics ceased being a "dismal science" with the rise of Keynesian theories during the Great Depression. But Keynes was no utopian, and his economics was originally conceived very much in a spirit of moderation. What Keynes said was that massive depressions were unnecessary and could be avoided by fairly simple governmental action which would help restore economic equilibrium. He anticipated that, once this was achieved, the capitalist system would resume its long-term rate of growth. That rate was, by our present standards, modest to the point of timidity: in the U.S., it meant an average annual increase in GNP of perhaps 2.5 percent. Paltry though that statistic seems to us today, it meant a doubling of national income every thirty years or so, an achievement no previous economic system could ever have imagined.

After World War II, the moderate optimism created by the Keynesian confidence that great depressions could be avoided became an immoderate and extravagant optimism. "Economic growth" replaced "economic stability" as the focus of attention, and economists began to assure us that growth rates of 4 percent or even 8 percent were possible, if only we did the right things, which, as it happens, turned out to be the inflationary things. These assurances seemed all the more plausible at the time because some nations—notably the Soviet Union and West Germany—were indeed achieving such impressive rates of growth. There was even a great deal of chatter in respectable academic circles that unless the United States could radically improve its performance, the Soviet economy would soon surpass it; and we were warned that all the "underdeveloped" nations (they had not yet been promoted to "developing" nations) would then promptly opt for communism. Those economists and social critics who were skeptical of this scenario were peremptorily informed that their thinking was out of date.

And so our present inflationary climate was born. The stock market boomed; at those projected rates of growth, you couldn't go wrong by buying common stock. Corporations plunged head over heels into debt; at those projected rates of growth, massive indebtedness seemed positively sensible, since the return on capital would easily cover repayment and leave a tidy profit besides. Individuals, too, began to go heavily into debt; what was wrong with pre-spending tomorrow's increased "guaranteed" income? And politicians began to pre-spend the "fiscal dividend" which the tax system, under these conditions of rapid and sustained economic growth, would pay out to the Treasury.

I vividly recall a dinner meeting, eight years ago, when a Washington official brought us the glad tidings that the major political problem facing the nation was how to spend that fiscal dividend (then estimated, I think, at $6 billion a year). When someone—not an economist—dared suggest that it was all just too good to be true and that life wasn't really like that, he was silenced by an uncomprehending stare.

And all of this took place in a decade when the media—television, especially—converted this nation into a vast echo chamber, in which fashionable opinions were first magnified and then "confirmed" through interminable repetition. Gradually it came to be believed that, in the immortal words of a 19th-century utopian socialist, "nothing is impossible for a government that *wants* the good of its citizens." As a matter of fact, this proposition doesn't even sound particularly utopian today; it sounds almost banal.

THE REALITY PRINCIPLE

The 1970s are slowly disillusioning us of all these fantasies, and it is pleasing to report that, just as the economists were the leaders of yesteryear's "revolution of rising expectations," so today they are the most eloquent in affirming the reality principle, in the traditional accents of their "dismal science." But such reversals of established opinion do not occur overnight, and bad habits are not so easily discarded. Corporation executives still feel compelled to promise their shareholders growth rates of at least 7 percent to 10 percent; though if stock prices are any indicator, no one is believing them, which is a good thing. Politicians, too, still feel that they are required to come up with new and glittering promises to the electorate at frequent intervals. It seems clear that the electorate, which has more common sense than economists, corporate executives, or politicians, doesn't believe them either. The media naturally calls this disbelief "apathy" and "cynicism," and deplores it.

I suspect that, had it not been for the insanities of the Watergate Affair, we would be much further along the sobering-up process than we now are. Mr. Nixon's overwhelming majority in 1972 can be fairly interpreted as a vote for political and economic sobriety. Indeed, so can Mr. Carter's primary victories over his more liberal competitors for the Democratic nomination. But many politicians are still suffering from cultural lag, and we shall have to give them some time to catch up. Meanwhile, it is to be hoped that our economists will stay "dismal" and thereby help revive the spirit of moderation which they had earlier helped to subvert.

14

SOME DOUBTS ABOUT

"DEREGULATION"

EVERYONE suddenly seems to be in favor of "deregulation": Presidents Ford and Carter, conservative economists, liberal Congressmen, the media, Ralph Nader, Common Cause, populist academics, the *Wall Street Journal*, etc. Such an odd consensus ought to be enough to cause one to have second thoughts about the whole business. And, indeed, there are very good grounds for such second thoughts. For upon examination there is far less to "deregulation" than meets the eye. And what substance there is, is of dubious merit.

The movement for "deregulation" may seem to be a healthy reaction against what Walter Lippmann called "the sickness of an overgoverned society." But in actuality it is not really anything of the sort. It is a movement directed almost exclusively against *some* of the activities of the *older* regulatory agencies: the Interstate Commerce Commission, the Civil Aeronautics Board, the Federal Power Commission, the Securities and Exchange Commission, and others. Not *all* such agencies, it is interesting to note. There seems to be little urge to dismantle the Food and Drug Administration or the Federal Trade Commission. And there appears to be no impulse whatsoever to apply "deregulation" to the activities of the *newer* regulatory bodies: the Environmental Protection Agency, the Occupational Safety and Health Administration, or the Consumer Products Safety Commission. On the contrary: the bureaucracy and red tape of these other agencies calmly and inexorably multiply, attracting little controversy, even as the movement for "deregulation" grows more popular.

So, while "deregulation" sounds as if it means de-bureaucratization, it turns out not to have that meaning at all. Or, more precisely, it is a very selective kind of de-bureaucratization. And there is reason to believe that it is the wrong kind, one whose ultimate consequences will be more government control over the economy rather than less.

The history of the current fervor for "deregulation" is an interesting one. The idea itself was born a couple of decades ago at the University of Chicago, specifically in its department of economics, and is associated with such distinguished names as George Stigler and Milton Friedman. Since the economics department at Chicago is famous for its orientation toward a free market economy, there is nothing surprising in its producing studies critical of government regulation. What is surprising is the direction this criticism took. Not only did it expose, with great cogency, the inefficiencies associated with government regulation; it further argued, and tried to prove, that all such regulatory agencies eventually become the captives of their business constituencies. Thus "regulation" really became a kind of governmental-business conspiracy against the commonweal.

It is this last thesis which, in more recent years, has enthusiastically been taken up by the Left, for fairly obvious reasons. Articles and books have been pouring forth from the academy, all purporting to reveal the workings of this conspiracy; and the idea that, when government regulates business, business ends up running government, has now become a commonplace of radical-populist thought. Indeed, some younger historians are now arguing that such agencies as the ICC came into existence at business's behest, and for the clear purpose of maximizing corporate profits. This explains why "deregulation" has become so popular among people who have never had a kind word to say for capitalism.

Now, there are two issues posed here: one involving historical fact, the other involving economic theory.

Whether the older regulatory agencies were from the beginning conceived as allies of "big business" (as the radicals say) or merely became such allies in the course of time (as the free-market economic historians assert) can be left to these parties to debate. Some recent scholarship (which I find more persuasive) argues that they are both wrong—that what seems obvious is not always false, that the more traditional view of such regulation as being a political reaction *against* "big business," and on the whole operating as a genuine restraint on it, is probably the correct one. In any case, I have yet to meet an executive in a regulated industry —railroads, say, or airlines—who had the impression that those regulators in Washington were really on his side.

The issue of economic theory is both more important and more troublesome, since it involves a conception of the "natural tendencies" of a capitalist economy. The Chicago school insists that oligopoly and monopoly either (1) are created by governmental policies, or (2) would dissolve under the corrosive effects of competition were it not for governmental policies. But there are other economists—the great Joseph Schumpeter was one—who believe (without animus toward capitalism) that free competition among firms can lead to the "survival of the fittest," and that these in the end will number a relatively few of the largest and most efficient firms. In other words, there is a question as to whether the free market, at least in certain areas, has a tendency to create a situation where only a handful of large corporations compete with one another, and where such competition is mitigated and internally moderated (especially as regards pricing) by the desire to protect the profitability of the industry as a whole.

It would be presumptuous of me to have too strong an opinion on this matter. I have the greatest respect for George Stigler and Milton Friedman. Still, I'll go so far as to say that there does seem to be *some* validity in the Schumpeter analysis. Conditions of entry into *some* capital-intensive industries are so difficult as to be, in effect, impossible, and though competition does exist within them, it is highly imperfect competition. If and where this is the case, enforcement of antitrust laws, and/or some kind or degree of government regulation, and/or legally sanctioned self-regulation by the industry in question, may turn out to be the only way to preserve what competition exists. In the longer run, it may be the only realistic alternative to some form of nationalization. And we are already witnessing, in such an area as stockbrokerage, how "deregulation" might end by creating a capital-intensive industry where one does not now exist.

THE ORIGINAL ARGUMENT

It seems reasonable, therefore, to worry about the consequences of unthinking "deregulation." The SEC may sincerely believe that its recent actions have opened the financial markets to greater competition, but what is visible is only a movement toward greater concentration. "Deregulation" of the airlines would probably have the same consequences; a more concentrated airline industry would surely lead to a nationalized airline industry. There really does seem to be substance in the traditional belief that the older regulatory agencies have both the purpose and the effect of preserving some competition where competition might otherwise diminish or disappear under the pressure of "natural" market forces. And it is well to recall that the original arguments for such regulation, in decades past, were that it would help save capitalism and "free enterprise" from "big business." This is not such an incredible notion. Indeed, if one thing is certain, it is that the more "big business" we have, the more "big government" we shall get.

To be sure, there is an excellent case for the *reform* of these older regulatory agencies. They have, over time, become encrusted to a scandalous degree with bureaucratic sloth, bureaucratic stupidity, and bureaucratic inefficiency. They do need an infusion of new blood and new thinking, especially economic thinking, to correct the traditional legalistic habits of mind which take more satisfaction in complicating problems than in resolving them.

And there is an even better case for turning our "deregulating" and "de-bureaucratizing" energies to the newer regulatory agencies. These did not come into existence, nor do they operate, in order to preserve capitalism. On the contrary, they overflow with unfriendly feelings against *all* business, not just "big business." Their aim is to substitute, wherever possible, their decision-making powers for those of the marketplace so as to improve the "quality of life." This is why they are so utterly indifferent to the burdensome costs of their interventions, most of which, inevitably, make the very existence of a small business almost an economic impossibility.

I am sure that the Chicago economists would be delighted to apply "deregulation" to these new agencies, and to the "new class" which created them and populates them. But were they to try to do so, I suspect that we would all suddenly discover that "deregulation" had gone out of fashion.

15

THE CREDIBILITY OF
CORPORATIONS

'TIS THE SEASON for scapegoating, and the large corporation is once again everyone's favorite candidate for ritual slaughter. In the debased version of democratic politics which prevails today, political demagoguery and popular paranoia—both, as it happens, so congenial to the melodramatic temperament of our mass media—demand that blame always and instantly be assigned to shadowy "profiteers." After all, if things go wrong, what other possible explanation is there? It can't be public opinion, which is always right, or the politicians, who are always dedicated to the commonweal, or misfortunes of historical circumstance, from which Americans are supposed to be exempt. So it has to be someone or something that has an interest in, say, higher prices for oil, as the oil companies unquestionably do.

In a sense, none of this is new. In any democracy, large and powerful organizations which are in business to make a profit will inevitably be regarded—have always been regarded—with distaste and suspicion. The power of the large corporation appears "irresponsible" precisely because of the anonymity which cloaks it: one doesn't know who is making all those decisions that affect our lives, or why, and in such a case the nastiest interpretation seems as plausible as any other. And when these decisions become dramatically costly to the average citizen, it is the nastiest interpretation that will come most naturally to mind.

Nor is this state of affairs wholly to be deplored. Within limits, the fear and dislike of "bigness" is a healthy democratic instinct, because it is indeed true that, as large organizations come to dominate our lives, each one of us loses a measure of freedom and sovereignty. But it is also true that large organizations are here to stay. No reasonable person can envisage dismantling these structures; their existence is the precondition for too many benefits to which we are strongly attached. So when hostility to "big business" goes beyond a certain limit, there is no alternative to some form of nationalization. A government-owned or government-operated enterprise is beyond reproach so far as concerns its motives. It is, as we blithely (and mindlessly) say, "publicly" owned and operated, and its rationale is "service," not profit. That this enterprise may then be less efficient, more bureaucratic, and not at all responsive to public needs somehow doesn't matter. The Post Office gets away with murder while AT&T is crucified for every fault, simply because in the one case management's motives are assumed to be "pure" while in the other they are by definition "impure."

There is already some talk about nationalizing the large oil companies, and it can be fairly predicted that, in every successive economic crisis, other industries will seem like logical candidates for "public" ownership. It is possible to think that this trend is irreversible, that it is inherent in the dynamics of a liberal democracy whose instinct for limited government becomes progressively weaker while its instinct for bureaucratically imposed "equality of sacrifice" (this the Post Office does accomplish) grows stronger. Still, it is also possible to think that this process can at least be slowed down, and that it may be within the power of the large corporations to do something for their own survival. So the question is: What is to be done?

Essentially, as I see it, the problem is one of candor and credibility, *not* of "public relations." Indeed, one of the reasons the large corporations find it so difficult to persuade the public of anything is that the public always suspects them of engaging in clever public relations, instead of simply telling the truth. And the reason the public is so suspicious is because our large corporations so habitually do engage in clever public relations instead of simply telling the truth.

For instance, what is one to make of a corporation which proudly announces that it has just completed the most profitable year in its history, and then simultaneously declares that its return on capital is pitifully inadequate, that it is suffering from a terrible cost-squeeze, and so on and on? In 1973—to take a dramatic, indeed watershed, year—most corporations were engaged in precisely this kind of double-talk. Is it any wonder they created so enormous a credibility gap?

Now, the truth is that 1973 was not so profitable a year for our large corporations. One would see this instantly if corporations reported their profits in *constant* dollars, i.e., corrected for inflation. Trade unions do this when they report their members' earnings to the world at large; *they* don't want to look like "profiteers" when they sit down at the bargaining table. Corporations, in contrast, do seem to be under a compulsion to look like "profiteers" even when they are not, in fact, operating at a particularly profitable level. The explanation for this bizarre behavior has to do with the prevailing standards of "successful management" in the corporate world.

It is not much of an exaggeration to say that these standards, over the past quarter-century, have come to be set by a relatively small number of speculators on Wall Street, who determine the price of the corporation's common stock. I say "speculators," not "shareholders," because the authentic shareholder of yesteryear is a vanishing breed. Most stock today is purchased by people and institutions whose sole intention is to hold it for a relatively brief period and then sell it at a profit. They do not "invest" in a company but are rather in the business of trading in its securities. These are the people to whom corporate managements are, in the end, responsible. In their annual reports, and in their advertising, corporations still like to sustain the legend that their legal owners are "shareholders," people who have invested their capital in the company and, over a lifetime, share in the company's fortunes for better or worse. In reality, the fate of corporate management is ultimately decided by a motley group of speculators, and just about the sole criterion of successful management is whether or not it has managed to establish a relatively fancy price for its securities in the stock market.

The result, inevitably, is consistent deception which varies only in degree. One of the reasons that the myth of an "affluent society" became so prevalent—a myth, which, in turn, gave birth to all kinds of popular fantasies about the standard of living that Americans are "entitled" to—is that corporations have helped propagate it by grossly overstating their earnings. They accomplish this by sleazy accounting, shrewd accounting, or technically honest but still misleading accounting. What we call "the revolution of rising expectations" is really but another version of an old-fashioned speculative fever on a mass scale. The modern corporation helps to engender and sustain this fever, and when reality dawns, as it always does, the corporation is sure to be held responsible for reality's shortcomings.

At a recent conference, attended by some dozen top executives of major corporations, I inquired why they don't take inflation into account when they compose their annual reports and state their profits. The only answer I got was that, if someone would start doing it, they would be quite content to follow, but that they were not about to take the lead in dispensing such bitter—if wholesome—medicine. These same executives, of course, are intensely and sincerely interested in "the social responsibility of corporations," and are quite willing to contemplate "bold initiatives" in training the ghetto poor, solving our urban problems, etc. In other words, they are eager to assume responsibilities for various and remote tasks they probably cannot accomplish, but loath to shoulder the responsibility for doing what can be easily done: i.e., giving the public a true picture of the condition of their enterprises. It is, on the whole, a neat prescription for corporate suicide.

THE MATTER OF STOCK OPTIONS

It is no secret that one of the reasons corporate executives are so concerned about the way Wall Street regards their securities is that so many of them are the owners of stock options, and therefore have a personal interest in the matter. But should such an interest be permitted to exist? Why should corporate executives be permitted to trade in the securities of their own firms? There may be something to be said for executives owning stock in their corporations, but to recognize the right of executives to *sell* stock in their own companies—however this stock is acquired—is to create the favorable conditions for scandals involving "insider trading." Would it not be reasonable to insist that no executive be permitted to sell any of his stock in his company as long as he holds office?

I will be told—I have been told—that any such restriction would make stock options meaningless, since corporate executives, not being wealthy men for the most part, have to sell their stock in order to get the money to exercise new stock options. But are stock options all that desirable anyhow? It seems to me that many corporate executives suffer from a confusion of identity; they think that they are entitled to entrepreneurial rewards instead of merely managerial ones. Which is to say, they think they have the right to become wealthy—that is the hope behind stock options—not simply to be well paid. (Former President Nixon apparently was the victim of this same confusion.) But corporate executives are *not* entrepreneurs; they do not take the risks of entrepreneurs and are not entitled to the rewards. They are employees of the corporation, just like the switchboard operator, and should expect the same kinds of benefits other employees get: a decent salary, an adequate pension, and the rest. If they wish to become wealthy, they ought to go into business for themselves.

It is, I would suggest, this same confusion between entrepreneurial rewards and management rewards that establishes salary levels for executives which, in the eyes of the public, are indecently high. I know it will be said that you have to pay a lot of money in order to get "the best available talent." But we are all aware it doesn't quite work that way. No corporation goes out shopping for executive talent, trying to obtain the best for the least amount of money. The levels of corporate salaries are fixed beforehand and the salary varies with the title, not with the man.

Who fixes these levels? Why, other corporate executives, of course, who are called "directors." That's a very cozy arrangement. One can be sure that if the salaries of professors, government officials, and plumbers were set by committees of professors, government officials, and plumbers, they would be much higher than they now are. Every profession and occupation tends to have a high opinion of itself. Besides, it can always be "demonstrated" that a high salary is really quite small in comparison with all the benefits which will accrue to the institution by reason of the splendid and well-rewarded talents that populate it.

But what if such benefits are not realized? This question is an urgent one, since we are clearly entering a period of some economic hardship for a great many Americans. How many corporate executives are going to cut their salaries because their firms are doing badly? And if they do cut them, by how much will they cut? One can foresee a corporation president proudly announcing to six million unemployed Americans that he is reducing his salary by 20 percent— say, from $200,000 a year to $160,000 a year—and then wondering why no one is impressed with his self-imposed "sacrifice."

There is much more that can, and should, and hopefully will be said—and, of course, debated—along these lines. But the point I wish to make is that the American corporation is in serious trouble, to which it is reacting in a largely frivolous way. Social responsibility begins at home, and if the large corporation wishes to gain the trust of the American public, it has to consider what kinds of changes will make it more worthy of this trust. It is true that the corporate image is in a worse condition than it deserves. But it is also true that this image is not going to be changed by the mirror-magic of "public relations."

16

THE OPEC CONNECTION

IF POLITICAL DECADENCE can be identified with "a failure of nerve"—that is to say, an unwillingness to confront and cope with reality—then the reaction of the West to the emergence of OPEC is about as clear a sign of decadence as one could imagine. In every possible way, we have sought to minimize, ignore, and otherwise evade the new facts of life that OPEC has presented us with.

The modes of evasion are various. Many hard-headed bankers, for instance, have promptly concentrated their attention (and ours) on the terms of trade. They announce that the "recycling" of OPEC's new-found wealth is proceeding better than had been anticipated, and that the economics of the problem are quite manageable. This, of course, is economic nonsense. Why should we be pleased that Saudi Arabia buys our goods with our dollars, instead of burying those dollars in the sand? Is it easier for us to produce goods than to print dollars? Is it cheaper?

What the bankers seem unable to realize is that we are talking about a net transfer of real wealth—a levy, a monopoly tax—and that whether we transfer this wealth in the form of goods or dollar bills is of no economic significance to the nation as a whole (even if it does make a difference to bankers). As a matter of fact, that very term, "recycling," helps disguise the economic reality of the transaction that is taking place. The word, as originally applied to problems of pollution, signified a process that produced a net economic gain: what had been waste matter was now being converted into a marketable commodity. But as applied to our relations with the OPEC countries, it obscures the fact that we are talking simply about their gain and our loss.

Or take the popular rhetoric about the importance of "conservation." Obviously, if we arrange our lives so as to use less energy, we shall need less of it, and we shall then seem to be paying a smaller levy to OPEC. But we will in fact be paying the original total levy, only we shall be taking some of it out of our own hides. "Conservation" means making ourselves poorer by doing without; it doesn't affect the costs to us of the OPEC monopoly, but simply reveals those costs openly.

There is much to be said in favor of paying the costs of OPEC in this candid, self-disciplined way. But to listen to some of the apostles of conservation one would think that it is one of those bitter-tasting medicines that is really good for us. That is because the conservationists of today—like their brethren, the environmentalists—are for the most part anachronistic hangovers of the 1960s. They still believe we live in an "affluent society," in which economics is no longer a significant problem as compared with something called the "quality of life." When they preach "conservation" they think that they are talking about sacrificing a few of the frills that decorate the American standard of living, and suggest that this may even be for our benefit. They fail completely to realize the profound crisis in world economics that OPEC has plunged us into. Continuing to pay for OPEC is not a matter of snipping off a few frills but of cutting to the bone.

The costs of OPEC, to the United States and to the West generally, are invariably underestimated and often unperceived. Thus, for instance, it is generally known that the United States' bill for oil imports in 1978 hovers in the vicinity of $40 billion. That is a lot of money, but when viewed as a percentage of our Gross National Product it does not seem wildly alarming.

But is that the full story? Certain factors seem to have been overlooked. For one thing, it does not make much sense to talk about the cost of oil to the United States and the cost of oil to the so-called Less Developed Countries (which, for this purpose, would include a nation such as Italy) in isolation from one another. Since 1973, the non-OPEC LDC's have increased their borrowing—mainly from the United States and Western Europe—by over $100 billion. Not all of this is the result of the increased price of oil, but much of it is. Does anyone really expect that the bulk of these loans will ever be repaid in full? Those countries are never going to be that flush. The loans will be renegotiated unto infinity, until at some point they will be canceled. In other words, we have huge hidden costs here, disguised by conventional bookkeeping. And those costs will increase, since the LDC's are going to have to keep on borrowing as their economies grow and as the price of oil is steadily raised by OPEC. And we shall have to continue to lend, lest those countries collapse utterly, with economic and political consequences that are beyond calculation.

In addition, there is the effect of the increased costs of energy on our existing capital stock. As Charles Schultz pointed out, when he was still at Brookings, those increased costs have reduced the value of our industrial equipment, since the technology incarnated in existing capital goods was premised on much cheaper energy. Now we are, in effect, experiencing an involuntary write-down of that technology and that equipment. In the same way, increasing energy costs make all capital stock less productive than it would otherwise have been, so we experience a decrease in productivity.

The costs of OPEC, therefore, are far, far greater than we

generally realize. And by our continuing refusal to face up to these costs and their implications, we have made matters even worse than they need have been. As Francis Kelly, of Blyth Eastman Dillon, has acutely observed, there are only four ways in which we could cope with those costs. The first is to print money, which we are doing. But the resulting inflation provides only a temporary relief which is a prelude to longer-term debility. The second is to place the burden directly on consumers by way of reduced real income and higher unemployment. No one dares avow such a policy, though it is to some extent surreptitiously followed. The third is to put the burden on the public sector by cutting government services. To the degree that such services are worthwhile, this is another cost for the consumer to bear. But, in any case, our politicians regard this possibility as unthinkably sacrilegious. The fourth is to pile those costs on the capital-formation sector, through reduced profitability. For the most part, this is the policy we have been following, with a predictable result: the eventual impoverishment of the American economy.

It is the OPEC connection that makes most current prescriptions of economic policy so irrelevant. The assumption behind all such prescriptions is that, if only the right advice is heeded, the American economy can return to a prosperous condition. But the OPEC levy, with its effects diffused through the world economy, makes such a prospect chimerical. That levy must be paid, not only today but tomorrow and the day after. We can pay it with inflation; we can pay it with unemployment, we can pay it by a general reduction in our standard of living—but pay we must. And the more successful we are in meeting those payments, the easier it will be for OPEC to increase its levy.

A THREAT TO WORLD COMMERCE

It is this same OPEC connection that is now threatening the whole structure of world commerce. As each nation seeks to evade its share of the cost and seeks to pass it on to others, a new spirit of protectionism is everywhere evident. To a very large degree, the extraordinary economic growth in the post-World War II decades was based on the growing volume of international trade and investment. The new protectionism is therefore economically self-defeating, but it is so attractive politically that it is hard to see what can prevent its gaining momentum.

Nor is there any easy escape from this OPEC connection. For the next decade or so we are "locked into" it. Even if we were to make Herculean efforts to develop alternative, economical sources of energy, putting aside all environmental considerations, the "lead time" necessary before they could make significant contributions to the economy brings us to 1985 or beyond. Nuclear power plants cannot be built overnight; neither can the vast transportation network needed to transport huge amounts of coal. And by 1985, the cost of oil imports to the consumer nations is estimated by Walter J. Levy at $300 billion! Who is going to pay that bill? And how?

The problem is OPEC. Though we can cope with OPEC in better or worse ways—and we have hitherto generally chosen the worse over the better—there is no way of coping that avoids oppressive economic costs. And, ultimately, political costs too: when a society finds itself in economic distress, it inevitably turns to government to do something about it. The OPEC monopoly doesn't merely violate free market principles; it will, if it endures, subvert all free market economies where (and to the extent that) they still exist.

The OPEC monopoly, like any other successful monopoly, is a political arrangement for economic ends. Coping with OPEC, therefore, is a matter of politics, not economics. Specifically, it is a problem for American foreign policy, economic, diplomatic, perhaps even military—yet it is not even on our foreign policy agenda. Until it appears on that agenda, the notion that we are somehow coping with OPEC is nothing but a costly and self-defeating illusion.

17

THE REPUBLICAN FUTURE

EVERY POLITICAL PARTY has its roots in some vision of an ideal nation. Left-wing parties are usually quite precise in defining this ideal—they are fond of "blueprints for the future"—and try to be equally precise in prescribing the means for achieving the ideal (redistribution of income, nationalization of industry, new governmental "initiatives," etc.). It is because this work of definition is an intellectual task that left-wing parties are always so interested in recruiting intellectuals. And it is because they are assigned so crucial a political function that intellectuals tend to find left-wing parties so congenial.

But the dilemma of left-wing parties is that their ideals are invariably utopian to begin with, and all that passionate precision turns out to be self-defeating. The trouble with an exact route to nowhere—and "nowhere" is the original, literal meaning of "utopia"—is that it doesn't get you any closer to home, no matter how long you travel. So left-wing politics has within it the seeds of its own frustration. And this frustration always takes the form of denouncing the party leadership for lacking sufficient devotion to the party's ideals and sufficient determination to realize them. This is what is happening in the Labor Party in Britain today, and in the Social-Democratic Party in Germany. We have also seen it happen in our own Democratic Party.

Something similar happens to conservative parties—but, in their case, because they tend to have only a blurred vision of a vague ideal. They are the party of "practical" men, uninterested in large ideas or in a precise elaboration of the relation of means to ends. Being so excessively "practical," they soon find themselves the prisoners of circumstances; they become political managers entirely, with no sense of political entrepreneurship. The problem of a conservative party in a democracy is not its inability to get elected. It usually does get elected, once the left has made a mess of things (as it inevitably will). But the victory turns out to be a hollow one. The clock is neither set back, nor is it pushed forward according to some new mode of political reckoning. All that happens is that the machinery is tinkered with so as to make it workable once again.

This situation, as it pertains to the American scene, was neatly summed up by the British journalist, Henry Fairlie, in an article in *The New Republic*. Since the end of World War II, Mr. Fairlie said, the Republican Party and the Democratic Party have occupied the White House for the same number of years, but no one thinks of these as Republican years. . . . The conservatives and the Republican Party just do not seem to be part of the history of this century in the way in which the Democratic Party so clearly has been.

To this, Republican leaders might defensively reply that those Republican presidents usually had to coexist with Democratic Congresses, and therefore had little power to accomplish their objectives. But this rejoinder doesn't dispose of the question, it merely reformulates it. *Why* do the American people seem willing to elect Republican presidents but not Republican Congresses? The answer, I would suggest, is that they will not return the Republican Party to power because they do not have clear and reassuring ideas as to (a) what the Republican vision of the American future is, and (b) how it will go about shaping that future.

And so we get conservative frustration, and rebellions against the party leadership, the most obvious recent case being the Reagan rebellion, which may well have cost the Republicans an election they might otherwise have won. But if Mr. Ford had been elected, would that have meant anything more than a slight pause in our march into a Democratic future? And if Mr. Reagan himself had been elected President, how much difference would even that have made? Would he have been able to create a conservative America, any more than he created a conservative California? That's the real trouble with the Republican Party: it loses even when it wins.

Whereas the Democratic left is frustrated because its ideals are inherently unrealizable, Republican conservatives are frustrated because their party has not been able, over these past decades, to articulate any coherent set of ideals and to suggest a strategy for achieving them. The Republican Party has functioned primarily as a critic of Democratic efforts to shape the American future. The criticisms have often been cogent. But finding fault with someone else's program is no substitute for a program of your own.

Why hasn't the Republican Party been able to construct a program of its own, in which the American people can have confidence? I would suggest two reasons. First, the party has never fully reconciled itself to the welfare state, and therefore has never given comprehensive thought to the question of what a *conservative welfare state* would look like. Second, because of their close historic association with the business community, Republican leaders tend to think like businessmen rather than like statesmen, and therefore bumble their way through their terms in office. Let me elaborate.

The idea of a welfare state is in itself perfectly consistent with a conservative political philosophy—as Bismarck knew, a hundred years ago. In our urbanized, industrialized, highly mobile society, people need governmental action of some kind if they are to cope with many of their problems:

old age, illness, unemployment, etc. They need such assistance; they demand it; they will get it. The only interesting political question is: *How* will they get it?

This is not a question the Republican Party has faced up to, because it still feels, deep down, that a welfare state is inconsistent with such traditional American virtues as self-reliance and individual liberty. Those virtues are real enough, and are a proper conservative concern. But the task is to create the kind of welfare state which is consistent, to the largest possible degree, with such virtues.

That is not an impossible task, though it would be foolish to pretend it is an easy one. It is a matter of relating means to ends. But before one can do that, one has to take the ends seriously. One has to believe that the American people really need some sort of medical insurance program, or old age assistance program. Because the Republican Party has never been able to make up its mind about this, it has left the initiative to liberal Democrats. It then finds itself in the position, when in office, of having to administer Democratic programs in the least extravagant way. That's no way for a party to govern.

The basic principle behind a conservative welfare state ought to be a simple one: wherever possible, people should be allowed to keep their own money—rather than having it transferred (via taxes) to the state—on condition that they put it to certain defined uses. Thus, the Republican Party should be demanding that the individual's medical insurance premiums be made tax-deductible. It should be insisting that individuals ought to be free to make additional contributions to their Social Security or pension funds, and that all such contributions should be tax-deductible. (One would then, of course, tax all retirement income, but this would be no great hardship.) It should be demanding that life insurance premiums be made tax-deductible, at least up to a specific point. Policies such as these have the obvious advantage of reconciling the purposes of the welfare state with the maximum degree of individual independence and the least bureaucratic coercion. They would also have the advantage of being quite popular.

So why hasn't the Republican Party been proposing them? The answer has to do with the businessman's mentality that prevails in the party.

I say "businessman's mentality," but a more accurate description would be "accountant's mentality." All of the reforms suggested above would cost the Treasury a lot of money. And all Republican administrations will be quick to explain that, desirable as such reforms might be, they are not feasible "at this time" because they would dangerously unbalance the budget. It is the way they look at the budget that hypnotizes Republican administrations into impotence.

Democrats are more interested in the shape of the budget than its size. Republicans are more interested in its size than its shape. One result of this situation is that Democrats care far less about fiscal integrity and fiscal responsibility than they ought; this is their weakness, for which they are intermittently chided by the electorate. The other result is that Republicans care more about balancing the books than about *what* is being balanced. And this is a far more serious weakness. Indeed, it is a fatal flaw. For it means that the Republican Party spends practically all of its time and energy trying to bring a Democratic budget into balance.

It is the Democratic Party that shapes the nation's future by shaping the federal budget. The self-assigned mission of the Republican Party is to administer this budget so that the nation doesn't go bankrupt. To perform this task, it is intermittently put in office by the electorate. No wonder conservatives become restless and rebellious under such an arrangement!

If the Republican Party were capable of thinking politically—i.e., thinking in terms of shaping the future—it would realize that its first priority is to shape the budget, not to balance it. Then it could go to the electorate with the proper political questions: *How* do you want the budget balanced? By more taxes for more governmental services? Or by lower taxes, lower governmental expenditures, and incentives for the citizen to provide for his own welfare?

Obviously, there is some risk in such a bold approach. The budget, for a while, would indeed be in a perilous condition if some such Republican programs were passed while Democratic programs were not cut back. But that is the only way to permit the American people to choose their future—by making the choice, not only a clear-cut one, but a necessary one.

Unless and until the Republican Party is willing to overcome its bookkeeping inhibitions and become a truly political party, it will be of only marginal significance which faction is in control, or which candidate it proposes.

18

"THE STUPID PARTY"

JOHN STUART MILL once remarked, from the vantage point of his own liberalism, that a conservative party always tends to be "the stupid party." But such a judgment need not be invidious or censorious. Conservative "stupidity," properly understood, is intimately connected with sentiments that are at the root of conservative virtues: a dogged loyalty to a traditional way of life; an instinctive aversion to innovation based on mere theoretical speculation; and a sense of having a fiduciary relation to the whole nation—past, present, and future.

There is always a kind of immunity to fashionable political ideas which is associated with conservatism, and a country that does not have a goodly portion of it is incapable of stable and orderly government. No political or social system can endure without engendering, in a perfectly organic way, this kind of conservative "stupidity." It is the antibody of the body politic.

But there will always come periods in the life of a nation when "stupidity" is not enough. At such times, funda-

mental questions of political philosophy emerge into the
public forum and demand consideration. The life of politics
then becomes enmeshed with the life of the mind, for better
or worse. Venerable clichés, long regarded as self-evident
truths, lose their moral standing as well as all power to persuade. Intellectuals, who are marginal to a healthy society,
suddenly become important political spokesmen. Everything
becomes controversial, and political argument between partisan theorists replaces customary political debate between
politicians. Obviously, when this happens, "the stupid party"
—which is always the less articulate party—finds itself at an
immense disadvantage. And that, it seems to me, is the situation of the Republican Party in the United States today.

Indeed, this has been the situation of the Republican Party
for more than half a century now, which helps explain why
it is today such a minority party. True, the Republican
Party has won its share of elections during this period,
but these successes masked an ever-increasing weakness. In
almost every case, a Republican victory has been the consequence of a Democratic default—of Democratic misman-
agement, of Democratic corruption, of Democratic factional-
ism. Through it all, the Democratic Party has more surely
secured its position as the majority party and the "natural"
governing party. Each Republican administration is marked
at birth as an interregnum, which is what it invariably grows
up to be.

A 20TH-CENTURY TRANSFORMATION

This is not a purely American affair, as developments in
Britain testify. It has to do with the transformation of democratic politics in the 20th century. This politics has become,
at one and the same time, a more naked expression of
group interests and a more ideological expression of political ideals. This may seem paradoxical, but it is not. It is in
the very nature of ideological politics in a democracy to
anchor itself in specific interests, to draw sustenance from
these interests, to mobilize these interests into a party, and
in the end to "use" them for its creative purposes.

The politics of "conservative stupidity," however, is uncomfortable with blunt appeals to interest groups, which it feels to be "divisive." True, when it is out of power the Republican Party can benefit, in a general way, from the dissatisfaction various interests may have with an incumbent administration. But it rarely feels the need to link itself firmly to any of them, to establish itself as their "natural" representative. And when in office, it rarely pays much attention to these interests, preferring to imagine itself as a "national" party whose responsibility is to be "fair" to all citizens.

Similarly, the Republican Party is made uneasy by too close an association with political ideas. In a better world, this would be a desirable, even admirable, trait. But in such a world, the conservative party would indeed be the "natural" governing party—losing an occasional election, to be sure, but then patiently waiting for the "common sense" of the citizenry to reassert itself. That is not the kind of world we live in, and a conservative party which tranquilly watches itself become the party of a minority of registered voters has carried "conservative stupidity" beyond the limits of political reason. Today, a conservative party has to "stand for" a perceived vision of a decent society; it has to be able to articulate the elements and rationale of this vision; and, when it has been in office, one should be able to say what it "stood for," win or lose. Republican administrations since World War II have been sadly lacking in this quality.

It really is ironic that the Democratic Party should have been able to persuade an apparent majority of the American people that it represents the "public interest," whereas the Republican Party is the party of "vested interests." It has been successful in this strategy precisely because it can incorporate its interest-group appeals into a large ideological perspective. But one has only to compare the Democratic and Republican platforms to see which party is more seriously engaged in interest-group politics. And one has only to observe the behavior of Republicans in office to see how negligent they are of their constituencies, actual or possible. Take the case of old people, for instance. Old people tend naturally to be conservative. They have lived long enough to be skeptical of politicians' easy promises about "creating a better world" today or tomorrow. And they have experienced enough fiscal adversity in the course of their own lives to appreciate the importance of fiscal integrity; they "know the value of a dollar," as one says. They ought, therefore, to be voting overwhelmingly for Republican candidates. But they do not, and the reason is simple: Republican administrations never show any particular concern for old people. Ever since its idiotic hostility to the original Social Security legislation, the Republican Party in office has never, on its own initiative, gone out of its way to do anything striking for the benefit of the elderly. On the contrary: it always ends up in the position of trying to pare existing benefits for these people.

When one inquires in Washington why this is the case, the answer is always in terms of "fiscal integrity." Programs for the elderly are very expensive; the budget is out of balance; economies must be made. But this is to substitute a narrow accounting perspective on reality for a truly political one, i.e., a comprehensive one. To begin with, the money saved by a Republican administration will promptly be spent by a Democratic Congress or a subsequent Democratic administration, to whom will accrue all the political credit. But more important, one cannot achieve fiscal integrity in government until one has a strong constituency in favor of it; and old people must be part of any such constituency. Spending money on old people may be bad for the budget in the short run, but it is a step toward eventual fiscal sobriety. If our senior citizens are not given any stake in the success of a conservative party, but on the contrary are constantly being alarmed and menaced by this party, where shall a conservative politics sink its roots?

THE "REAL" BUSINESS COMMUNITY

Or take the case of "the business community," with which the Republican Party is supposed to have an intimate association. In fact, that intimacy is mainly with the executives of a few hundred large corporations, not with the several million small businesses, which Republican administrations tend to ignore. Such intimacy, in turn, is largely the result of substituting a narrow economic perspective on reality for a comprehensive political one. Our large corporations are crucial economic institutions, and their condition is of great significance for the kind of macroeconomic thinking that goes on in the Council of Economic Advisers, the Treasury, and the Office of Management and Budget. But they have, if anything, a negative value as a political constituency. They suggest a combination of privilege and power which a democracy will always be suspicious of, and they can offer precious few votes. Meanwhile, the *real* business community (real in political terms), made up of smaller business proprietors, benefits hardly at all from a conservative administration and is given little stake in conservative successes. Just contrast the consideration with which the Democrats treat trade unions to the petty, grudging concessions which the Republicans make to small business, and the point is only too obvious.

Much the same point can be made about other elements that might add up to a conservative constituency: farmers, homeowners (actual or prospective), and others. There is a possible conservative majority out there—unless a nation is in the process of disintegration—but it has to be welded together out of disparate parts; it has to be created, not just assumed. And it can only be created through the unifying power of political ideas.

There are many conservative thinkers in this country now trying to provide such ideas. I happen to have grave reservations about many of those ideas. Too often they are engaged in futile protest against the principles of the welfare state, instead of trying to construct a conservative welfare state. But such disagreement is less important than the fact that all such ideas float around the periphery of the Republican Party. No one seems to take them seriously.

The world would doubtless be a nicer and healthier place if large ideas were kept at a distant remove from political power. The close conjunction is a dangerous one. But the world is what it is. It is a world of media, a world where habit and custom are weak before the forces of communication. It is, therefore, a world where ideas and their articulation are indispensable to effective conservative government, because it is only such ideas that can provide definition and coherence to the conservative constituency. "Political stupidity," alas, will no longer suffice.

19

ON CONSERVATISM

AND CAPITALISM

THESE DAYS, Americans who defend the capitalist system, i.e., an economy and a way of life organized primarily around the free market, are called "conservative." If they are willing to accept a limited degree of government intervention for social purposes, they are likely to be designated as "neo-conservative." Under ordinary circumstances these labels would strike me as fair and appropriate. Capitalism, after all, is the traditional American economic and social system; unlike the nations of Europe, we have never known any other. And people who wish to defend and preserve traditional institutions are indeed conservative, in the literal sense of that term.

But the circumstances surrounding the use of such labels today are *not* ordinary; they are almost paradoxical. To begin with, the institutions which conservatives wish to preserve are, and for two centuries were called, *liberal* institutions, i.e., institutions which maximize personal liberty vis-à-vis a state, a church, or an official ideology. On the other hand, the severest critics of these institutions—those who wish to enlarge the scope of governmental authority indefinitely, so as to achieve ever greater equality at the expense of liberty—are today commonly called "liberals." It would certainly help to clarify matters if they were called, with greater propriety and accuracy, "socialists" or "neo-socialists." And yet we are oddly reluctant to be so candid.

In part, this lack of candor is simply the consequence of a great many "liberals" being demagogic or hypocritical about their political intentions. It really is absurd that Bella Abzug should call herself a "liberal" when her political views are several shades to the left of Harold Wilson, Helmut Schmidt, Olof Palme, or probably even Indira Gandhi. Obviously, however, she is not about to reject the label, which is so useful to her. Instead, when asked, she may blandly assert that she is truly an enlightened defender of the free enterprise system. One would have to be naive to blame her, and others like her, for saying it; we can only blame ourselves for believing it.

It is clear that, in addition to such routine political deception, there is an enormous amount of a most curious self-deception going on. I find it striking that the media, and members of the business community too, should consistently refer to John Kenneth Galbraith as a "liberal" when he has actually taken the pains to write a book explaining why he is a socialist. And even Michael Harrington, who is the official head of a minuscule socialist party, will often find himself being introduced as "a leading liberal spokesman."

Why does this happen? And why, especially, do conservatives permit it to happen? Why should those who defend liberal institutions have yielded the term "liberal" to those who have no honorable intentions toward these institutions or, indeed, toward liberty itself?

The answer, I think, has to do with the fact that the idea of "liberty" which conservatives wish to defend, and which our liberal institutions are supposed to incarnate, has become exceedingly nebulous in the course of the past century.

This puts conservatives in the position of being, or seeming to be, merely mindless defenders of the status quo. Indeed, to many they seem merely intransigent defenders of existing privilege, issuing appeals to "liberty" for such an ulterior purpose alone. This, in turn, has permitted "liberals" to impress their own definition of "liberty" on public opinion.

This "liberal" definition has two parts. First, it entails ever-greater governmental intervention in certain areas—economics, educational administration, the electoral process, etc.—to achieve greater equality, itself now identified with "true liberty." Second, it entails less governmental intervention in those areas—religion, school curricula, culture, entertainment, etc.—which have to do with the formation of character, and in which it is assumed that "the marketplace of ideas" will "naturally" produce ideal results.

The success which this "liberal" redefinition—a combination of moralistic egalitarianism and optimistic "permissiveness"—has achieved means that, in the United States today, the law insists that an 18-year-old girl has the right to public fornication in a pornographic movie—but only if she is paid the minimum wage. Now, you don't have to be the father of a daughter to think that there is something crazy about this situation, and the majority of the American people, if asked, would certainly say so. Nevertheless, conservatives find it very difficult to point out where the craziness lies, and to propose an alternative conception of liberty. As the saying goes, you can't beat a horse with no horse; and right now conservatives are horseless.

Ever since the beginnings of modern capitalism in the 18th century, two very different conceptions of liberty have emerged. The first was the "libertarian" idea. It asserted that God and/or nature had so arranged things that, by the operations of an "invisible hand," individual liberty, no matter how self-seeking, could only lead ultimately to humanity's virtuous happiness. "Private vices, public benefits" was its motto—and still is.

The second idea of liberty may be called the "bourgeois" idea. It asserted that liberty implied the right to do bad as well as the right to do good, that liberty could be abused as well as used—in short, that a distinction had to be made between liberty and "license." The making of this distinction was the task of our cultural and religious institutions, especially the latter. It was these institutions which infused the idea of liberty with positive substance, with "values," with an ethos. The basic belief was that a life led according to these values would maximize personal liberty in a context of social and political stability, would ensure—insofar as this is humanly possible—that the exercise of everyone's personal liberty would add up to a decent and good society. The practical virtues implied by the "bourgeois" values were not very exciting: thrift, industry, self-reliance, self-discipline, a moderate degree of public-spiritedness, and so forth. On the other hand, they had the immense advantage of being rather easily attainable by everyone. You didn't have to be a saint or a hero to be a good bourgeois citizen.

It did not take long for the culture emerging out of bourgeois society to become bored with, and hostile to, a life and a social order based on such prosaic bourgeois values. Artists and intellectuals quickly made it apparent that "alienation" was their destiny, and that the mission of this culture was to be anti-bourgeois. But so long as religion was a powerful force among ordinary men and women, the disaffection of the intellectuals was of only marginal significance. It is the decline in religious belief over the past 50 years—together with the rise of mass higher education, which popularized the culture's animus to bourgeois capitalism—that has been of decisive importance.

ADAM SMITH'S MISTAKE

The defenders of capitalism were, and are, helpless before this challenge. Businessmen, after all, had never taken culture seriously. They have always rather agreed with Adam Smith when he wrote:

> Though you despise that picture, or that poem, or even that system of philosophy which I admire, there is little danger of our quarreling on that account. Neither of us can reasonably be much interested about them.

He could not have been more wrong. What rules the world is ideas, because ideas define the way reality is perceived; and, in the absence of religion, it is out of culture—pictures, poems, songs, philosophy—that these ideas are born.

It is because of their indifference to culture, their placid philistinism, that businessmen today find themselves defending capitalism and personal liberty in purely amoral terms. They are "libertarians"—but without a belief in the providential dispensations of God or nature. Capitalism, they keep insisting, is the most *efficient* economic system. This may be true if you agree with Adam Smith when he said: "What can be added to the happiness of man who is in health, who is out of debt, and has a clear conscience?" But if you believe that a comfortable life is not necessarily the same thing as a good life, or even a meaningful life, then it will occur to you that efficiency is a means, not an end in itself. Capitalist efficiency may then be regarded as a most useful precondition for a good life in a good society. But one has to go beyond Adam Smith, or capitalism itself, to discover the other elements that are wanted.

It was religion and the bourgeois ethos that used to offer this added dimension to capitalism. But religion is now ineffectual, and even businessmen find the bourgeois ethos embarrassingly old-fashioned. This leaves capitalism, and its conservative defenders, helpless before any moralistic assault, however unprincipled. And until conservatism can give its own moral and intellectual substance to its idea of liberty, the "liberal" subversion of our liberal institutions will proceed without hindrance.

20

ON CORPORATE

PHILANTHROPY

WHEN Henry Ford II resigned from the board of the Ford
Foundation, he was moved to remind it that it was "a creature
of capitalism." And he went on to suggest delicately to the
trustees and staff that "the system that made the foundation
possible very probably is worth preserving."

Those words captured the attention of the media, which
perceived an obvious irony in a Ford defending capitalism
against the foundation which Ford money established.
Those same words also created reverberations within the
academic and business communities, exciting latent and powerful anxieties about the relations between the two realms.

Since there is going to be, and already has been, a great
deal of hypocritical nonsense uttered about this matter, it
may be useful to do some sorting out. The facts themselves
are not really in dispute, but the proper inferences to be
drawn from these facts most certainly are.

To begin with, it is a fact that the majority of the large
foundations in this country, like most of our major univer-

sities, exude a climate of opinion wherein an anti-business bent becomes a perfectly natural inclination. One does not wish to exaggerate or be dogmatic about this situation. Those foundations and universities are not homogeneous or totalitarian institutions; not all divisions and departments have identical attitudes, and these attitudes themselves are not consistently sovereign.

Thus—and this is a suitable place to declare an interest— the Ford Foundation has been helpful to my own journal, *The Public Interest,* and has made some modest grants to the American Enterprise Institute, with which I am associated. Nevertheless, it is fair and accurate to say that most of the time the Ford Foundation seems more interested in supporting people and activities that display a habitual animus to the business community. Henry Ford II was not suffering from delusions of persecution.

There is not really any puzzle or paradox in this state of affairs. Foundations and universities are for the most part— though not exclusively—populated by those members of the "new class" who sincerely believe that the large portion of human virtue is to be found in the public sector, and the larger portion of human vice in the private.

If one reads a publication like the *Foundation News,* one gets a pretty unambiguous impression as to the attitudes that prevail. Thus, in 1976, the board of the Council of Foundations passed a resolution urging all foundations "to recognize the urgent obligation to help bring about constructive social change." One would have to have spent these past decades on another planet to believe that "constructive social change" might involve limiting governmental powers rather than expanding them. In our universities, in our foundations, and in our media too, "constructive social change" is always something that government does for and to people, never something that people do for and to themselves—and most definitely nothing that American business does for or to anyone.

Since foundations and universities are the idea-germinating and idea-legitimizing institutions of our society, this bias—the word may here be used descriptively rather than

polemically—is a serious problem for those of us who are
concerned for the preservation of a liberal society under
limited government. After all, these are the ideas that our
children encounter in their textbooks, in their teachers, and
on their television screen. It would seem both right and
proper to worry about them.

Yet any such expressions of concern are quickly countered
by accusations that, should such concern become widespread, "academic freedom" would be endangered. This is
a red herring. True, it would be dangerous if angry citizens
thought they had the right to prescribe foundation policies,
or the content of a university curriculum, or the composition
of the faculty. There is even danger in businessmen trying to
endow chairs of "free enterprise" on a university campus.

In such cases the liberal ideal of a university, where freedom of thought is respected and where no system of thought
—no ideology, to put it bluntly—is given a privileged or
official status, is violated. Economists in a university, after
all, are supposed to teach economics, not free enterprise or
socialism. The fact that many professors of economics violate
their obligation to teach economics, and teach ideology instead, is indeed a problem, but not one that can be solved by
aggravating the condition to a degree where everyone *legiti-
mately* teaches his own ideology.

On the other hand, it does not follow that businessmen or
corporations have any obligation to give money to institutions whose views or attitudes they disapprove of. It is absurd to insist otherwise. Yet this absurdity is consistently set
forth by college presidents, and in the name of "academic
freedom." When David Packard and William Simon made
the perfectly reasonable suggestion that corporations look
before they give, and discriminate among friends, neutral
and foe in their philanthropy, they were denounced in the
most vehement terms by universities which seemed to think
they had some kind of *right* to that money.

They have no such right. If they want money from any
particular segment of the population, it is their job to earn
the good opinion of that segment. If they are indifferent to
that good opinion, they will just have to learn to be indif-

ferent to the money too. That's the way it is, and that's the way it's supposed to be in a free society where philanthropy is just as free as speech.

Many businessmen—most, I imagine—will find this line of thought congenial enough, but will still end up uneasy and confused. Where do we go from here, they will ask? For the sad truth is that the business community has never thought seriously about its philanthropy, and doesn't know how.

Some corporate executives seem to think that their corporate philanthropy is a form of benevolent charity. It is not. An act of charity refines and elevates the soul of the giver, but corporations have no souls to be saved or damned. Charity involves dispensing your own money, not your stockholders'. When you give away your own money, you can be as foolish, as arbitrary, as whimsical as you like. But when you give away your stockholders' money, your philanthropy must serve the longer-term interests of the corporation. Corporate philanthropy should not be, and cannot be, disinterested.

One such corporate interest, traditionally recognized, is usually defined as "public relations," but can more properly be described as meeting one's communal responsibilities. This involves donations to local hospitals, welfare funds, and other benevolent organizations active in the community where the corporation resides. In a sense, this philanthropy is *mandated* by community opinion, and there are few interesting or controversial decisions about it for the executives to make.

In addition to such mandated philanthropic expenditures, however, there are the *controllable* expenditures. These latter reflect a movement beyond communal responsibility to "social responsibility." Different corporations may well have different conceptions of such "social responsibility," and there is nothing wrong with that. But most corporations would presumably agree that any such conception ought to include as one of its goals the survival of the corporation itself as a relatively autonomous institution in the private sector. And this inevitably involves efforts to shape or reshape the climate of public opinion, a climate that is created by our scholars, our teachers, our intellectuals, our publicists: in short, by the New Class.

How are corporations to proceed in this direction? Well, one preliminary step, already mentioned, would be to decide *not* to give money to support those activities of the "new class" which are inimical to corporate survival.

A more positive step, of course, would be for corporations to give support to those elements of the "new class"—and they exist, if not in large numbers—which do believe in the preservation of a strong private sector. For the "new class," fortunately, is not an utterly homogeneous entity. It contains men and women who are not necessarily "pro business," and who may not be much interested in business at all, but who *are* interested in individual liberty and limited government, who *are* worried about the collectivist tendencies in the society. The large foundations regard their views as being somewhat short of "respectable" and they tend to be ignored by the business community, which is often unaware of their existence.

"How can we identify such people, and discriminate intelligently among them?" corporate executives always inquire plaintively. Well, if you decide to go exploring for oil, you find a competent geologist. Similarly, if you wish to make a productive investment in the intellectual and educational worlds, you find competent intellectuals and scholars—"dissident" members as it were, of the "new class"—to offer guidance. Yet few corporations seek any such advice on their philanthropy. How many large corporations make use of academic advisory committees for this purpose? Almost none, so far as I can determine.

This is a melancholy situation, for in any naked contest with the "new class," business is a certain loser. Businessmen who cannot even persuade their own children that business is a morally legitimate activity are not going to succeed, on their own, in persuading the world of it. You can only beat an idea with another idea, and the war of ideas and ideologies will be won or lost within the "new class," not against it. Business certainly has a stake in this war, but for the most part seems blithely unaware of it.

21

THE SHAREHOLDER

CONSTITUENCY

AT the annual meeting of Sperry Rand in 1974, the chairman of that corporation urged the company's 100,000 shareholders to start lobbying with the federal government in order to create a more pro-business climate in Washington. As quoted in the *Wall Street Journal*, Mr. J. Paul Lyet said: "When a business manager talks to a politician, he listens politely; but when thousands of stockholders and employees speak up, he listens attentively."

Yes, of course—only it's not quite that simple. Mr. Lyet was pointing to a terribly important problem, but with a somewhat wavering finger. The problem is: Where does the modern corporation find its political constituency? The wavering is caused by a failure to realize that, in a democracy, constituencies are not born but created, and once created they need constant, attentive cultivation. This is something all politicians understand with ease. In contrast, corporate management seems hardly to understand it at all.

No institution in our society can endure without a constituency—a substantial number of people who are loyal to
the institution and who will quickly rally to its defense when
it is in trouble. Yet the modern corporation is just about the
only major institution of our society which does not have
such a constituency. Traditionally, it has never felt the need
for one. Instead, it was able to rely for self-defense upon two
bulwarks. The first was the courts, which used to regard the
corporation as a "person" and gave its assets constitutional
protection as a form of "private property." The second was its
own corps of lobbyists, who could quietly persuade legislators, by one means or another, of the unwisdom of various
anti-business proposals.

Both of these bulwarks have now crumbled. The courts
today clearly regard the corporation as a kind of social,
rather than private, property. Short of outright confiscation,
there is almost nothing legislators can do to the corporation
which will not be upheld by the courts. As for the lobbyists,
they have very little "clout" these days as compared with the
bureaucracy and its allies in the media, with organized
labor, organized consumer groups, organized environmental groups, etc. Most of their time and energy is
spent in carrying out adult education programs among
legislators and their staffs—an absolutely vital task but one
which cannot, in the nature of things, show glowing results in
the way of academic achievement. Education, as we know,
depends upon motivation, and not all legislators are motivated by a pure love of learning.

So the corporation today is largely defenseless: a nice,
big, fat, juicy target for every ambitious politician, and a
most convenient scapegoat for every variety of organized
discontent. The hostility toward the large corporation is
not new, it has been visible for about a century now. But
what *is* new is the corporation's utter defenselessness against
this hostility. There it is, a wealthy and powerful institution
that is utterly vulnerable to a political takeover bid. Naturally, the competition is keen.

The corporation, as never before, needs a constituency.
And though, in some instances, employees or customers may

realistically be regarded as belonging to such a constituency, in just about all instances it is the stockholders to
whom the corporation will naturally turn. Management, after
all, is supposedly elected by the stockholders. It is through
this political process that management derives its legal and
moral legitimacy—not, as some think, from "performance."
The stockholders already are a constituency in theory; the
question is how to make them a constituency in fact. What
management is so reluctant to realize is that this requires
forethought, hard work, and more than a little self-sacrifice.

Essentially the attitude of most managements is that it
would be nice if stockholders formed a constituency, so long
as this constituency was no bother to management. But
that's not the way the process of political representation
works. As I have already suggested, you first have to create
the constituency; then you have to nourish it; and finally
you have to be responsive to it.

CREATING A CONSTITUENCY

A constituent is a citizen, i.e., someone who resides in your
community and has a stake in its future. A person who is
merely passing through, whether a tourist or traveling sales-
man, is not a constituent. The trouble with regarding shareholders as a constituency is that this important distinction
does not exist either in law or practice. Some shareholders
are indeed corporate citizens, i.e., they are *investors*, who
buy for the long term and therefore have a responsible
concern for the corporation's long-run prosperity. Many
shareholders, however, are only *speculators*, who buy the
stock but not the company, and are only interested in selling
their stock at a profit as soon as circumstances permit. These
latter do not think like a constituency and will never act like
one. Their instinct, in time of trouble, will always be to abandon ship.

The first job of management, therefore, is to create a corporate constituency by favoring the investor as against the
speculator. There are various ways of doing this, no doubt,

and all should be explored. But one recommends itself for its elegant simplicity. That is, to give extra stock dividends to the investor, e.g., a 5 percent stock dividend for each five years that the stock is held. The net effect would be to offer the investor both greater downside protection and upside potentialities, all at the expense of the speculator.

I am told that, as things now stand, changes in the law and/or SEC regulations may be necessary to achieve this reform (though no one seems certain). But this should not be too hard to accomplish: ours is a society which looks more benignly on investors than on speculators, and discrimination in favor of the former is likely to be quite popular.

NOURISHING A CONSTITUENCY

Once your shareholders are more predominantly investors in the company, rather than speculators in its stock, their loyalty must be cultivated. This is a political exercise which will involve the top management of the company, and not merely the public relations department. Shareholders will need to be candidly and fully informed of how the company is doing, what the company is doing, and why. Since these are people who are going to be around for a long time, there is no point in "selling" them flashy—and frequently deceptive—year-to-year results. That demagogic strategy might work for a while. But adversity is always around the corner, and a management which misleads is a management that had better have a second career to fall back on.

It really is extraordinary how little attention management now pays to its shareholders. In general, it pays less attention than the average college does to its alumni (who are an important part of *its* constituency). How many corporations send out regular newsletters to their shareholders, in addition to the quarterly reports? How many corporations arrange for their management to meet with groups of shareholders in various cities—to report, answer questions, and discuss? How many corporations invite shareholders to visit and inspect their plants and facilities? This is the sort of thing colleges routinely do for their alumni or for parents of their students. I know of no corporation that cultivates its own natural constituency to any comparable degree.

BEING RESPONSIVE TO A CONSTITUENCY

The neglect of shareholders by management is not accidental. For people at the top, autocracy is always a more convenient and less bothersome system than representative government. It is also, in many ways, a genuinely more efficient system in that the decision-making process is less complicated, more rational. Indeed, the idea of "shareholder participation" is a nightmare from which management is always trying to awake.

Nevertheless, if you want a constituency that will support you against unreasonable government regulation and harassment, you have to pay the price for it. And the price is some diminution of management's prerogatives. Thus, Mobil Oil's decision to try to merge with Marcor may or may not have been a prudent one, from a purely economic point of view. But was it really prudent of Mobil to make no effort whatsoever to discover how its own shareholders felt about this prospect? That kind of autocratic decision-making only serves to cast doubt on the legitimacy of corporate management itself, and to invite even further government involvement in the affairs of all corporations.

It is safe to predict that corporate management will enthusiastically greet the idea of having a constituency behind it. It is also safe to predict that this same management will move quickly to ensure that this constituency is more symbolic than real: something to evoke when necessary, and to forget about when possible. That won't work. If management is serious about preserving the integrity of the corporation as a legitimate institution of the private sector, it has to be prepared to shoulder new and burdensome responsibilities of an unfamiliar kind. And there is no way it can shift this burden onto anyone or anything else.

PART THREE

What Is
"Social Justice"?

22

UTOPIANISM,

ANCIENT AND MODERN

MEN are dreaming animals, and the incapacity to dream makes a man less than human. Indeed, we have no knowledge of any human community where men do fail to dream. Which is to say, we know of no human community whose members do not have a vision of perfection—a vision in which the frustrations inherent in our human condition are annulled and transcended. The existence of such dreaming visions is not, in itself, a problem. They are, on the contrary, a testament to the creativity of man which flows from the fact that he is a creature uniquely endowed with imaginative powers as an essential aspect of his self-consciousness. Only a madman would wish to abolish men's dreams, i.e., to return humanity to a purely animal condition, and we are fortunate in having had—until recently, at any rate—little historical experience of such madness. It is true that, of late, certain

writers—notably Norman O. Brown—hold out the promise of
such regression as a kind of ultimate redemption. But even
their most admiring readers understand that this is largely
literary license, rather than a serious political agenda.

On the other hand, and far more common, there are also
madmen who find it impossible to disentangle dreams from
reality—and of this kind of madness we have had, alas, far
too much experience. Indeed, it would not be an exaggeration to say that a good part of modern history takes place
under the sign of this second kind of madness, which we
familiarly call "utopianism."

I am using the term, "madness," advisedly and not merely
to be provocative. The intellectual history of the past four
centuries consists of islands of sanity floating in an ocean of
"dottiness," as the British call it. We don't see this history in
this way, and certainly don't study it in this way, because—
I would suggest—we have ourselves been infected by this
pervasive "dottiness." Just look at the cautious and respectful way our textbooks treat the French utopian theorists of
the 19th century: Saint-Simon, Comte, Fourier, and their
many loyal disciples. It is no exaggeration to say that all of
these men were quite literally "touched in the head" and that
their writings can fairly be described as the feverish scrib-
blings of disordered minds. Fourier, for instance, divided
humanity into no less than 810 distinct character types and
then devised a social order that brought each character type
his own special brand of happiness. He also believed that,
in the ideal world of the future, the salty oceans would
benevolently turn themselves into seas of lemonade, and that
men would grow tails with eyes at the tip. Saint-Simon and
Comte were somewhat less extreme in their lunacies—but not
all that much. To read them, which so few actually do today,
is to enter a world of phantasmagoria. Oh yes, one can cull
"insights," as we say, from their many thousands of pages.
But the inmates of any asylum, given pen and paper, will
also produce their share of such "insights"—only it doesn't
ordinarily occur to us that this is a good way of going about
the collecting of insights. It is only when people write about
politics in a large way that we are so indulgent to their

madness, so eager to discover inspired prophecy in their fulminations.

It is not too much to say that we are all utopians now, in ways we no longer realize, we are so habituated to them. Further than that: we are even utopian when we think we are being very practical and rational. My own favorite instance of such subterranean utopianism is in an area where one is least likely to look for it. I refer to the area of city planning.

William H. Whyte, Jr., in his excellent book, *The Last Landscape,* has pointed out that, if you examine the thousands of plans which now exist for shiny, new, wonderful cities, there is always one thing that is certain to be missing. That one thing is—a cemetery. In a properly planned city, the fact that people die is taken to be such an unwarranted intrusion into an otherwise marvelous equilibrium that city planners simply cannot face up to it. After all, if people die and are replaced by new and different people, then the carefully prescribed "mix" of jobs, of housing, of leisure-time activities—all this is going to be upset. Modern city planning, whether in the form of constructing New Towns or Cities Beautiful, is inherently and radically utopian in that it aims to bring history to a stop at a particular moment of perfection. The two traditions of urban planning I have just mentioned disagree in their attitude toward modern technology and modern industrial society—the one wishing to minimize their influence, the other wanting to exploit their potentialities to the utmost. But both are, as a matter of historical fact, descended from various 19th century utopian-socialist movements, and neither of them can bear to contemplate the fact that men are permanently subject to time and changing circumstances.

That is why city planners are so infuriated when someone like Jane Jacobs comes along and points out that the absence of old buildings in their model cities is a critical flaw because old buildings, with their cheap rents, are needed by the small entrepreneur, the bohemian intellectual, the dilatory graduate student, the amateur scholar, and eccentrics of all kinds. These are the people who give urban life its color, its vitality, its excitement—and who, moreover, play an indispensable role in the dynamics of urban growth and decay. But growth and decay are precisely what most offend the utopian cast of mind, for which time is an enemy to be subdued. And this is why the dimension of time is so rigorously excluded from modern city planning—and from modern architecture too, which derives from the same utopian tradition. Ask a city planner or an architect whether his work will grow old gracefully, and he finds your question incomprehensible. His is the perfection of art, which is immune to time, which does not age or wither or renew itself. That human beings and human societies do age and wither and renew themselves is for him only an immense inconvenience, and he cannot wait until our social sciences shall have resolved that problem.

This utopian cast of mind I have been describing is quite rational, only it has ceased to be reasonable. And this divorce between rationality and reasonableness, which is characteristic of so many forms of madness, is also a crucial feature of modern utopianism.

Rationality has always been taken to be a criterion of utopias. This, in turn, means that utopian dreaming is a very special kind of dreaming. All of us are aware, for instance, that there is a difference between a vision of paradise or heaven on the one hand, and a vision of utopia on the other. The Old and New Testaments—or the Koran, for that matter —do not present us with utopias. It would be ridiculous to take literally or seriously any specific remarks that are found in these documents concerning the social or economic structure of heaven, or the mode of governance to be found there. Similarly, all depictions of man in his unfallen condition are not meant to be analytically scrutinized. Dreams of this order do tell us something about the nature of man, but only in the most general and allusive way. They are a kind of myth, a kind of poetry, not a kind of political philosophy. And that is why all religions take such a very dim view of those among their adherents who give too much detailed attention to such myths. It is taken as a sign of either mental instability or willful heresy when someone begins speculating in some detail about how things really were in Paradise, or how they are likely to be in Heaven. To ask questions—or worse, to give answers—about, say, the relation between the sexes in Paradise or Heaven is to transgress the boundaries of acceptable discourse. Such speculation is ordinarily forbidden, or at least frowned upon, by religious authorities.

Utopian thinking, in contrast, is a species of philosophical thinking, and arises historically at that moment when philosophy disengages itself from myth and declares its independent status. Which is to say, of course, that it is first observable among the Greeks. Plato's *Republic* is the first utopian discourse we know of, a work of the philosophic imagination. There are myths in *The Republic*, of course, but they are recounted as myths, not as authoritative history. Moreover, *The Republic* is constructed before our eyes, step by step, by dialectical discourse among reasoning men. Though the end result will certainly strike many of us as being quite an absurd picture of an ideal society, there is nothing illogical in it, nothing miraculous, nothing superhuman. It is a possible society, violating none of the laws of nature and inhabited solely by men who are governed by recognizably human motives and passions.

All this is clear, and yet this clarity is but the occasion for a larger mystery which scholars have been exploring for two millennia now. What was Plato's intention? Was he being solemn throughout or playful throughout? How seriously did he mean us to take his ideal society? And if he did mean us to take it seriously, *in what way* did he want us to take it seriously?

These questions continue to be debated today, and will doubtless be debated forever. The view of Plato's utopia which I find most plausible—a view derived from the writings of Professor Leo Strauss—is that it is primarily a pedagogic construction. After all, Plato was neither a fool nor a madman—we could take Aristotle's word for that, even if his other dialogues did not make it evident—and he was not likely to confuse a philosopher's imaginings with the world as it is. Even if he did believe that the society described in *The Republic* would be the best of all possible societies—and we

must assume he did believe it, since he says so—he almost
surely did *not* believe that it was ever likely to exist. For it
to come into existence, as he makes plain, you would need
a most improbable conjunction of circumstances: an absolutely wise man given absolute power to construct a new
social order—to do it without hindrance or restriction of any
kind. This is not a logical impossibility; if it were, there
would have been no point at all in writing *The Republic*. On
the other hand, it is so unreal a possibility that a reasonable
man would not allow it to govern his particular attitude
toward any particular society at any particular time. As
Professor Strauss puts it, Plato's utopia exists in words,
not in deeds. The one existence is as authentically human as
the other, but there is a world of difference between them.

This is, I should say, the basic attitude of all classical, pre-
modern utopian thinking. Constructing a utopia was a useful act of the philosophical imagination. Contemplating such
a constructed utopia—studying it, analyzing it, arguing over
it—was a marvelous exercise in moral and political philosophy. Both the construction and the contemplation were an
elevating affair, leading to self-improvement of mind for
those talented few who were capable of it. It also provided
one with an invaluable perspective on the essential limitations of one's own society—a philosophical wisdom about
things political that was superior to the reigning conventional
political wisdom. But all of this was, in the highest sense of
the term, "academic." Utopias existed to produce better political philosophers, not better politics. True, the existence of
better political philosophers *might*, at some point, have a
benevolent effect upon the society in which they lived. But
the odds were overwhelmingly against it, and in his practical conduct of life the supreme virtue for the philosopher, as
for everyone else, was prudence.

All of this is most perfectly and beautifully exemplified in
the last of the classical utopias, Sir Thomas More's treatise
which introduced the word itself, "utopia," into our Western
languages. More's *Utopia* stands as an indictment of the
gross imperfections in the social and political orders of his
day. It was a most subversive document, but its aim was to

subvert only young students of political philosophy, who could read the Latin in which it was written, and who could then be spiritually transported into the "good place" (the literal meaning of the Greek term, *eutopos*), the "no-place" (the literal meaning of *outopos*) which was the philosopher's realm of freedom. More himself, as we know, went into the service of King Henry VIII in order, as he explicitly informs us, to minimize the evils which a ruler may introduce into the world as it is. In loyally serving King Henry, he never repudiated his utopian vision: he never apparently had the sense he was in any way "compromising" it; and he certainly never pretended that he was engaged in "realizing" it. He simply thought that, as a political philosopher with a superior vision of the ideal, he might prudently influence the politics of his time toward somewhat more humane ends. He failed utterly, as we know, and paid for his failure with his life. But he was not at all surprised that he failed, nor was he shocked to discover the price of his failure. A less utopian statesman than the author of *Utopia* is hard to find. And yet there was not an ounce of cynicism in him. His nobility of character consisted precisely in the fact that, even as he could imagine the world as it might be, he could also live and work in the world as it was, trying to edge the latter ever so slightly toward the former, but experiencing no sour disillusionment at his ultimate lack of success. Such a perfect combination of detachment from the world and simultaneous attachment to it is as exemplary as it is rare.

After Sir Thomas More, we are in the modern era, the era of utopian-*ism*. By utopian*ism* I mean that frame of mind which asserts that utopias are *ideals to be realized*—to be realized in deed and not merely in words, in historical time and not merely in the timelessness of speculative thought. This conception of utopia is so familiar to us, and so congenial to us, that when *we* call someone "utopian" we mean no more than that he is unduly optimistic about the time necessary to achieve the ideal, or perhaps unduly enthusiastic about his particular version of the ideal. The notion that a utopia is an ideal to be realized does not strike us as inherently unreasonable; we ask only that men be not too exigent in demanding their perfect society here and now. *That,* we say, is to be "utopian." In contrast, the ancients tell us that to demand a perfect society in the foreseeable future is to be mad; while to expect a perfect society to exist at all, at any time, is to be utopian. By the standards of the ancients, the modern era and its modern societies are suffused with quite unreasonable expectations, and have therefore an equally unreasonable attitude toward political reality. We confuse words with deeds, philosophical dreams with the substantial actualities of human existence. And, of course, the ancients anticipated that from such a dire confusion only disaster could result.

Just how it happened that the utopian mode of thought emerged so strongly in the 16th and 17th centuries is something that our historians can only partially explain. Perhaps we ought not to demand more than partial explanations from them; such a mutation of the human spirit is, one might say, as inexplicable as it was unpredictable. Still, it does seem clear that certain identifiable trends of thought, all in their different ways, contributed to the event. These trends can be identified as millenarianism, rationalism, and what Professor Hayek calls "scientism."

Millenarianism is an intrinsic aspect of the Judeo-Christian tradition, and without it there would be no such thing as the *history* of Western civilization, as distinct from the *chronicles* of Western peoples. It is from the millenarian perspective that both Judaism and Christianity derive their very special sense of history as a story with a beginning, a middle, and an end—a conception of historical time that is not to be found in Oriental thought, which seeks and finds ultimate perfection only in a denial of time's meaning, and in a transcendence of time by the contemplative and withdrawn individual. The dynamics of Western civilization are organically linked to this profound belief in "the end of time" as a prospective historical event. This belief always created immense problems for the religious authorities, and Church and synagogue responded with efforts to impose reasonable limitations upon this millennial expectation. In both Judaism and Christianity those who attempted to "hasten the end," whether through magic or politics, were defined as heretics and were expelled from the religious community. This did not prevent such heresies from bubbling up, again and again, but the church did contain them, or even assimilate them (as in the case of the Franciscan movement), for more than a thousand years. In the 16th century, however, as religious authority fragmented under the impact of what we call the Reformation, these millennial expectations overflowed, and have never been entirely subdued since. What we now call the "prophetic" element in Judaism and Christianity became the intellectually and even popularly dominant element. Indeed, in the United States today you can claim prophetic status and justify any excess of prophetic fervor on the basis of nothing more than an introductory course in sociology.

What makes modern millenarianism so powerful—one is tempted to say irresistible—is its association with modern scientific rationalism and modern technology. Scientific rationalism also emerges in the 16th century, persuading us that reality can be fully comprehended by man's abstract reason, and that therefore whatever exists should be capable of being rationally explained in a clear and consequential way. As applied to all social institutions, this came to mean—it is, indeed, the essential meaning of that period we call the Enlightenment—that existing institutions could be legitimized only by reason: not by tradition, not by custom, not even by the fact that they seemed to be efficacious in permitting men to lead decent lives, but only by reason. It was against this mode of thought, an inherently radical-utopian mode of thought, that Edmund Burke polemicized so magnificently. It was against this radical-utopian temper that modern conservatism emerges. Modern conservatism found it necessary to argue what had always been previously assumed by all reasonable men: that institutions which have existed over a long period of time have a reason and a purpose inherent in them, a collective wisdom incarnate in them, and the fact that we don't perfectly understand or cannot perfectly explain why they "work" is no defect in them but merely a limitation in us. Most ordinary people, most of the

time, intuitively feel the force of this conservative argument.
But these same ordinary people are defenseless intellectually
against the articulated and aggressive rationalism of our intellectual class—and this explains why, when modern men do
rebel against the unreasonableness of modern rationalism,
they are so likely to take refuge in some form of irrationalism.
The 20th-century phenomenon of fascism is an expression
of exactly such an exasperated and irrational rebelliousness
against the tyranny—actual or prospective—of a radical-
utopian rationalism.

But neither millenarianism nor rationalism would, by itself, have been able to sustain the utopian temper had it not
been for the advent of modern technology, with its large
promise of human control over human destiny. There is
nothing dreamlike about technology: it works—and because
it works, it gives plausibility to the notion that modern man
is uniquely in the position of being able to convert his
idealized dreams into tangible reality. It also gives plausibility to the notion that, because the development of technology—of man's control over both nature and man—is progressive, therefore human history itself can be defined as
progressive, as leading us from an imperfect human condition
to a perfected one. The ancient Hebrews, the Greeks, and the
Christians all felt that there was a diabolical aspect to the
power of technology; they saw no reason to think that men
would always use this power wisely, and thought it quite
probable that we would use it for destructive ends. But modern technology, emerging in a context of millenarian aspirations and rationalist metaphysics, was not bothered—at least
not until recently—by such doubts. Francis Bacon's *New
Atlantis* is the first truly modern utopia—a society governed
by scientists and technologists which, it is clear, Bacon
thought could easily exist in fact, and which he proposed as
a very possible and completely desirable future.

As one looks back over these past centuries, the wonder is
not that there has been so much change and tumult, but
rather that there has been so much stability. The main cur-
rents of modern thought are all subversive of social stability,
and yet the bourgeois-liberal societies of the last two hun-

dred years managed somehow to keep triumphantly afloat. They did this, essentially, by diffusing power—economic power, social power, political power—throughout the body politic, so that the utopian spirit was constantly being moderated by the need to compromise various interests, various enthusiasms, and even various utopian visions. No modern liberal society has failed to express its faith in the potential of science and technology to improve radically the human condition. No modern liberal society has failed to insist that its institutions are created by—and legitimated by—human reason, rather than by mere tradition or custom, and certainly not by divine revelation. And no modern liberal society has ever explicitly rejected the utopian goals and the utopian rhetoric which are spawned by the millenarian spirit. These goals and this rhetoric, indeed, are by now clichés: "a world without war," "a world without poverty," "a world without hate"—in short, a world without any of the radical imperfections that have hitherto characterized every world actually inhabited by man. But what rendered these beliefs less explosive than, in their pure form, they are, was the liberal individualism that bourgeois society insisted they accommodate themselves to. In short, what made bourgeois society so viable was the *domestication* of modern utopianism by liberal individualism.

It was a viability, however, that was always open to question. The trouble with living in a bourgeois society which has domesticated its utopian spirit is that nothing is permitted to go wrong—at least very wrong, for very long. In all pre-modern societies, a mood of stoicism permeated the public and private spheres. Life is hard, fortune is fickle, bad luck is more likely than good luck and a better life is more probable after death than before. Such stoicism does not easily cohabit with the progressive spirit, which anticipates that things naturally will and *ought* to get better. When they don't—when you are defeated in a war, or when you experience a major malfunctioning of your economic system—then you are completely disoriented. Bourgeois society is morally and intellectually unprepared for calamity. Calamity, on the other hand, is always ready for bourgeois society—as it has always been ready, or always will be ready, for every other society that has existed or will exist.

When calamity strikes, it is never the utopian temper that is brought into question—that is literally an unimaginable possibility—but rather the liberal individual polity in which this temper has been housed. At such a moment, indeed, the utopian spirit flares up in anger, and declares, in the immortal words of the 19th-century French utopian socialist, Etienne Cabet, ". . . Nothing is impossible for a government that *wants* the good of its citizens." This sentiment expresses neatly what might be called the *collectivist imperative* which always haunts bourgeois-liberal society—and which can never be entirely exorcised, since it derives from the utopian world-view that all modern societies share. Once it is assumed that history itself works toward progressive improvement, and that we have the understanding and the power to guide this historical dynamic toward its fruition, it is only a matter of time before the state is held responsible for everything that is unsatisfactory in our condition. There is, after all, nothing else that could be held responsible.

Having made that statement, I must quickly modify it. For more than a century, bourgeois-liberal society *did* have one powerful inner check upon its utopian impulses, and that was the "dismal science" of economic theory. Classical economic theory insisted that, even under the best of circumstances, the mass of the people could expect only small, slow increments of improvement in their condition—and, under the worst of circumstances, could anticipate an actual worsening of their condition. The cornerstone of this theory was the Malthusian hypothesis that the pressure of population among poorer people would tend to wipe out the gains of economic growth. This hypothesis was accepted by most thinking men of the 19th century, and helped shape a climate of opinion in which great expectations could not easily flourish, except on the margins of society where all sorts of intellectual eccentricities were naturally to be found. But the discovery by modern economists that technological innovation had rendered Malthusianism false—that increasing productivity could easily cope with population growth—removed this formidable check upon the utopian temper. Indeed, economics itself now became a discipline which constantly challenged the conventional limits of economic possibility. And in this challenge, the role of the state was crucial. Whereas it was once thought that the state had to accommodate itself, like everyone else, to the iron laws of economics, it now became common to think that the state could pretty much write the laws of economics to suit itself. Our liberation from Malthusian economics—one of the truly great intellectual accomplishments of this past century— was quickly perceived by journalists, politicians, and even many among our better-educated people as a liberation from all economic constraint. The result is that the idea that ". . . Nothing is impossible for a government that *wants* the good of its citizens," once a radical proposition, now sounds rather conventional. I don't know that any American politician has actually said it, in so many words. But a great many politicians are strongly implying it—and it is even possible that more than a few of these politicians actually believe it.

The strength of this collectivist imperative is such that it feeds on itself—and most especially (and more significantly) on its own failures. These failures are as immense as they are obvious, and yet it is astonishing how little difference they seem to make. One would have thought that the catastrophic condition of agriculture in the Soviet Union, China, and Cuba would have brought these economies into universal disrepute. Yet no such thing has happened. These regimes are extended infinite moral and intellectual credit for their utopian ideals, and their credit ratings seem little vulnerable to their poor economic performance. Similarly, in the Western democracies, the tremendous expansion of government during these past three decades has not obviously made us a happier and more contented people. On the contrary, there is far more sourness and bitterness in our lives, public and private, than used to be the case; and these very governments, swollen to enormous size, are visibly less stable than they were. Nevertheless, the response to this state of affairs among our educated classes is to demand still more governmental intervention—on the theory that a larger dose of what should be good for us will cure the illness caused by a smaller dose of what should have been good for us. The ordinary people, whose common world always anchors them more firmly in common sense, are skeptical of such a prescription, but they have nothing to offer in its place, and will in the end have to go along with it.

But what about the liberal-individualist ethos? Is that not today, as it was a century ago, an authentic alternative? Some eminent thinkers say it is, and I would like nothing better than to agree with them. But, in truth, I cannot. The liberal-individualist vision of society is not an abstract scheme which can be imposed on any kind of people. For it to work, it needs a certain kind of people, with a certain kind of character, and with a certain cast of mind. Specifically, it needs what David Riesman calls "inner-directed" people—people of firm moral convictions, a people of self-reliance and self-discipline, a people who do not expect the universe to be offering them something for nothing—in short, a people with a non-utopian character even if their language is shot through with utopian clichés. The kind of person I am describing may be called the *bourgeois citizen*. He used to exist in large numbers, but now is on the verge of becoming an extinct species. He has been killed off by bourgeois prosperity, which has corrupted his character from that of a *citizen* to that of a *consumer*. One hears much about the "work ethic" these days, and I certainly appreciate the nostalgic appeal of that phrase. But the next time you hear a banker extolling the "work ethic," just ask him if he favors making installment buying illegal. When I was very young, it was understood that the only people who would buy things on the installment plan were the irresponsibles, the wastrels, those whose characters were too weak to control their appetites. "Save now, buy later," is what the work ethic used to prescribe. To buy now and pay later was the sign of moral corruption—though it is now the accepted practice of our affluent society. A people who have mortgaged themselves to the hilt are a dependent people, and ultimately they will look to the state to save them from bankruptcy. The British have a wonderful colloquial phrase for installment purchasing: they call it buying on "the never-never." The implication is that through this marvelous scheme you enter a fantasy world where nothing is denied you, and where the settling of all accounts is indefinitely postponed. This is a consumer's utopia. And more and more, it is as such a consumer's utopia that our bourgeois society presents itself to its people.

The transformation of the bourgeois citizen into the bourgeois consumer has dissolved that liberal-individualist framework which held the utopian impulses of modern society under control. One used to be encouraged to control one's appetites; now one is encouraged to satisfy them without delay. The inference is that one has a *right* to satisfy one's appetites without delay, and when this "right" is frustrated, as it always is in some way or other, an irritated populace turns to the state to do something about it. All this is but another way of saying that 20th-century capitalism itself, in its heedless emphasis on economic growth and ever-increasing prosperity, incites ever more unreasonable expectations, in comparison with which the actuality of the real world appears ever more drab and disconcerting. It doesn't matter what economic growth is actually achieved, or what improvements are effected—they are all less than satisfying. Ours is a world of promises, promises—and in such a world everyone, to some degree or another, automatically feels deprived.

Let me give you an illustration that, I think, makes the point nicely. The historic rate of growth of the American economy, over the past century and a half, has averaged about 2.5 percent a year. By historic standards, this is a fantastic and unprecedented achievement; it means that the national income doubles every twenty-eight years. But is this a source of gratification to us? Do we go around complimenting ourselves on doing so well? One can answer these questions by asking another: What if the President of the United States were to declare tomorrow that it was his firm intention to sustain this rate of growth of 2.5 percent a year? What would be the reaction? I think one can safely say that most Americans would think he was being pretty niggardly and mean-spirited. And there would be no shortage of politicians who would point out that 3 percent was really a much nicer number, and 5 percent nicer still. Does anyone doubt that they would be listened to? The proof that they would be is the fact that no President, in our lifetime, is going to mention that 2.5 percent figure. It's too *real* a number, and is therefore offensive to our inflamed political sensibilities.

But one cannot continue in a condition in which reality is always offending our expectations. That is an unnatural condition, and sooner or later people will be seeking relief from it. Oddly enough, even though utopianism gives rise to the collectivist impulse, the collectivist state seems to be one way in which the fires of utopianism are dampened. The institutionalization of utopianism is itself an answer to utopianism. Thus the Christian Church had its origins in a utopian impulse, but the Church then functioned to control and pacify this impulse. The Church solved the problem of the Second Coming by announcing that it had already happened, and that the Church itself was its living testimony. Similarly, in Russia and China today, the regimes of these nations, born out of secular messianism, announce that there is no further need for messianism since their states are its incarnation in the here and now, and there is nothing further to be messianic about. This gives these regimes a double attraction to many people in the West: they affirm utopianism while offering a deliverance from it. This explains what is at first sight a paradox: the fact that so many of our Western intellectuals will simultaneously follow a utopian thinker like Herbert Marcuse in denouncing the bourgeois status quo and at the same time praise Maoist China or Soviet Russia where Marcuse's works are forbidden to be published. Indeed, Marcuse himself is involved in this paradox! The paradox dissolves, however, if one realizes that the utopian impulse, in the end, must actively seek its own liquidation because it is impossible to sustain indefinitely; the psychological costs become too great. Utopianism dreams passionately of a liberation from all existing orthodoxies—religious, social, political—but, sooner or later, it must wearily and gratefully surrender to a new orthodoxy which calms its passions even as it compromises its dreams. The interesting question is whether the various emerging forms of collectivist orthodoxies in our time have the spiritual resources to establish a new order in which men can achieve some kind of human fulfillment. The evidence, so far, is that they do not; they seem to be morally and intellectually bankrupt from the outset. Marxism may be the official religion of Russia and China, but it is a religion without theologians—there isn't a Marxist philosopher worthy of the name in either country—and it is a religion whose holy scriptures, the works of Marx, Engels, and Lenin, are unread by the masses. These orthodoxies are sustained *only* by coercion—which means they are pseudo-orthodoxies, exuding an odor of boredom which is also the odor of decay.

Where does that leave us—we who inhabit the "free world"—the post-bourgeois bourgeois world? It leaves us, I should say, with a dilemma—but a dilemma which is also an opportunity. The opportunity is simply the opportunity of taking thought, of reflecting upon our condition, of trying to understand how we got where we are. This does not sound like much—and yet it is much, much more than it sounds. For the real antidote to utopianism is a self-conscious understanding of utopianism. A utopianism which knows itself to be utopian is already on the way to denying itself, because it has already made that first, crucial distinction between dream and reality. And once that distinction is made—as it was made in classical, pre-modern philosophy—both the legitimacy of the dream and the integrity of reality can be preserved.

The modern world, and the crisis of modernity we are now experiencing, was created by ideas and by the passions which these ideas unleashed. To surmount this crisis, without destroying the modern world itself, will require new ideas—or new versions of old ideas—that will regulate these passions and bring them into a more fruitful and harmonious relation with reality. I know that it will be hard for some to believe that ideas can be so important. This underestimation of ideas is a peculiarly bourgeois fallacy, especially powerful in that most bourgeois of nations, our own United States. For two centuries, the very important people who managed the affairs of this society could not believe in the importance of ideas—until one day they were shocked to discover that their children, having been captured and shaped by certain ideas, were either rebelling against their authority or seceding from their society. The truth is that ideas are *all*-important. The massive and seemingly-solid institutions of any society—the economic institutions, the political institutions, the religious institutions—are always at the mercy of the ideas in the heads of the people who populate these institutions. The leverage of ideas is so immense that a slight change in the intellectual climate can and will—perhaps slowly, but nevertheless inexorably—twist a familiar institution into an unrecognizable shape. If one looks at the major institutions of American society today—the schools, the family, the business corporation, the federal government—we can see this process going on before our eyes.

But just as it is ideas that alienate us from our world, so it is ideas which can make us at home in the world—which can permit us to envision the world as a "homely" place, where the practice of ordinary virtues in the course of our ordinary lives can indeed fulfill our potential as human beings. In such a world, dreams complement reality instead of being at war with it. The construction of such a world is the intellectual enterprise that most needs encouragement and support today. It will, on the surface, look like a mere academic enterprise, involving as it does a re-examination and fresh understanding of our intellectual and spiritual history. But such a re-examination and fresh understanding is always the sign that a reformation is beginning to get under way. And a reformation of modern utopianism, I think we will all agree, is what we are most desperately in need of. Only such a reformation can bring us back to that condition of sanity, to that confident acceptance of reality, which found expression in Macaulay's tart rejoinder to Francis Bacon: "An acre in Middlesex is better than a principality in Utopia."

23

ABOUT EQUALITY

THERE would appear to be little doubt that the matter of equality has become, in these past two decades, a major political and ideological issue. The late Hugh Gaitskell proclaimed flatly that "socialism is about equality," and though this bold redefinition of the purpose of socialism must have caused Karl Marx to spin in his grave—he thought egalitarianism a vulgar, philistine notion and had only contemptuous things to say about it—nevertheless most socialist politicians now echo Mr. Gaitskell in a quite routine way. And not only socialist politicians: in the United States today, one might fairly conclude from the political debates now going on that capitalism, too, is "about equality," and will stand or fall with its success in satisfying the egalitarian impulse. To cap it all, a distinguished Harvard professor, John Rawls, recently published a serious, massive, and widely acclaimed work in political philosophy whose argument is that a social order is just and legitimate *only* to the degree that it is directed to the redress of inequality. To the best of my knowledge, no serious political philosopher ever offered such a proposition before. It is a proposition, after all,

that peremptorily casts a pall of illegitimacy over the entire
political history of the human race—that implicitly indicts
Jerusalem and Athens and Rome and Elizabethan England,
all of whom thought *in*equality was necessary to achieve a
particular ideal of human excellence, both individual and
collective. Yet most of the controversy about Professor
Rawls's extraordinary thesis has revolved around the question of whether he has demonstrated it with sufficient ana-
lytical meticulousness. The thesis itself is not considered
controversial.

One would think, then, that with so much discussion
"about equality," there would be little vagueness as to what
equality itself is about—what one means by "equality." Yet
this is not at all the case. I think I can best illustrate this
point by recounting a couple of my editorial experiences at
the journal, *The Public Interest*, with which I am associated.

It is clear that some Americans are profoundly and sincerely agitated by the existing distribution of income in this
country, and these same Americans—they are mostly professors, of course—are constantly insisting that a more equal
distribution of income is a matter of considerable urgency.
Having myself no strong prior opinion as to the "proper"
shape of an income-distribution curve in such a country as
the United States, I have written to several of these professors
asking them to compose an article that would describe a
proper redistribution of American income. In other words,
in the knowledge that they are discontented with our present
income distribution, and taking them at their word that
when they demand "more equality" they are not talking
about an absolute leveling of all incomes, I invited them
to give our readers a picture of what a "fair" distribution
of income would be like.

I have never been able to get that article, and I have come
to the conclusion that I never shall get it. In two cases, I was
promised such an analysis, but it was never written. In the
other cases, no one was able to find the time to devote to it.
Despite all the talk "about equality," no one seems willing to
commit himself to a precise definition from which statesmen
and social critics can take their bearings.

As with economists, so with sociologists. Here, instead of income distribution, the controversial issue is social stratification, i.e., the "proper" degree of intergenerational social mobility. The majority of American sociologists seem persuaded that American democracy has an insufficient degree of such mobility, and it seemed reasonable to me that some of them—or at least one of them!—could specify what degree would be appropriate. None of them, I am sure, envisages a society that is utterly mobile, in which *all* the sons and daughters of the middle and upper classes end up in the very lowest social stratum, where they can live in anticipation of *their* sons and daughters rising again toward the top, and then of their grandsons and granddaughters moving downward once again! On the other hand, there is much evident dissatisfaction with what social mobility we do have. So why not find out what pattern of social mobility would be "fair" and "just" and "democratic"?

I regret to report that one will not find this out by consulting any issue of *The Public Interest.* I further regret to report that nowhere in our voluminous sociological literature will one find any such depiction of the ideally mobile society. Our liberal sociologists, like our liberal economists, are eloquent indeed in articulating their social discontents, but they are also bewilderingly modest in articulating their social goals.

Now, what is one to infer from this experience? One could, of course, simply dismiss the whole thing as but another instance of the intellectual irresponsibility of our intellectuals. That such irresponsibility exists seems clear enough, but *why* it exists is not clear at all. I do not believe that our intellectuals and scholars are genetically destined to be willfully or mischievously irresponsible. They are, I should say, no more perverse than the rest of mankind, and if they act perversely there must be a reason, even if they themselves cannot offer us a reason.

I, for one, am persuaded that though those people talk most earnestly about equality, it is not really equality that interests them. Indeed, it does not seem to me that equality per se is much of an issue for anyone. Rather, it is a surrogate for all sorts of other issues, some of them of the highest importance; these involve nothing less than our conception of what constitutes a just and legitimate society, a temporal order of things that somehow "makes sense" and seems "right."

A just and legitimate society, according to Aristotle, is one in which inequalities—of property, or station, or power—are generally perceived by the citizenry as necessary for the common good. I do not see that this definition has ever been improved on, though generations of political philosophers have found it unsatisfactory and have offered alternative definitions. In most cases, the source of this dissatisfaction has been what I would call the "liberal" character of the definition: it makes room for many different and even incompatible kinds of just and legitimate societies. In some of these societies, large inequalities are accepted as a necessary evil, whereas in others they are celebrated as the source of positive excellence. The question that this definition leaves open is the relation between a particular just and legitimate society and the "best" society. Aristotle, as we know, had his own view of the "best" society: he called it a "mixed regime," in which the monarchical, aristocratic, and democratic principles were all coherently intermingled. But he recognized that his own view of the "best" regime was of a primarily speculative nature—that is to say, a view always worth holding in mind but usually not relevant to the contingent circumstances (the "historical" circumstances, we should say) within which actual statesmen have to operate.

Later generations found it more difficult to preserve this kind of philosophic detachment from politics. The influence of Christianity, with its messianic promises, made the distinction between "the best" and "the legitimate" ever harder to preserve against those who insisted that *only* the best regime was legitimate. (This, incidentally, is an assumption that Professor Rawls makes as a matter of course.) The Church tried—as an existing and imperfect institution it had to try—to maintain this distinction, but it could only do so by appearing somewhat less Christian than it had promised to be. When the messianic impulse was secularized in early modernity, and science and reason and technology took over the promise of redemptive power—of transforming this dismal world into the wonderful place it "ought" to be— that same difficulty persisted. Like the Church, all the political regimes of modernity have had to preserve their legitimacy either by claiming an ideal character which in obvious truth they did not possess, or by making what were taken to be "damaging admissions" as to their inability to transform the real into the ideal.

The only corrective to this shadow of illegitimacy that has hovered threateningly over the politics of Western civilization for nearly two millennia now was the "common sense" of the majority of the population, which had an intimate and enduring relation to mundane realities that was relatively immune to speculative enthusiasm. This relative immunity was immensely strengthened by the widespread belief in an afterlife, a realm in which, indeed, whatever existed would be utterly perfect. I think it possible to suggest that the decline of the belief in personal immortality has been the most important *political* fact of the last hundred years; nothing else has so profoundly affected the way in which the masses of people experience their worldly condition. But even today, the masses of people tend to be more "reasonable," as I would put it, in their political judgments and political expectations than are our intellectuals. The trouble is that our society is breeding more and more "intellectuals" and fewer common men and women.

I use quotation marks around the term "intellectuals" because this category has, in recent decades, acquired a significantly new complexion. The enormous expansion in higher education, and the enormous increase in the college-educated, means that we now have a large class of people in our Western societies who, though lacking intellectual distinction (and frequently lacking even intellectual competence), nevertheless believe themselves to be intellectuals. A recent poll of American college teachers discovered that no fewer than 50 percent defined themselves as "intellectuals." That gives us a quarter of a million American intellectuals on our college faculties alone; if one adds all those in gov-

ernment and in the professions who would also lay claim
to the title, the figure would easily cross the million mark!
And if one also adds the relevant numbers of college students,
one might pick up another million or so. We are, then, in a
country like America today, talking about a mass of several
millions of "intellectuals" who are looking at their society
in a highly critical way and are quick to adopt an adversary posture toward it.

It is this class of people who are most eloquent in their
denunciations of inequality, and who are making such a
controversial issue of it. Why? Inequality of income is no
greater today than it was twenty years ago, and is certainly
less than it was fifty years ago. Inequality of status and opportunity have visibly declined since World War II, as a
result of the expansion of free or nearly-free higher education. (The percentage of our leading business executives
who come from modest socioeconomic backgrounds is much
greater today than in 1910.) Though there has been a
mushrooming of polemics against the inequalities of the
American condition, most of this socioeconomic literature is
shot through with disingenuousness, sophistry, and unscrupulous statistical maneuvering. As Professor Seymour Martin
Lipset has demonstrated, by almost any socioeconomic indicator one would select, American society today is—as best
we can determine—*more* equal than it was one hundred years
ago. Yet, one hundred years ago most Americans were boast-
ing of the historically unprecedented equality that was to be
found in their nation, whereas today many seem convinced
that inequality is at least a problem and at worst an intolerable scandal.

The explanation, I fear, is almost embarrassingly vulgar
in its substance. A crucial clue was provided several years ago
by Professor Lewis Feuer, who made a survey of those American members of this "new class" of the college-educated—engineers, scientists, teachers, social scientists, psychologists, etc.—
who had visited the Soviet Union in the 1920s and 1930s, and
had written admiringly of what they saw. In practically all
cases, what they saw was power and status in the possession of
their own kinds of people. The educators were enthusiastic

about the "freedom" of educators in the USSR to run things as they saw fit. Ditto the engineers, the psychologists, and the rest. Their perceptions were illusory, of course, but this is less significant than the wishful thinking that so evidently lay behind the illusions. The same illusions, and the same wishful thinking, are now to be noticed among our academic tourists to Mao's China.

The simple truth is that the professional classes of our modern bureaucratized societies are engaged in a class struggle with the business community for status and power. Inevitably, this class struggle is conducted under the banner of "equality"—a banner also raised by the bourgeoisie in *its* revolutions. Professors are genuinely indignant at the expense accounts which business executives have and which they do not. They are, in contrast, utterly convinced that *their* privileges are "rights" that are indispensable to the proper workings of a good society. Most academics and professional people are even unaware that they are among the "upper" classes of our society. When one points this out to them, they refuse to believe it.*

The animus toward the business class on the part of members of our "new class" is expressed in large ideological terms. But what it comes down to is that our *nuovi uomini* are persuaded they can do a better job of running our society and feel entitled to have the opportunity. This is what *they* mean by "equality."

Having said this, however, one still has to explain the authentic moral passion that motivates our egalitarians of the "new class." They are not motivated by any pure power-lust; very few people are. They clearly dislike—to put it mildly—our liberal, bourgeois, commercial society, think it unfit to survive, and seek power to reconstruct it in some unspecified but radical way. To explain this, one has to turn to the intellectuals—the real ones—who are the philosophical source of their ideological discontent.

---

* One of the reasons they are so incredulous is that they do not count as "income"—as they should—such benefits as tenure, long vacations, relatively short working hours, and all of their other prerogatives. When a prerogative is construed as a "right," it ceases to be seen as a privilege.

Any political community is based on a shared conception of the common good, and once this conception becomes ambiguous and unstable, then the justice of any social order is called into question. In a democratic civilization, this questioning will always take the form of an accusation of undue privilege. Its true meaning, however, is to be found behind the literal statements of the indictment.

It is interesting to note that, from the very beginnings of modern bourgeois civilization, the class of people we call intellectuals—poets, novelists, painters, men of letters—has never accepted the bourgeois notion of the common good. This notion defines the common good as consisting mainly of personal security under the law, personal liberty under the law, and a steadily increasing material prosperity for those who apply themselves to that end. It is, by the standards of previous civilizations, a "vulgar" conception of the common good: there is no high nobility of purpose, no selfless devotion to transcendental ends, no awe-inspiring heroism. It is, therefore, a conception of the common good that dispossesses the intellectual of his traditional prerogative, which was to celebrate high nobility of purpose, selfless devotion to transcendental ends, and awe-inspiring heroism. In its place, it offered the intellectuals the freedom to write or compose as they pleased and then to sell their wares in the marketplace as best they could. This "freedom" was interpreted by—one can even say experienced by—intellectuals as a base servitude to philistine powers. They did not accept it two hundred years ago; they do not accept it today.

The original contempt of intellectuals for bourgeois civilization was quite explicitly "elitist," as we should now say. It was the spiritual egalitarianism of bourgeois civilization that offended them, not any material inequalities. They anticipated that ordinary men and women would be unhappy in bourgeois civilization precisely because it was a civilization of and for the "common man"—and it was their conviction that common men could only find true happiness when their lives were subordinated to and governed by uncommon ideals, as conceived and articulated by intellectuals. It was, and is, a highly presumptuous and self-serving argument to offer—though I am not so certain that it was or is altogether false. In any case, it was most evidently not an egalitarian argument. It only became so in our own century, when aristocratic traditions had grown so attenuated that the only permissible anti-bourgeois arguments had to be framed in "democratic" terms. The rise of socialist and communist ideologies made this transition a relatively easy one. A hundred years ago, when an intellectual became "alienated" and "radicalized," he was as likely to move "Right" as "Left." In our own day, his instinctive movement will almost certainly be to the "Left."

With the mass production of "intellectuals" in the course of the 20th century, traditional intellectual attitudes have come to permeate our college-educated upper-middle classes, and most especially the children of these classes. What has happened to the latter may be put with a simplicity that is still serviceably accurate: they have obtained enough of the comforts of bourgeois civilization, and have a secure enough grip upon them, to permit themselves the luxury of reflecting uneasily upon the inadequacies of their civilization. They then discover that a life that is without a sense of purpose creates an acute experience of anxiety, which in turn transforms the universe into a hostile, repressive place. The spiritual history of mankind is full of such existential moments, which are the seedbeds of gnostic and millenarian movements—movements that aim at both spiritual and material reformations. Radical egalitarianism is, in our day, exactly such a movement.

The demand for greater equality has less to do with any specific inequities of bourgeois society than with the fact that bourgeois society is seen as itself inequitable because it is based on a deficient conception of the common good. The recent history of Sweden is living proof of this proposition. The more egalitarian Sweden becomes—and it is already about as egalitarian as it is ever likely to be—the more *enragés* are its intellectuals, the more guilt-ridden and uncertain are its upper-middle classes, the more "alienated" are its college-educated youth. Though Swedish politicians and journalists cannot bring themselves to believe it, it should be

obvious by now that there are *no* reforms that are going to
placate the egalitarian impulse in Swedish society. Each reform only invigorates this impulse the more, because the
impulse is not, in the end, about equality at all but about
the quality of life in bourgeois society.

In Sweden, as elsewhere, it is only the common people
who remain loyal to the bourgeois ethos. As well they might:
it is an ethos devised for their satisfaction. Individual liberty
and security—in the older, bourgeois senses of these terms—
and increasing material prosperity are still goals that are
dear to the hearts of the working classes of the West. They
see nothing wrong with a better, bourgeois life: a life without uncommon pretensions, a life to be comfortably lived by
common men. This explains two striking oddities of current
politics: (1) The working classes have, of all classes, been
the most resistant to the spirit of radicalism that has swept
the upper levels of bourgeois society; and (2) once a government starts making concessions to this spirit—by announcing its dedication to egalitarian reforms—the working
class is rendered insecure and fearful, and so becomes more
militant in *its* demands. These demands may be put in terms
of greater equality of income and privilege—but, of course,
they also and always mean greater inequality vis-à-vis other
sections of the working class and those who are outside the
labor force.

Anyone who is familiar with the American working class
knows—as Senator McGovern discovered—that they are far
less consumed with egalitarian bitterness or envy than are
college professors or affluent journalists. True, they do believe that in a society where so large a proportion of the
national budget is devoted to the common defense, there
ought to be some kind of "equality of sacrifice," and they are
properly outraged when tax laws seem to offer wealthy people a means of tax avoidance not available to others. But
they are even more outraged at the way the welfare state
spends the large amounts of tax moneys it does collect.
These moneys go in part to the nonworking population
and in part to the middle-class professionals who attend to
the needs of the nonworking population (teachers, social

workers, lawyers, doctors, dieticians, civil servants of all description). The "tax rebellion" of recent years has been provoked mainly by the rapid growth of this welfare state, not by particular inequities in the tax laws—inequities, which, though real enough, would not, if abolished, have any significant impact on the workingman's tax burden. After all, the 20 billion dollars—a highly exaggerated figure, in my opinion—that Senator McGovern might "capture" by tax reforms would just about pay for his day-care center proposals, which the working class has not displayed much interest in.

Still, though ordinary people are not significantly impressed by the assertions and indignations of egalitarian rhetoric, they cannot help but be impressed by the fact that the ideological response to this accusatory rhetoric is so feeble. Somehow, bourgeois society seems incapable of explaining and justifying its inequalities and how they contribute to or are consistent with the common good. This, I would suggest, derives from the growing bureaucratization of the economic order, a process which makes bourgeois society ever more efficient economically, but also ever more defenseless before its ideological critics.

For any citizen to make a claim to an unequal share of income, power, or status, his contribution has to be—and has to be seen to be—a human and personal thing. In no country are the huge salaries earned by film stars or popular singers or professional athletes a source of envy or discontent. More than that: in most countries—and especially in the United States—the individual entrepreneur who builds up his own business and becomes a millionaire is rarely attacked on egalitarian grounds. In contrast, the top executives of our large corporations, most of whom are far less wealthy than Frank Sinatra or Bob Hope or Mick Jagger or Wilt Chamberlain, cannot drink a martini on the expense account without becoming the target of a "populist" politician. These faceless and nameless personages (who is the president of General Electric?) have no clear title to their privileges—and I should say the reason is precisely that they are nameless and faceless. One really has no way of knowing what they

are doing "up there," and whether what they are doing is in
the public interest or not.

It was not always so. In the 19th century, at the apogee of
the bourgeois epoch, the perception of unequal contributions
was quite vivid indeed. The success of a businessman was
taken to be testimony to his personal talents and character—
especially character, than which there is nothing more personal. This explains the popularity of biographies of successful entrepreneurs, full of anecdotes about the man and with
surprisingly little information about his economic activities.
In the 20th century, "entrepreneurial history," as written in our universities, becomes the history of the firm
rather than the biography of a man. To a considerable extent, of course, this reflects the fact that most businessmen
today are not "founding fathers" of a firm but temporary
executives in a firm: the bureaucratization of modern society empties the category of the bourgeois of its human content. To the best of my knowledge, the only notable biography
of a living businessman to have appeared in recent years was
that of Alfred P. Sloan, who made his contribution to General Motors a good half century ago.

Nor is it only businessmen who are so affected. As the
sociological cast of mind has gradually substituted itself for
the older bourgeois moral-individualist cast of mind, military men and statesmen have suffered a fate similar to that
of businessmen. Their biographies emphasize the degree to
which they shared all our common human failings; their
contributions to the common good, when admitted at all, are
ascribed to larger historical forces in whose hands they
were little more than puppets. They are all taken to be
representative men, not exceptional men.

But when the unequal contributions of individuals are
perceived as nothing but the differential functions of social
or economic or political roles, then only those inequalities
absolutely needed to perform these functions can be publicly
justified. The burden of proof is heavy indeed, as each and
every inequality must be scrutinized for its functional pur-
port. True, that particular martini, drunk in that place, in

that time, in that company, might contribute to the efficiency and growth of the firm and the economy. But would the contribution really have been less if the executive in question had been drinking water? *

So this, it appears to me, is what the controversy "about equality" is really about. We have an intelligentsia which so despises the ethos of bourgeois society, and which is so guilt-ridden at being implicated in the life of this society, that it is inclined to find even collective suicide preferable to the status quo. (How else can one explain the evident attraction which totalitarian regimes possess for so many of our writers and artists?) We have a "New Class" of self-designated "intellectuals" who share much of this basic attitude—but who, rather than committing suicide, pursue power in the name of equality. (The children of this "New Class," however, seem divided in their yearnings for suicide via drugs, and in their lust for power via "revolution.") And then we have the ordinary people, working-class and lower-middle-class, basically loyal to the bourgeois order but confused and apprehensive at the lack of clear meaning in this order—a lack derived from the increasing bureaucratization (and accompanying impersonalization) of political and economic life. All of these discontents tend to express themselves in terms of "equality"—which is in itself a quintessentially bourgeois ideal and slogan.

It is neither a pretty nor a hopeful picture. None of the factors contributing to this critical situation is going to go away; they are endemic to our 20th-century liberal-bourgeois society. Still, one of the least appreciated virtues of this society is its natural recuperative powers—its capacity to change, as we say, but also its capacity to preserve itself, to adapt and survive. The strength of these powers always as-

---

* As Professor Peter Bauer has pointed out, the very term "distribution of income" casts a pall of suspicion over existing inequalities, implying as it does that incomes are not personally *earned* but somehow *received* as the end product of mysterious (and therefore possibly sinister) political-economic machinations.

tonishes us, as we anticipate (even proclaim) an imminent
apocalypse that somehow never comes. And, paradoxically
enough, this vitality almost surely has something to do with
the fact that the bourgeois conception of equality, so vehe-
mently denounced by the egalitarian, is "natural" in a way
that other political ideas—egalitarian or anti-egalitarian—
are not. Not necessarily in all respects superior, but more
"natural." Let me explain.

The founding fathers of modern bourgeois society (John
Locke, say, or Thomas Jefferson) all assumed that biological
inequalities among men—inequalities in intelligence, talent,
abilities of all kinds—were not extreme, and therefore did
not justify a society of hereditary privilege (of "two races,"
as it were). This assumption we now know to be true, demonstrably true, as a matter of fact. Human talents and abilities, as measured, do tend to distribute themselves along a
bell-shaped curve, with most people clustered around the
middle, and with much smaller percentages at the lower and
higher ends. That men are "created equal" is not a myth or
a mere ideology—unless, of course, one interprets that phrase
literally, which would be patently absurd and was never the
bourgeois intention. Moreover, it is a demonstrable fact that
in all modern, bourgeois societies, the distribution of income
is also roughly along a bell-shaped curve, indicating that in
such an "open" society the inequalities that do emerge are
not inconsistent with the bourgeois notion of equality.
    It is because of this "natural tyranny of the bell-shaped
curve," in the conditions of a commercial society, that contemporary experiments in egalitarian community-building
—the Israeli kibbutz, for instance—only work when they
recruit a homogeneous slice of the citizenry, avoiding a
cross-section of the entire population. It also explains why
the aristocratic idea—of a distribution in which the right-
hand section of the bell curve is drastically shrunken—is so
incongruent with the modern world, so that modern versions
of superior government by a tiny elite (which is what the
communist regimes are) are always fighting against the eco-

nomic and social tendencies inherent in their own societies. Purely egalitarian communities are certainly feasible—but only if they are selective in their recruitment and are relatively indifferent to economic growth and change, which encourages differentiation. Aristocratic societies are feasible, too —most of human history consists of them—but only under conditions of relative economic lethargy, so that the distribution of power and wealth is insulated from change. But once you are committed to the vision of a predominantly commercial society, in which flux and change are "normal" —in which men and resources are expected to move to take advantage of new economic opportunities—then you find yourself tending toward the limited inequalities of a bourgeois kind.

This explains one of the most extraordinary (and little-noticed) features of 20th-century societies: how relatively invulnerable the distribution of income is to the efforts of politicians and ideologues to manipulate it. In all the Western nations—the United States, Sweden, the United Kingdom, France, Germany—despite the varieties of social and economic policies of their governments, the distribution of income is strikingly similar. Not identical; politics is not entirely impotent, and the particular shape of the "bell" can be modified—but only with immense effort, and only slightly, so that to the naked eye of the visitor the effect is barely visible.* Moreover, available statistics suggest that the distribution of income in the communist regimes of Russia and Eastern Europe, despite both their egalitarian economic ideologies and aristocratic political structure, moves closer every year to the Western model, as these regimes seek the kind of economic growth that their "common men" unquestionably desire. And once the economic structure and social structure start assuming the shape of this bell-shaped curve, the political structure—the distribution of political power— follows along the same way, however slowly and reluctantly.

---

* It must be kept in mind, of course, that retaining the shape of the curve is not inconsistent with *everyone* getting richer or poorer. The bell itself then moves toward a new axis.

The "Maoist" heresy within communism can best be understood as a heroic—but surely futile—rebellion against the
gradual submission of communism to the constraints of the
bell-shaped curve.

So bourgeois society—using this term in its larger sense, to
include such "mixed economies" as prevail in Israel or
Sweden or even Yugoslavia—is not nearly so fragile as its
enemies think or its friends fear. Only a complete reversal of
popular opinion toward the merits of material prosperity
and economic growth would destroy it, and despite the fact
that some of our citizens seem ready for such a reversal, that
is unlikely to occur.

The concern and distress of our working- and lower-
middle classes over the bureaucratization of modern life can,
I think, be coped with. One can envisage reforms that
would encourage their greater "participation" in the corporate structures that dominate our society; or one can envisage reforms that would whittle down the size and power of
these structures, returning part way to a more traditional
market economy; or one can envisage a peculiar—and, in
pure principle, incoherent—combination of both. My own
view is that this last alternative, an odd amalgam of the prevailing "Left" and "Right" viewpoints, is the most realistic
and the most probable. And I see no reason why it should
not work. It will not be the "best" of all possible societies.
But the ordinary man, like Aristotle, is no utopian, and he
will settle for a "merely satisfactory" set of social arrangements and is prepared to grant them a title of legitimacy.

The real trouble is not sociological or economic at all. It is
that the "middling" nature of a bourgeois society falls short
of corresponding adequately to the full range of man's spiritual nature, which makes more than middling demands upon
the universe, and demands more than middling answers. This
weakness of bourgeois society has been highlighted by its intellectual critics from the very beginning. And it is this weakness that generates continual dissatisfaction, especially among
those for whom material problems are no longer so urgent.
They may speak about "equality"; they may even be obsessed

with statistics and pseudo-statistics about equality; but it is a religious vacuum—a lack of meaning in their own lives, and the absence of a sense of larger purpose in their society—that terrifies them and provokes them to "alienation" and unappeasable indignation. It is not too much to say that it is the death of God, not the emergence of any new social or economic trends, that haunts bourgeois society. And *this* problem is far beyond the competence of politics to cope with.

24

WHAT IS

"SOCIAL JUSTICE"?

I RECENTLY received a letter from a magazine which is preparing a special issue on the distribution of income in the United States. The letter asked for my thoughts on such questions as: "How should a society determine wages and salaries? Does our society do a fair job of distributing income?" And so on.

The issue to which these questions are addressed is certainly a crucial one. It is nothing less than the issue of "social justice"—or what used to be known, among political philosophers, as "distributive justice." The change in terminology, as it happens, has its own significance; in politics, the language we use to ask questions is always more important than any particular answer. "Distributive justice" is a neutral phrase; it points to a problem without suggesting any particular solution. "Social justice," however, is a loaded phrase: it blithely suggests that "society" ought to determine the distribution of income. This assumption is now so common that few people realize how controversial its implications are.

The social order we call "capitalism," constructed on the basis of a market economy, does *not* believe that "society" ought to prescribe a "fair" distribution of income. "Society," in this context, means government; "society" is voiceless until the political authorities speak. And the kind of liberal society historically associated with capitalism was, from its very beginnings, hostile to any political or "social" definition of distributive justice.

It is the basic premise of a liberal-capitalist society that a "fair" distribution of income is determined by the productive input—"productive" as determined by the market—of individuals into the economy. Such productivity is determined by specific talents, general traits of character, and just plain luck (being at the right place at the right time). This market-based distribution of income will create economic incentives and thereby encourage economic growth. As a result of such economic growth, everyone will be better off (though not necessarily equally better off). The economic growth that ensues may itself shape society in ways not everyone might like. But a liberal-capitalist order does not—except in extraordinary circumstances—concede to any authority the right to overrule the aggregate of individual preferences on this matter.

In contrast, non-capitalist societies—whether pre-capitalist or post-capitalist—have a very different conception of "fairness," based on one's contribution *to the society*, not merely to the economy. In such non-capitalist societies, economic rewards are "socially" justified, as distinct from being economically justified. Thus, in the Middle Ages it was thought to be fair to compel ordinary people to support the church and the clergy, whose activities were deemed to be of major social significance and social value. Similarly, in the Soviet Union today, the Communist Party does not have to defend its budget on any economic grounds: the value of its contribution to the polity as a whole is put beyond question. Such societies, of course, place no high valuation on individual liberty.

NO "PURE" TYPES OF SOCIETY

Obviously, there is no such pure type as "a capitalist society" or "a non-capitalist society." All non-capitalist societies recognize, to one degree or another, the importance of economic activity and material welfare. They therefore will allow differential rewards—again, to one degree or another—based on one's skill at such activity.

Similarly, all capitalist societies recognize, to one degree or another, that there is more to life than economic growth or material welfare, and they therefore make some provision for differential rewards based on one's skill at literary criticism, music, and philosophy. Ohio State University, for example, is exactly such a provision.

Still, though "pure" types may not exist, the types themselves do, in however impure a form. And there are three important points to be made about these different conceptions of a good society and the principles of "fairness" in income distribution by which they operate.

(1) There is no rational method which permits us to determine, *in the abstract*, which principle of distribution is superior. It is absurd to claim that capitalism, anywhere, at any time, is superior to non-capitalism, or vice versa. Any such judgment is bound to be contingent, i.e., based on the particular society's history and traditions, on the attitudes and social habits of its citizenry, and the like. There is no point in arguing that a particular society "ought" to be capitalist or socialist if the overwhelming majority of the people are not of a mind to be bound by the different kinds of self-discipline that these different political philosophies require, if they are to work. And this, of course, holds true for all large political ideals. Which is why Jefferson, living in Paris before the French Revolution, could write—in all good republican conscience—that the French people were not

"ready" for republican self-government, and that it would be a mistake for them to try to establish it immediately.

(2) A distribution of income according to one's contribution to the society—to the "common good"—requires that this society have a powerful consensus as to what the "common good" is, and that it also have institutions with the authority to give specific meaning and application to this consensus on all occasions. Now, when you have such a consensus, and such authoritative institutions, you do not have—cannot have—a liberal society as we understand it. It can certainly be a good society (if the values behind the consensus are good); but it will not be a liberal society. The authorities which represent the "common good," and which distribute income in accordance with their conception of the common good, will—with a clear conscience—surely discriminate against those who are subversive of this "common good." They may, if they are broad-minded, tolerate dissidents, but they will never concede to them equal rights —even if equality is a prime social value. The dissidents, after all, may be those who believe in inequality.

(3) A liberal society is one that is based on a *weak* consensus. There is nothing like near-unanimity on what the "common good" is, who contributes to it, or how. There is not utter disagreement, of course; a liberal society is not—no society can be—in a condition of perpetual moral and political chaos. But the liberty of a liberal society derives from a prevalent skepticism as to anyone's ability to know the "common good" with certainty, and from the conviction that the authorities should not try to define this "common good" in any but a minimal way. That minimal definition, in a liberal society, will naturally tend to emphasize the improvement of the material conditions of life—something that very few people are actually against. A liberal society, therefore, will be very tolerant of capitalist transactions between consenting adults because such transactions are for mutual advantage, and the sum of such transactions is to everyone's material advantage. And, consequently, a liberal society will think it reasonable and "fair" that income should, on the whole, be distributed according to one's productive

input into the economy, as this is measured by the market-place and the transactions which occur there.

LIBERTY AS A VALUE

In sum, the distribution of income under liberal capitalism is "fair" if, and only if, you think that liberty is, or ought to be, the most important political value. If not, then not. This distribution of income under capitalism is an expression of the general belief that it is better for society to be shaped by the interplay of people's free opinions and free preferences than by the enforcement of any one set of values by government.

But there have always been many people in this world who do not believe that liberty is the most important political value. These people are sincere dogmatists. They believe they know *the* truth about a good society; they believe they possess *the* true definition of distributive justice; and they inevitably wish to see society shaped in the image of these true beliefs. Sometimes they have prized religious truth more than liberty; sometimes they have prized philosophic truth more than liberty (e.g., the Marxist philosophy); and sometimes they have prized equality more than liberty. It is this last point of view that is especially popular in some circles—mainly academic circles—in the United States today.

Thus Professor Ronald Dworkin, one of our most distinguished liberal legal philosophers, has recently written that "*a more equal society is a better society even if its citizens prefer inequality.*" (Italics mine.) From which it follows that "social justice" may require a people, whose preferences are corrupt (in that they prefer liberty to equality), to be coerced into equality. It is precisely because they define "social justice" and "fairness" in terms of equality that so many liberal thinkers find it so difficult genuinely to detest left-wing (i.e., egalitarian) authoritarian or totalitarian regimes. And, similarly, it is precisely because they are true believers in justice-as-equality that they dislike a free society, with all its inevitable inequalities.

As one who does like a free society, I have to concede to these people the right to hold and freely express such opinions. But I do find it ironical that their conception of "social justice" should be generally designated as the "liberal" one. Whatever its other merits, an authentic attachment to liberty is not one of them.

25

TAXES, POVERTY,

AND EQUALITY

IT WAS not so long ago—in 1958, to be exact—that John Kenneth Galbraith could casually observe, in the course of analyzing *The Affluent Society*, that "few things are more evident in modern social history than the decline of interest in inequality as an economic issue." Obviously, times have changed, though in what way or for what reason it is not at all clear. The question of inequality is now widely regarded as an urgent one, especially in connection with our present system of taxation, which many hold responsible for a distribution of income deemed to be flagrantly unequal and hence inequitable. No one has a kind word to say for our tax structure; everyone appears utterly convinced that it is in a miserable condition and that drastic surgery is as necessary as it is desirable.

In this atmosphere of feverish discontent, meaningless rhetoric and misleading statistics flourish. They are so common that most of us simply nod at them, in some kind of vague assent or toleration: the urge to scrutinize has withered away. Thus, *The New Republic*'s eminent columnist, TRB, could calmly inform his readers (on June 22, 1974) that "wealth at the rate of $10 billion annually is now flowing from the lowest three-fifths of America's income groups to the richest one-fifth." That *sounds* precise and authoritative enough. But if one stops to think, one is prompted to wonder what this "flowing" means and just how it is happening. It cannot mean what it seems to mean: that the distribution of income in this country is all of a sudden becoming more radically unequal, to the benefit of the very rich, than it had been. Such a statement would simply be false, and no reputable economist, of whatever political persuasion, has sanctioned it. Presumably, TRB had some more arcane bit of economic intelligence in mind. Or perhaps he was merely giving an extremely loose interpretation of something he read, somewhere. But what is absolutely certain is that the readers of *The New Republic* are not going to bother him with demands for an explanation. On this subject, they—like most of us—are credulous to the point of numbness.

The fact is that the partisan use of statistics in the modern world seems to have outdistanced the ability of even well-informed and educated citizens to cope with them. Thus, one reads that the top 20 percent of families, which receive a little over 40 percent of total income, now pay 50 percent of total taxes, and the top 5 percent, which receive 16 percent of total income, pay 25 percent of total taxes. This statistic is accurate and conveys the impression that our present tax system distributes the tax burden rather fairly. One also reads that the top 20 percent pay in taxes about the same proportion (33 percent) of their income as the lowest 20 percent. This statistic, too, is accurate in its own way and, while not contradicting the first, conveys a quite opposite impression. One can do quite marvelous things with statistics, and the sad truth is that most of us are utterly defenseless against their inherent persuasive power.

Similarly, one can make (many do make) much of the fact

—and it is a kind of fact—that families with annual incomes
below $2,000 pay 50 percent of their income in taxes. That
sounds horrendous—until one is made aware of the com-
plications lurking in the background. To begin with, we
are not talking about *income* tax, from which these families
are exempt. Nor are we even talking about such familiar
"regressive" taxes as the sales tax, which obviously cannot
amount to 50 percent of expenditure. (Among such low-
income families, expenditure can be assumed to be identical
with income.) No, we are talking about payments which most
of us do not regard as "taxes" at all, e.g., that portion of our
rent which represents the landlord's real estate tax. And it
further helps to put this statistic in perspective if we realize
(1) that in most cases this income is not *earned* income but
represents tax-free (of income tax, that is) transfer payments from the government in the first place (welfare, social
security, unemployment insurance, etc.); and (2) that not
all of these families with incomes below $2,000 a year are
really poor. A 24-year-old married graduate student, who
earns $1,800 as a research assistant or teaching assistant,
and who also receives financial support from his and his
wife's parents, or who borrows on the basis of his (or her)
future earning prospects, is not so much terribly poor as
very young. Now, none of these qualifications should be
taken to imply that we do not have a problem of poverty in
the United States. They do suggest, however, that mixing
up the problem of poverty with the problem of tax equity
is not very enlightening, though the political and rhetorical
advantages of such confusion are evident enough.

As with income distribution, so with the distribution of
wealth. TRB, in the aforementioned column, declared indignantly that "fewer than 1 percent of the people currently own over 50 percent of the corporate stock in the
country." And, from other recent and reputable publications one can cull similar statistics: that 2 percent of individual stockholders own about two thirds of all stock held
by individuals, or that the top 1 percent of adult American
wealth holders own roughly 25 percent of all personal prop-

erty and personal financial assets. Now, there is no doubt
that wealth is unequally distributed in the United States
but it is also certain that wealth is not nearly so concentrated
as those statistics would lead the casual reader to think. The
phrase "corporate stock" brings to mind the stock of General Motors or IBM; one is not likely to think of all those
thousands of small or tiny businesses where stock is owned
mainly by an individual founder or members of his family,
and where the value of the stock may be modest or even
negligible. Who owns what proportion of "the total corporate stock" tells you far less than it seems to. Similarly, the
percentage of "all stock owned by individuals" slides around
the fact that a significant percentage (35 percent is a common estimate) of the stock of the larger corporations is
owned by institutions—pension and profit-sharing funds, mutual insurance companies, mutual funds—which are surro-
gates for individuals who, in their own name, own no stock
at all.* In other words, *the mode of stock ownership by less
wealthy people is collective rather than individual,* so that
statistics on individual stock ownership exaggerate the degree of concentration. And much the same thing is true
for "personal financial assets": for most working-class and
middle-class people, *impersonal ownership* of financial assets
is more important than personal ownership. These assets are
mainly in their pension plans—and also, of course, in Social
Security and Medicare (the equivalent of an annuity and
a medical insurance policy, respectively), which are not
counted as "assets" at all but which, if capitalized and included in the statistics, would significantly reduce the degree of inequality in the ownership of "wealth." We have
gone to great pains to create a "welfare state," but our

---

* Thus, the Sears Roebuck pension and savings fund owns 20 percent
of all outstanding shares of the company. The value of the common stock
owned by all pension and savings funds amounts to about 15 percent of
the total market value of all shares of all companies listed on the New
York Stock Exchange. The assets of these funds are growing at the rate
of 14 percent a year—i.e., they will quadruple by 1985. "Social ownership" of the "means of production" is proceeding faster than anyone
realizes—only not in ways that either socialists or capitalists anticipated.

statistics on the distribution of wealth utterly ignore the existence of the institutions of the welfare state, and of the claims
upon the nation's wealth which these institutions "own."

To repeat, the ownership of wealth in the United States
is unequally distributed—somewhat more unequally than income, most economists estimate. But those isolated and scary
statistics—all technically correct—which convey the notion that
this country is "owned" by a tiny oligarchy of rich people
are the stuff of paranoid fantasies, not of economic or social
reality.

THE "FACTS" AND THE "TRUTH"

The basic facts about the distribution of income in the United
States over the past decades are well known, and are set forth
in the following table, constructed by the Council of Economic Advisers in February 1974:

	1947		1972
Bottom 20% of population received	5.1%	of total income	5.4%
Top 20% of population received	43.3%	of total income	41.4%
Top 5% of population received	17.5%	of total income	15.9%

Over the past 25 years, there has been a slight shift of
(pre-tax) income away from the very rich to the middling
ranks, not—in any significant degree—to the poor. That is
what the statistics show. They also show, beyond question, a
substantial and persistent degree of inequality in the distribution of income. So far, so uncontroversial. However, as
is almost always the case, the statistical "facts" may as easily
obscure as reveal the "truth" of the matter.

To begin with, there is always the question of the subjec-
tive impression created by objective statistics. In this case,
especially, there is the way most of us react to any statistics
concerning "the top 5 percent" or "the top 20 percent" of the
income-receiving population. It is in the nature of a demo-

cratic, affluent society that quite well-to-do people never do *feel* as well-off as they statistically are. Later on, it will be suggested why this is so; but, for the moment, it suffices to say that most people, when they think of the "top 5 percent" or the "top 20 percent," promptly have visions of the Great Gatsby, or the Rockefellers, or at least the executives of major corporations. It comes as a great shock to them to discover they may very well, without knowing it, be thinking of themselves. The "top 5 percent" consists of all households with incomes over $30,000 a year. The "top 20 percent" consists of all households with incomes over $20,000 a year. Most of these "rich" people are people who, in the ordinary course of events, are regarded as "middle-class": our doctor, our dentist, our lawyer, our accountant, our children's professors, perhaps ourselves. This confusion of socioeconomic perspectives creates a special problem for politicians, who start out with the idea of "taxing the rich" and end up with a "middle-class tax rebellion" on their hands.

But there really is much more to it than that. These objective statistics are not only easily misread, they are also, *objectively*, very misleading. They grossly exaggerate the degree of income inequality in the first place, because, like all such cross-sectional statistical pictures snapped at a moment in time, they overlook a very significant human and social phenomenon: age, and the relation of age to the income we receive.

Young people earn less than mature adults in the prime of their working lives. Old people, over 65, earn less than younger adults in the prime of their working lives. We all know this and take it to be perfectly natural and proper and inevitable. *But the table cited above, like most such tables on the distribution of income, does not "know" this.* It simply does not take age into account.

Just how important the question of age is in determining the distribution of income may be seen from a look at the 25 percent of all households that earn less than $5,000 annually. In 10 percent of these households, the head is under 25 years of age. In 46 percent, the head is over 65. Only 22 percent of these households have more than two people. The conclusion is inescapable that the conventional cross-sectional "picture" of income distribution in the United States significantly overstates the degree of income inequality.*

Moreover, once we are alerted to the importance of age in affecting the distribution of income, we become aware of some odd and paradoxical connections between demography and the distribution of income. Thus the postwar baby boom, by increasing the proportion of young workers, is clearly making the distribution of income today at least slightly more unequal than would otherwise be the case. The same is true for the postwar boom in higher education: it has increased the number of households consisting of married graduate students (including medical students, law students, etc.) who have (temporarily) lower incomes than if they were working at full-time jobs—and who can expect to have much better than average incomes eventually.

Social policies further complicate the relationship between age and income. More generous Social Security payments to the aged encourages them to retire from full-time (and better-paid) work at an earlier age. Medicare for the aged increases (one hopes) their longevity, which is good for the people but bad (in terms of equality) for the income distribution curve. It is facts such as these which make it so senseless to demand, as many of our egalitarians are now doing, that no "person" or "household" should have an income of less than 60 percent of the national median. The categories of "person" and "household," which disregard age and specific circumstance, are just too vague for any serious discussion of the "fairness" of income distribution.

Lester Thurow, in his analysis of income inequality in *The Public Interest* (No. 31, Spring 1973), does take age partially into account. He points out that the top 14.5 per-

---

* Presumably the same is true for the distribution of wealth. The London *Economist* (June 22, 1974), after estimating that 10 percent of Britain's population owns 40 percent of all personal wealth, reckons that since "the old are bound to have larger savings than the young because they have been longer at it . . . the age distribution of the population alone accounts for the concentration of 30 percent of wealth in so few hands."

cent of adult, white, fully-employed males earn 28 percent of total earnings for this group. And he suggests that this fairly modest degree of inequality—modest in view of the differences in occupation, from doorman to surgeon—serve as an appropriate goal for a redistribution of income among the population as a whole. To which one may say: (1) Since men have to be young before they become adult, and become old after passing through their prime, it is not obvious that *this* pattern of income distribution among adult males should or can serve as a model for the population as a whole at any single point in time; and (2) Thurow's own statistics do not distinguish between the younger man beginning his career and the mature man at the height of his earning power, so the degree of inequality among white, fully-employed, adult males is certainly even less—perhaps substantially less—than he estimates.

So where does all this leave us? Well, it leaves us with the distinct impression that the "truth" about income distribution in the United States is far more complex and confusing than the "facts," as ordinarily presented, would imply. That incomes are unequal, is clear enough. That they are less unequal than indignant critics assert, is certain. Is the inequality that does exist too large? That question admits of no easy answer. Christopher Jencks, in his study, *Inequality*, reports: "The average white child born into the most privileged fifth of white American families could look forward to an annual income 75 percent greater than the average child born into the least privileged fifth of white families." * He also reports that income differences between brothers who have been raised in the same home are almost as great as the difference between any two individuals chosen at random. Jencks, who is a socialist, was frankly surprised to discover so little inequality—though, as an absolute egalitarian, he still thinks it is too much. Others will be immensely reassured to find that traditional "equality of opportunity" still

* The inclusion of black children would certainly worsen the statistics. But the issue here is not the inequalities suffered by blacks, which are real enough and beyond dispute, but the extent of inequality throughout American society as a whole.

works so well. Obviously, the issue of how much inequality is consistent with a "fair" distribution of income in a democracy is anything but a simple matter of arithmetic.

OF TAXES AND "LOOPHOLES"

So far we have been talking about pre-tax incomes. What is the effect of our tax system upon the distribution of income? The question is easy to ask, much less easy to answer. Not only do we have a very complex system of taxation, so that its impact is diffused in ways very difficult to trace or measure, but we also have a complex economic and social system, and the interaction of these two complexities is such as to defeat the capabilities of the most powerful computer. Take the apparently simple matter of defining "income." In a welfare state, much of our tax money—in fact, 20 percent of our gross national product—goes to the support of services and grants which are not ordinarily counted as "income," but which are intended to function as income supplements. Here again, a good portion of the "income" of the less well-to-do, and most especially of the poor, is *impersonal income:* subsidized housing, food stamps, Medicaid, free legal services, scholarships for poor students, etc. There is little doubt that when the effects of such expenditures and "transfer payments" are taken into account, the post-tax distribution of income in the United States is less unequal than the pre-tax distribution.*

* The effects of the welfare state, in its totality, upon income redistribution are exceedingly difficult to calculate; there are so many different programs, in cash and kind, with so many different consequences for people in different circumstances. Robert J. Lampman has made the most sophisticated analysis, and his findings are as follows:
   Some 20 percent of the American population have an "original income"—i.e., before Social Security, unemployment insurance, welfare, or any other transfers in cash or kind—which puts them below the official poverty line. Their total "original income" represents 3 percent of national income. As a result of transfers in cash and kind (e.g., food stamps, low-cost housing, Medicare and Medicaid, etc.), this 20 percent of the population increases its share of the national income from 3 percent to 9 percent. As a result of cash transfers alone, about one third of these people are taken out of poverty.
   Obviously, we have not abolished poverty in the United States. Equally

Most of the controversy over our tax system concerns itself with the progressive income tax, and expresses the disappointments of those who expected this tax to be more redistributive than it is. Indeed, among some such people the disappointment is so keen that they declare the progressive income tax to be one huge fraud, in that there is nothing progressive about it. This is patently false. As Roger Freeman has shown, the only class for which the income tax is not progressive is the middle class—i.e., those earning $7,000 to $20,000 a year. This class has 60 percent of the nation's adjusted gross income, but bears only 54 percent of the income tax liability. In contrast, those over $20,000 have 21 percent of adjusted gross incomes but bear 36 percent of total tax liability.*

But why, then, does the progressive income tax not result in an obvious and substantial redistribution of income? The explanation is manifold: (1) To begin with, and as has already been mentioned, much of the redistribution that does occur takes the form of services and subsidies on the part of the state which do not show up in conventional income statistics. (2) To some degree, the progressive character of the income tax is counterbalanced by the non-progressive character of other taxes (e.g., the sales tax and the Social Security tax). (3) Most important, the expectations about the redistributive consequences of the progressive income tax were unrealistic in the first place—there just are not enough "rich" people, and their share of the national income is just not large enough for the progressive income tax to have massive results by way of redistribution.

It would be nice, from the point of view of egalitarians, if our income structure resembled an inverted pyramid, in which a slice from the top yielded a visible dividend for everyone else. But, in actuality, our income structure is

---

obviously, we have made substantial progress in that direction. Recent increases in Social Security will undoubtedly make these statistics look even better.

* See Roger A. Freeman, *Tax Loopholes: the Legend and the Reality*, an AEI-Hoover Institution study (May 1973).

diamond-shaped; a slice from the very top yields a barely
visible dividend for everyone else—and, if you start slicing
further down, you quickly find that you are taxing large
numbers of people who do not think of themselves as "rich"
and who will tell their elected representatives, in no uncertain terms, that their tax burden is heavy enough already.
Senator McGovern discovered this fact of economic life when
he proposed his "demogrant" scheme (a $1,000 tax credit
per person), to be financed by tax reforms that would affect "the rich." In its final version, this scheme required
that 35 percent of the American population pay more taxes
than they do now. That is a "minority," true; but it is evidently far too large a minority for a politician to trifle with.

But what about all those "loopholes" which permit the
wealthy to evade their share of the tax burden—the sort of
thing that Philip M. Stern writes about in his much-discussed
book, *The Rape of the Taxpayer: Why You Pay More While
the Rich Pay Less*, or that Michael Harrington has in mind
when he declares (*Saturday Review*, October 21, 1972) : "The
unconscionable fact is that the Internal Revenue Code is a
perverse welfare system that hands out $77 billion a year,
primarily to the rich"?

Alas, this vast and passionate literature about how the rich
maneuver without cost through our tax system tells us more
about the prevalence of egalitarian passions in our democracy than about our tax system.* This $77 billion figure is

* It also tells us something about the uses of political demagoguery in
a democracy. Back in 1969, Joseph Barr, a former Democratic Representative with a keen eye for a headline, became acting Secretary of the
Treasury for 31 days. In that period, he caused a sensation by announcing, two days before leaving office, that 155 taxpayers with an adjustable
gross income of $200,000 or more had paid no income tax in 1967. He
offered no explanation, but merely created the impression that some
ghastly inequity in our tax system made this possible. Subsequently, the
matter was analyzed by Roger Freeman and others, and it was revealed
that Barr either didn't understand the tax laws or wished deliberately to
mislead. Thus, the incomes he was talking about were "adjusted gross
incomes," not "net incomes," i.e., not income after costs that might have
been incurred in earning that income. (For example, he counted the income received from investing a large sum of borrowed money but not
the interest that had to be paid on that loan.) The failure to make this
distinction explains why 55 out of the 155 paid no taxes. The other hundred are explained by the fact that they earned their money abroad and

derived from a Brookings study by Joseph Pechman, which showed—in the course of proposing a simplified recasting of our tax system—that *all* tax exemptions and allowances total $77 billion dollars.* Repeat: *all* tax exemptions and allowances, for everyone. Mr. Pechman never said—a serious scholar, he never would say—that these deductions and allowances benefit the rich exclusively. He never even said that they benefit the rich "primarily." It is others who made that intellectual leap from bare statistics to gaudy indictment.

As a matter of fact, if all these exemptions and allowances were repealed, some 55 percent of that $77 billion dollars would be derived from families earning under $25,000 a year. In addition, some 10 million families who earn less than $10,000 a year, and who now pay no tax because of these exemptions and allowances, would be added to the tax rolls. So there is no question at all of any total repeal of these "loopholes" which include (it is worth a reminder) such things as personal exemptions, deductions for all dependents, the tax-exempt status of social security, unemployment insurance, workmen's compensation, veteran's disability benefits, various tax privileges for the blind and the handicapped, all charitable deductions, and all sorts of other exemptions and allowances in the tax laws that no one thinks of as "loopholes."

The real issue raised by Pechman and others is whether a portion of this $77 billion—$10 to $15 billion dollars is the figure most often arrived at—which mainly does benefit the well-to-do, can be "captured" by tax reform. The "loopholes" which such a tax reform would be directed at include (1) taxation of capital gains at special, lower rates; (2) the tax-

---

paid foreign taxes on it (sometimes larger than the American tax they might have paid), or because they made a generous charitable gift (e.g., to a university or a museum) larger than their income for that year, or because they had tax-loss carry-forwards from previous financial disasters. It is worth noting that there are some 15,000 people at the above-$200,000 income level, and they paid taxes in 1967 at a rate of 44 percent on adjusted gross income. Nevertheless, Barr made his point: most Americans are now convinced that it is easy for the very rich to pay no taxes at all.

* For a brilliant and definitive discussion of this whole topic, see Professor Boris I. Bittker's article, "Income Tax 'Loopholes' and Political Rhetoric," in the *Michigan Law Review*, Vol. 71 (May 1973).

free status of interest on municipal and state bonds; (3) the "depletion allowance" for oil and other extractive industries; (4) the exclusion of unrealized capital gains from income tax on death of the taxpayer; (5) the tax-deductibility of interest on home mortgages; and, depending on who is composing the list, a few other miscellaneous items.*

One thing can promptly be said about any such agenda for tax reform: it will certainly end up "recapturing" far less than $15 billion, or anything like it. The trouble is that the easy and obviously desirable reforms (e.g., ending depletion allowances or taxing unrealized capital gains in death) raise only a little money (a billion dollars or so in the case of depletion of allowances) or a relatively modest sum (perhaps $3 to $4 billion in the case of taxing capital gains at death). In contrast, the reforms that might raise more substantial sums will either never be enacted by Congress or will be enacted in such a way as to fall short of this goal: Congress is not about to affront American homeowners by ending the tax-deductibility of interest payments on their mortgages; nor is it likely to tangle with the nation's governors and mayors by ending the tax-exempt status of state and municipal bonds; nor is it going to tax more heavily the capital gains realized by middle-class homeowners or small businessmen. Congress might fiddle around with these issues so as to squeeze out a little extra revenue from the more affluent beneficiaries; but we should then be talking about, say, $6–$8 billion in extra revenue.

The really interesting question about these and other "loopholes" is not how much extra tax money can be squeezed back through them: several billion dollars probably can, which would certainly be useful but which would have only a slight effect on the federal budget, and no noticeable effect on the post-tax distribution of income. The more interesting question is how they ever came to be regarded as "loopholes" at all. By far the most important feature of the discussion of this whole matter is not the numbers and the details, but

---

* Since this chapter was written, depletion allowances have been radically restricted, and capital gains made more taxable, by the Tax Reform Act of 1976.

rather the way in which the question itself has come to be
defined. It is a way suggestive of implications for our understanding of the role of taxation in a democratic and liberal
society with a "mixed economy."

WHO OWNS THE MONEY?

Why do we have a complicated tax system rather than a simple one? The reasons are neither obscure nor sinister. The
first has to do with equity. If it is "fair"—as we would all
doubtless agree—for people in comparable circumstances to
pay comparable taxes, then those whose circumstances differ
should pay different taxes. But people with the same incomes
can be in radically various circumstances. Their number of
dependents can vary; their medical needs can vary; their
willingness to support public charities can vary; and so on.
The tax laws try to take such circumstances into account,
and often tie themselves into elaborate knots in the process.

The second reason derives from the fact that the tax laws
have the purpose, not only of raising revenues, but also of
offering incentives for the channeling of personal expenditures toward what are deemed to be socially desirable ends.
The encouragement of public philanthropy, the stimulation
of capital investment, home ownership rather than home
renting—all these are taken to be things which are good for
the society as a whole, and which the tax laws should therefore help rather than hinder or even be indifferent to. Some
economists look upon these provisions as "distortions" of
what would otherwise be an elegantly simple mechanism for
raising revenues, and as undesirable intrusions of social values into individual decision making. Most citizens, however,
take it for granted that one of the responsibilities of government is precisely to affirm and sustain social values, and find
it impossible to imagine a government that adopts a posture
of absolute neutrality as to how people choose to spend their
money—which means, ultimately, how people live.

Now, one may accept the legitimacy of both of these
goals—equity and social purpose—and of government's responsibility for moving us closer to them, but nevertheless insist

that the tax system ought not to be used for these purposes.
After all, there is an alternative: one can levy taxes for the
sole purpose of raising revenues, and then one can subsidize,
by various legislative programs, all those individuals who
have special needs and problems, and all those activities
which government takes a benign view of. In short, take the
complexities out of the tax system and transfer them to the
political process. The advantage sought is one of precision.
Because tax provisions are necessarily so general, they frequently benefit people who do not really need any assistance
and whom Congress may never really have intended to assist
(e.g., the rich homeowner). Also, the more complicated the
tax system, the greater the risk that the affluent may end up
paying less in the way of taxes than was anticipated. A system of specific subsidies, on the other hand, can be more
accurately targeted—at least in theory. In fact, however, anyone who seriously contemplates the prospect of Congressional legislation covering all of these areas might be pardoned for surmising that the legislation embodying such
subsidies would be infinitely more complex than our existing tax laws, and he might also be pardoned for being uneasy
at the new powers (e.g., financing private universities and
all other philanthropies) which would be concentrated in
Washington.

Many economists and tax experts—Stanley Surrey, most
notably—nevertheless do favor subsidies rather than tax incentives, and argue persuasively for them. But in the course
of making these arguments, a very interesting rhetorical transformation takes place. They begin to think and talk as
if the basic decision to subsidize had already been made,
only the subsidies are now incarnated in the tax system
rather than in positive legislation. So they come quickly to
refer to all exemptions and allowances in our tax laws as
"tax subsidies" or even "tax expenditures." But note what
happens when you make this assumption and start using
such terms. *You are implicitly asserting that all income
covered by the general provisions of the tax laws belongs of
right to the government, and that what the government de-*

cides, by exemption or qualification, not to collect in taxes constitutes a subsidy. Whereas a subsidy used to mean a governmental expenditure for a certain purpose, it now acquires quite another meaning, i.e., a generous decision by government not to take your money.

When a man makes a tax-deductible gift to charity, whose money has he given away? Traditionally, it has been thought that he gives away his own money, and that the tax deduction exists only to encourage him to give away his own money for such a purpose. Today, however, one hears it commonly said that he has only in part given away his own money; in actuality, he has also given away some "public" money. This "public" money consists of that sum which, were no such deductions permitted by law, he would have to pay in taxes. It is then said—indeed, it is now a cliché—that the object of his philanthropy (a museum, say) is *"in effect"* being subsidized by public moneys.

What we are talking about here is no slight terminological quibble. At issue is a basic principle of social and political philosophy—the principle that used to be called "private property." The conversion of tax incentives into "tax subsidies" or "tax expenditures" means that "in effect" a substantial part of everyone's income really belongs to the government—only the government, when it generously or foolishly refrains from taxing it away, tolerates our possession and use of it. To put it another way, when you start talking glibly of some $70 billion of legal deductions and allowances as "tax subsidies," you have already in imagination socialized that amount of personal and corporate income.

That is the real significance of all the brouhaha about "loopholes." There are, in fact, very few "loopholes" in our tax laws, in the sense that Congress—either through oversight or sheer sloppiness—*unintentionally* ends up taxing some people or some activities less than it thought it had. What has happened is that Congress, in its wisdom or lack of it, has decided that, for reasons of equity or social purpose, certain classes of people or certain classes of activities ought not to be taxed as heavily as other classes of people and ac-

tivities.* This has traditionally been interpreted as a decision
not to take money from people who own it. Today, a major
intellectual effort is under way to reinterpret it as a decision
to *give* money to people who, for one reason or another, are
thought to deserve it.

By now, most public discussion of tax reform takes place on
the assumption that, since there are no limits to the government's taxing powers, all the people's monies have already in
principle been transferred to government, and the only question is how government should return a portion of these
monies to the people. The one group of the population which
remains unpersuaded of this belief is the majority of the
people itself. This helps explain what otherwise seems an
oddity: that in all opinion polls which ask people whether
they prefer a state sales tax or a state income tax, the majority invariably opt for the "regressive" sales tax. Why?
Well, with a sales tax, you pay taxes on what you spend,
i.e., you have some power in deciding what taxes on your
own income you wish to incur. The income tax, in contrast,
has come to suggest to people that the government does not
really believe they own their income after all. It is therefore
the least popular of taxes.

TAXING THE CORPORATION

The hidden agenda behind the more extreme attacks upon
the "inequities" of our tax system—a socialization in words

---

* Sometimes the decision will favor affluent people as well as poor
people: the personal exemption, interest payments on mortgages, charitable deductions, etc., are all of this kind. Such universal legislation,
covering rich and poor alike, has always been regarded as appropriate to
a democratic community living under the "rule of law." But, inevitably,
it gives rise to the accusation that the rich are favored unequally and
therefore inequitably. Thus a Rockefeller who gives $100,000 to a mu-
seum reduces his taxes by perhaps $70,000; whereas someone who makes
$12,000 a year, and gives $10 to his favorite charity, reduces his tax by
perhaps $2. But this is, of course, simply the reverse side of the pro-
gressive income tax. If you are rich, you pay a higher percentage of your
income in taxes—and, inevitably, every legitimate deduction saves you a
higher percentage in taxes. To argue that this is "unfair" is to assume
that the only legitimate purpose of the tax system is to take money from
the wealthy and give it *to the government*—not to anything or anyone
else.

which will subtly effect a nationalization in fact—is nowhere
more obvious than in the case of corporate taxation. Many
ardent reformers insist that corporations, by one devious
means or another, slyly escape their "fair share" of the
tax burden. Indeed, anyone who now challenges this proposition is regarded as simply being a "spokesman for business," whose ideas are tainted by narrow self-interest. But
the matter of corporate taxation is more complicated, and
the issues involved are far more subtle, than one would
gather from a cursory reading of our newspapers and
magazines.

To begin with, there is the not irrelevant question of just
whom or what we are taxing when we tax a corporation. Indeed, there is a powerful argument to the effect that corporations, by their very nature, do not ordinarily pay taxes
so much as *collect* them. After all, where does a corporation
get the money to pay its taxes? There are only three possible
sources. (1) It can get it from its stockholders by holding
down or cutting their dividends, in which case we are talking about a concealed tax on dividend income. (2) It can
get it from its customers in the form of higher prices—in
which case, we are talking about a concealed sales tax. In
the normal course of events, these are the ways corporations
do raise their tax money; or, to be precise, these are the
means of collecting them.

But if, for any reason, a corporation cannot lower or omit
its dividend or raise its prices without crippling the business, it does indeed pay taxes instead of merely collecting
them. It then (3) gets the money from retained earnings
which would otherwise be reinvested in new plant, new
processes, etc. It is this last source of tax moneys which is of
special interest to many reformers. This is because it gets to
the heart of a crucial question: What is the role of the private
sector in financing capital outlays and thereby determining (to
some degree) the shape of our economic and social system?
The key difference between the system of liberal capitalism
and the system of state capitalism which some call "socialism"
revolves around this very issue of control over investment. In
our "mixed economy," this control is shared by the private

and public sectors: we do not wish to give either of them un-
fettered control over our destinies. The consequence—and, one
can only suppose, the purpose—of any sharp increase in the
tax burden of corporations would be to shift such control mas-
sively toward the political authorities.

No one disputes the proposition that to get economic growth
you need capital investment. At the moment, in the United
States, that need is close to desperate. The share of real
corporate profits in the national income has fallen steadily over this past decade. Moreover, a substantial portion of
these profits is now allocated to meet anti-pollution, safety,
and other standards set by law—desirable ends, but which
do reduce the availability of capital for reinvestment in the
production of those marketable goods whose prices make
up the Labor Department's cost-of-living index, as well as its
standard-of-living estimates. The upshot is that corporations
find themselves squeezed for capital. In this situation, if you
call for still more severe corporate taxation, there are only
two possible explanations. The first is that you have a mindless animosity toward the very idea of corporate profits;
this seems to be the case with some trade union leaders.*
The second is that you have a very mindful, if unexpressed,
preference for an economic system where all or most of the
major investment decisions are made by government. This
latter class of people, in the United States at any rate, usually
think of themselves as "liberals." Were they living in Britain or Germany, they would identify themselves as "social
democrats"—i.e., as socialists of a moderate persuasion. But
since "socialism" is a chimera anyway, and always and everywhere means neither more nor less than some form of state
capitalism, they may be fairly described as liberal state-
capitalists.

Corporate taxes in the United States are right now among
the highest in the world—higher than in Japan, higher

* Trade union thinking and attitudes on this question were apparently
firmly set in the early 19th century, when it was generally believed by
social reformers that improving the conditions of the working class was
entirely a function of the *distribution* of wealth, and that the problem
of *production* (i.e. economic growth) had vanished because the industrial
revolution had once and for all established an "affluent society."

than in Germany. So is our tax on capital gains. And the tax money which our government collects does not ordinarily go into state-owned productive enterprises; it ends up in programs which stimulate consumption rather than investment. So it is fair to say that, as things now stand, the growth of the American economy is being frustrated by taxation plus regulation, while the state itself takes little or no responsibility for sustaining an adequate level of investment. It requires about $30,000 in capital investment to support one job in manufacturing. This money may come from either the private or public sector, but it must come from somewhere. One suspects that there are quite a few people in this country who are not displeased by the current difficulties of the private sector, since it might permit the enactment of various "basic reforms" that would enhance the power of the public sector.*

EQUITY OR EQUALITY?

The intellectual history of the income tax, which has yet to be fully written, is a fascinating subject for a student of modern capitalism and modern social thought.† The idea of the income tax is quite old, having been advocated by many

---

* It has been argued quite persuasively that *any* income tax, individual or corporate, is the wrong kind of tax from the perspective of economic growth. Leonard E. Kust explains why:

> . . . Let us compare one dollar spent on consumption with one dollar saved and invested at five percent. In the absence of an income tax, it takes one dollar, of course, to do either. After a 50 percent income tax, it takes two dollars of income to spend one dollar, but it takes four dollars of income to produce the same after-tax yield as five percent did on one dollar before the tax (*Tax Review*, July, 1973).

In short, any income tax double-taxes savings and investment—since it taxes both the money invested and the return on investment—as against consumption. Some kind of expenditure tax would seem to be preferable from a purely economic point of view. But since this is politically unthinkable in a liberal democracy, the point is academic, if interesting.

† The best treatment still is that superb book, *The Uneasy Case for Progressive Taxation*, by Walter J. Blum and Harry Kalven, Jr. (University of Chicago Press, 1953). Louis Eisenstein's *The Ideologies of Taxation* (New York, 1961) is also valuable.

19th-century liberals. But these gentlemen had in mind a *proportionate* income tax, not a *progressive* one, and they perceived the former as a "fair" device for raising needed revenues, not for achieving any redistribution of income. What made it "fair" was the principle of proportionality itself, which is traditionally identical with the definition of distributive justice (from each his due, to each his due). The idea that a wealthier person should pay higher taxes in proportion to his wealth seemed to be the epitome of equity. A flat tax of, say, 15 percent, on everyone's income—at least the income of those above the subsistence level, it was always agreed—achieved this neat result: the rich paid more to the degree that they were richer.

Advocates of a progressive rather than proportionate income tax in the 19th century were all socialists, and their candid aim was the expropriation of the rich. The *Communist Manifesto* urged the enactment of "a heavy progressive or graduated income tax" for exactly this reason. To this, liberals replied that (1) there was no way of defining an "equitable" rate of progression—it would all dissolve into politics; and (2) this politics would in turn dissolve into demagogy, as politicians began to promise vast benefits to the people on the assumption that only a tiny portion of the rich would pay for them. The objection was prescient, and for a while convincing. But only for a while. As state expenditures grew larger and larger—mainly for military purposes, then for social welfare programs—and as taxes became heavier and heavier, the idea of a progressive income tax became attractive to liberals too.

The liberal argument for progressive taxation still, however, based itself on the grounds of equity, not equality. But there was the potential for confusion here, because the argument for equity was put in terms of "equality of sacrifice." That is to say, within the liberal economists' utilitarian calculus of pleasures and pains, it could be asserted that, as one became wealthier, there was a declining utility attached to each increment of wealth—or, to put it more simply, as one became richer one could only spend money in rather frivolous ways, since there is only so much that *can* be spent to

meet "basic" needs. Equity required, therefore, that money
spent frivolously should be taxed at a higher rate than
money spent seriously (i.e., for food, shelter, etc.). This argument, in a somewhat vulgarized form, is still the main
pillar on which the theory of progressive taxation rests. We
call it taxation by "ability to pay."

Now, this argument from "equal sacrifice" or "ability to
pay" has some serious problems inherent in it. To begin with,
it assumes that the rich spend all their money, rather than
saving and investing it; in other words, it ignores the question of capital accumulation and economic growth. More important, the logic of the argument moves ineluctably from
equity to equality. So long as *any* inequalities of income
exist, marginal expenditures will never be equal in utility;
therefore unequal rates of taxation will still be called for to
achieve "true equality of sacrifice." This is so obvious that
one can only suspect that liberal advocates of the progressive
income tax, prior to World War I, understood it full well and
that they did indeed wish to use the income tax for purposes
of achieving a more equal distribution of income and wealth,
but for prudential reasons thought it advisable not to say so.

In our day, of course, the idea that the income tax should
have redistributive effects is no longer shocking; one can
even say it is on its way to becoming part of the conventional political wisdom. Unhappily, for its advocates, however, it is an idea that, in its more extreme forms, runs up
against the realities of our democratic, affluent society.

One of these realities is economic—that diamond-shaped
distribution of income already referred to. It is a fact that
the progressive aspect of the American income tax accounts
for approximately 15–20 percent of all revenues raised by
the income tax; the rest derives from the initial, proportional
rate. It follows from this fact that further taxation of the
rich through an increase in the rates of progression will not
yield enormous revenues. Clearly it would yield *some* revenues—enough, say, to pay for a modest national health insurance scheme—but at some cost to savings, investment, and
economic growth. It is because they dimly perceive this fact
of modern economic life—not only in the United States but

in all industrialized countries—that our more militant reformers of late have begun candidly to avow pure egalitarian
principles as the basis for a "just" social policy. They may as
well; the arguments about taxation according to "ability to
pay" have already approached their redistributive limits.

A second reality which efforts to redistribute via the income tax encounter is economic-social-political, all in one.
This is the fact that, in a democratic, affluent society, marginal amenities—one dares hardly call them privileges—become very expensive. As everyone becomes better off, it takes
ever larger increments of income for any single family to
become still better off. In New York City, in 1900, any upper-
middle-class family could afford a maid, private schools, a
townhouse (or at the very least a spacious apartment), and
perhaps a season ticket to the Metropolitan Opera. In New
York City today only the really affluent can afford these
things—and rarely can they afford all of them. The things that
are cheap in a democratic, affluent society are the things that
are mass-produced—products or services where economies of
scale are important. The things that are expensive are "minority tastes" and those services where economies of scale do
not apply, i.e., the very things one wants to purchase with
additional income. What this means is that practically any
family in the United States today that earns less than $30,000
a year finds that its "needs" are always pressing against its
after-tax income. And this, in turn, means that the argument
from "ability to pay" no longer has the moral force and persuasive power it used to, and that even the liberal middle
class feels that progressive taxation has gone quite far enough.

INFANTILE LIBERALISM——A DEMOCRATIC DISORDER?

It is generally regarded as bad form to analyze the motives of
social reformers. One usually concedes the sincerity of their
moral passion while questioning the efficacy of their proposals. This is reasonable enough, most of the time. But when
that moral passion becomes intellectually petrified into a
specific ideology, then sincerity can become transformed

into a peculiar kind of fanaticism. At that point, the purpose of reform becomes not a change of conditions which will satisfy the ostensible need, but rather the creation of circumstances which will legitimize in perpetuity the reforming passion itself. To that species of infantile communism which calls for permanent revolution, many of our liberals today respond with a kind of infantile liberalism which calls for permanent reform.

Listen, for instance, to Professor Eugene Smolensky, a distinguished economist who certainly regards himself as a liberal rather than a radical of any kind:

Over any long period of time, humanitarianism and egalitarianism must converge, since the concept of minimally decent is as relative to time and place as is the share of income going to the bottom tenth of the population. Thus, more than 60 per cent of Americans in the very prosperous year of 1929 would be categorized as impoverished by the official definition of poverty adopted in 1962. If a new exponent of the Great Society were to be elected president in 1976, I would expect a new official definition of poverty in 1977 based on some new concept of minimally decent, which would put us right back to 1960—with 20 per cent of families in poverty (*Annals of the American Academy of Political and Social Science*, September 1973).

Note, this is not a plain prediction but also a bland prescription. That, as society becomes more affluent, the conception of an appropriate "poverty line" will drift upwards, is inevitably and properly the case. But that the concept of poverty should be continually and vigilantly redefined so that 20 percent of the population is always "poor" is a function of ideology, not of sociology or economics or social science.

One may reasonably inquire: Is such a view primarily interested in the material well-being of poor people or the moral well-being of liberal reformers? Is it concerned mainly with a world in which poverty becomes less of a problem or rather one in which it is a permanent provocation? Most of us would think that any society which made steady progress in improving the conditions of the poor, but which resolutely kept denouncing itself for having failed to do so, is more than a little neurotic. Yet that is exactly the kind of society

218 WHAT IS "SOCIAL JUSTICE"?

that many social critics today appear to regard as normal
and desirable. Since these people are themselves perfectly
sane, and often very intelligent, there is only one possible
explanation: they are, perhaps unconsciously, considerably
more interested in the perpetuation of a critical attitude
toward liberal-capitalist society than in any particular set of
objective accomplishments. How else is one to interpret this
extraordinary phenomenon of people demanding various reforms but announcing beforehand that the achievement of
those reforms will in no way satisfy them?

One effect of this state of mind is to encourage intellectual irresponsibility, even frivolity. If your critical posture
toward the social reality is predetermined, no matter what
the exact nature of that reality, you really need not think
through your criticism of it. Thus, the well-known and usually astute sociologist, Lewis Coser, can write:

The elimination of poverty in America will not be attained even
when almost all of its citizens have moved above one of the statistical poverty lines. It will occur only when the present distribution
of income is changed so that the bottom portion of the income distribution is shifted into the middle category (*Dissent,* October
1971).

This *seems* to be saying that all those with below-median
incomes ought to be lifted up to the median level—but that,
of course, is an arithmetical absurdity, since a new median
would then be established, with half the population still
below and half still above. It *might* be interpreted to mean
that Professor Coser prefers to replace the present diamond-
shaped income distribution with that of a rather squat pyramid—but that is exactly the kind of income distribution (most
at the bottom, few at the top) which characterizes a poor
country like India, and which egalitarian reformers regard
as horrendously inequitable. But to look for any kind of precise meaning in this formula is to miss the point. The whole
purpose of the formula is to be sufficiently vague and ambiguous to legitimate a permanent posture of indignant disapproval
of whatever actually exists.

It is this characteristic of this class of social critics which
causes them to pay so little attention to two of the most im-

portant facts about the "abolition of poverty" which we have, in recent years, rediscovered. The first is that any effort to encapsulate the specific problem of poverty into the general problem of income inequality leads to an irresolvable intellectual muddle. This is because both the poor and the rich are a minority of the population, whereas the distribution of income affects the entire population. Thus, let us suppose that, miraculously, all those now in the $8,000–$15,000 income bracket were overnight transferred into the $15,000–$22,000 bracket. Has American society then become more equal or less? From the point of view of the poor it can be argued that it has become less equal; from the point of view of everyone else it has become more equal. Both perspectives are valid, but you cannot hold them simultaneously. Similarly, if as a result of a monumental stock market crash, the percentage of those in the top 10 percent ($25,000 or over) were halved, with some 10 million people moving downward to the $20,000–$25,000 bracket, would American society then be more equal? The answer is yes, but the condition of the poor would not have improved at all. That is why the only sensible way to approach the problem of poverty is through some "official poverty line"—a standard which is independent of the distribution of income. The advantage in trying to define poverty and inequality as a single problem is that it does offer a broad scope for selecting, at any time, those particular statistics with which you can "demonstrate" that things are getting worse, even if they seem to be getting better.

The other important fact is that *the way in which you "abolish poverty" can be as important as the statistical abolition itself.* This is the lesson of the "welfare explosion" of the past decade. In New York City, we have "abolished poverty" in the sense that welfare benefits are sufficiently generous to lift all recipients above the official poverty line.* Other cities are considerably less generous. But is it noticeable

---

* Indeed, if you include nonmonetary benefits, in New York City a family of four on welfare has an annual income greater than one-half the median family income in the city—a situation which some reformers have long regarded as the ultimate goal in the "war against poverty."

that the poor in New York City are better off than the poor
elsewhere? No, it seems not to be noticeable, or to have been
noticed, or to be so. The reason is that the welfare system
encourages various social pathologies—broken families, illegitimacy, drug addiction—which easily overwhelm the single statistical fact of "the abolition of poverty." Such an
"abolition of poverty" through transfer payments—i.e., through
a redistribution of income—does work for the aged, the sick,
the handicapped; it seems to be counterproductive for all
others. Dependency, for those who are not by nature and
necessity dependent, can have demoralizing consequences. The
bare statistics on the distribution or redistribution of income
ignore this crucial sociological fact—which is why, once again,
it is a good idea not to confuse the issue of poverty with the
issue of a more equal distribution of income.

As Bertrand de Jouvenel has pointed out, whereas riches
used to be a scandal in the face of poverty, today poverty
is a scandal in the face of affluence. There is, therefore, an
unquestionable moral necessity to assist the poor—in whatever way actually assists them. But when you redefine poverty in purely comparative terms—i.e., in terms of the distribution of income, of the "relative deprivation" of those
who have less as against those who have more—you have
eliminated the moral dimension entirely. Then, a melioristic
sentiment becomes converted into a passion for equality, a
passion that can be based on envy and greed as easily as on
a sense of moral obligation and moral deserts. The abolition
of poverty, or at least its amelioration, ought to be an in-
spiriting program, one which makes the entire polity feel
better because it is doing good. The compulsory redistribution of income via taxation, however, in order to satisfy a
sense of "relative deprivation," is little more than a prescription for eternal class war. For, our liberal reformers tell us,
so long as there is *any* inequality, there will be a consciousness of "relative deprivation." Not, they hasten to add (for
the most part), that absolute equality of everyone is an
appropriate goal. It is only the unending struggle toward this
inappropriate goal which they endorse as somehow representing the quintessence of liberal morality.

The idea of "relative deprivation" can be viewed either descriptively or normatively. As a description of what human beings are like, there is substance to it (alas). Firemen do go out on strike, and put at hazard the entire community, for the sake of a few dollars a week which will put them on a par with policemen. But it is quite another matter to accept it and endorse it as a perfectly normal and even desirable human attitude on the part of those who have less toward those who have more. This is blandly to legitimize envy, greed, and rapacity in the name of an ideal equality.

As Tocqueville emphasized long ago, equality is a natural "political passion" in a democracy. But, he went on to say, this passion can take two very different forms. It can become "a manly and legitimate passion for equality which rouses in all men a desire to be strong and respected" and which "tends to elevate the little man to the rank of the great"; or it can become "a debased taste for equality, which leads the weak to want to drag the strong down to their level and which induces men to prefer equality in servitude to inequality in freedom." The spirit of liberal reform originally—in the Progressive era, for example, as represented by Theodore Roosevelt and Woodrow Wilson—stood for equality in the first sense: it wanted to "level up," as we say. But since World War II, it is the passion for a perpetual "leveling down" that has come to prevail. It is not the improvement of the poor that matters any longer, it is punitive action against the rich that most gratifies the spirit of reform.

Is this an exaggeration? Well, it is interesting to observe the range of possible reforms which would be very helpful to poorer people, which would even work toward at least some slight diminution of after-tax inequality of incomes, and which do not rouse any enthusiasm at all among most of our reformers: children's allowances, for instance; or tax deductibility for the first $500 of life insurance premiums; or making tax-free the first $100 of interest on a savings account. All of these would primarily benefit those with low or modest incomes. The trouble is that, being of universal application, they would also marginally benefit the rich. And that is enough to make them unacceptable in liberal eyes.

In contrast, an increase in the present 50 percent maximum tax on earned incomes would receive instant and loud approval. But all that this would do is to make "more equal" those who earn $50,000 a year and those who make $100,000. Why should this be of any great interest to liberal reformers?

In part, the answer has to do with the version of the democratic passion for equality which now is predominant in liberal circles. When so thoughtful a man as Christopher Jencks can solemnly write that any "inequality (in ability) that derives from biology (genes) ought to be as *repulsive* as inequality that derives from early socialization"—and when he can write this without provoking massive ridicule among his Harvard colleagues, who presumably believe in intellectual and aesthetic (or even athletic) excellence—it is clear that a mindless egalitarianism has been calmly absorbed into an infantile liberalism. But this is not the entire answer. For behind this egalitarian impulse there lies another, and perhaps stronger impulse, already referred to, which tells us much about the past and future of liberal democracy.

THE "DIRTY LITTLE SECRET"

Large disparities of income, leading in turn to large concentrations of wealth, and these leading in turn to large *inherited* concentrations of wealth—such, it has long been recognized, can pose a very special problem for a democracy. The primal nightmare of a democracy is the emergence of an oligarchy that would, through the power associated with wealth, perpetuate itself, and eventually constitute a kind of aristocracy. So the question of the distribution of wealth is a proper concern for any democratic society. Whether, in the United States today, this question is acute is a matter of opinion and controversy. Since our economic historians tell us that, over the past 150 years, the distribution of wealth has probably become less unequal, it is not obvious that the subject should exercise us unduly. But let us assume, for the moment, that we decided it *was* acute enough (or was widely perceived to be acute enough) for us to do something about it. What might we do?

The question, oddly enough, is quite easy to answer: we should discourage the inheritance of large fortunes. This is a quite traditional liberal idea—Montesquieu and Jefferson would both have approved of it—nor is it such a difficult task. All we have to do is decide—and legislate—that no large fortune should outlast the lifetime of the man who made it, but rather that such a large fortune should dissolve into much smaller fortunes upon his death. Thus, we could make it a matter of public policy and law that no individual could inherit, in a lifetime, more than one million dollars, and any possessor of a large fortune must distribute it, prior to death or by testament, to his children, his relatives, his friends, anyone, with no one receiving more than that maximum legacy, which would be tax-free. (Institutional donations, of course, could be of any size.) Should he fail to do so, the government would levy a 100 percent tax on the undistributed portion of his estate.

There would seem to be many advantages to such a policy. It does not discourage the incentive to invest and make money; anyone can still become enormously rich in his lifetime. Moreover, the foreknowledge that he would have to distribute his riches means that the wealthy man would, in his lifetime, be the recipient of much flattering attention and many honors. He would, in addition, have the pleasure associated with the plenary power of disposing of his wealth as he saw fit—rewarding some, failing to reward others. No large fortune would outlast a generation; but there would still be enough wealthy people around to support charities, private educational institutions, unpopular political causes, and minority cultural tastes—in other words, to act as a useful counterbalance to the ever-increasing weight of government and the public sector. Even the children of the rich would benefit, since it has long been recognized that the inheritance of large sums of money tends to distort the motivations and corrupt the characters of young people.

It can be predicted that any such proposal would provoke the hostility of the wealthy, who really do—it is perfectly natural—have dreams of their families moving through oligarchy to eventual aristocracy. But it can also be predicted that any such proposal would be contemptuously dismissed by a great many liberal reformers. Why? The explanation is simple: when modern liberals talk about "the redistribution of income," they rarely mean a simple redistribution among individuals; more often they mean a redistribution *to the state*, which will then take the proper egalitarian measures. No proposal for the redistribution of large fortunes will get liberal support unless that money goes into the public treasury, where liberals will have much to say as to how it should be spent. That is the "dirty little secret"—the hidden agenda —behind the current chatter about the need for "redistribution." The talk is about equality, the substance is about power.

As M. de Jouvenel observed, in his neglected classic, *The Ethics of Redistribution:*

The more one considers the matter, the clearer it becomes that redistribution is in effect far less a redistribution of free income from the richer to the poorer, as we imagined, than a redistribution of power from the individual to the State. . . . Insofar as the State amputates higher incomes it must assume their saving and investment functions. . . . Insofar as the amputated higher incomes fail to sustain certain social activities, the State must step in, subsidize these activities, and preside over them. Insofar as income becomes inadequate for the formation and expenses of those people who fulfill the more intricate or specialized social functions, the State must see to the formation and upkeep of this personnel.

Is this not, in effect, what has been happening over the past half-century? The distribution of income and wealth within the private sector has been affected only modestly by the rise in the variety and extent of taxation. But the distribution of income and wealth as between the private and public sectors has been affected enormously. True, much of the money diverted to the public sector ends up in programs and expenditures that benefit low-income groups, and much of it, too, provides benefits for all of us. But what should not be overlooked is that this movement of money, to and fro, has helped create and now sustains whole classes of professionals, in both the public and quasi-public sectors, that have a profound interest in the growth and prosperity of the public sector (and an instinctive animus toward the private sector). This interest is both material and ideological. It is a question of jobs and status and power. But it is also a question of using the state for the purpose of "realizing one's ideals," i.e., achieving indirectly what it is so difficult to persuade a democratic majority to endorse directly.

Taxation, poverty, and equality are all and always proper subjects for concern and reformist action. But the first step toward effective reform is to disentangle these three themes. And this first step cannot itself be taken unless one appreciates and makes allowance for the powerful (if usually subterranean) movement of opinion among proponents of reform toward some form of liberal state capitalism, as distinct from our present "mixed economy." For it is this movement of opinion which is responsible for the original entanglement and which has a profound interest in its continuance.

26

OF POPULISM AND TAXES

WHAT is populism and why is everyone suddenly saying
such nice things about it? The answer to that last question,
at least, is easy enough: when a populist spirit is abroad in
the land, most Americans are always eager to say nice things
about it. After all, populism as a political movement is in-
disputably based on popular passions and popular resent-
ments, and very few commentators today are willing to adopt
a critical posture toward it, lest they stand accused of the
awful ideological error of "elitism." During the 1950s, the late
Richard Hofstadter (among others) could explore the connections in American history between political populism
and political paranoia—the belief that the world is being
misdirected by some kind of mischievous conspiracy against
the "common man." The perception of such a connection permits one to understand some of the more interesting aspects
of American populist movements: their tendency toward
xenophobia and racism for one thing, their extraordinary in-
eptitude at significant institutional reform for another. But,
in recent years, Hofstadter's work has been nibbled at by a

flock of younger historians who are maddened by his very
detachment from populist clichés. In America, intellectuals
are now more consistently populist than the populace itself.
Political populism is a natural temptation for a democratic
people, but the populist idea seems to have become something
like a secular religion for the democratic intellectual, who is
convinced that "the people" represent a holy congregation
and, therefore, that their indignation is the wrath of God. Indeed, when the American people sensibly resist the populist
temptation—when they exhibit a preference for a politics of
calm deliberation over a politics of passionate resentment—
they are likely to be rebuked by their intellectuals for their
disgusting "apathy."

What is populism? Oddly enough, I believe the classical
Marxist definition is the most accurate: populism in America
is the radicalism of the petit-bourgeois sensibility—the radicalism of the traditional-minded and nostalgia-ridden "common man," a radicalism of the sullen, the bewildered, the
resentful, the anxious, the frustrated. It is, Marxism goes on
to say, a "false" class consciousness in that it is myth-ridden
and essentially "escapist"; it is therefore a very dangerous
form of radicalism because, in the end, it is more likely to
be captured by unscrupulous right-wing demagogues than by
proper socialist theoreticians. This interpretation of populism
is doubtless schematic and even melodramatic, as Marxist
interpretations tend to be. But I think it to be more valid
than not, and I would remark that the ease with which so
many of yesterday's quasi-Marxist radicals have transformed
themselves into today's self-styled "populists" is a sad commentary on the condition of American political thinking in
the 1970s.

Still, when all this has been said, considerably less than
everything has been said. Populism may be a natural temptation in a democracy, but large numbers of citizens are not
likely to succumb to this temptation unless circumstances
move them to do so. *Vox populi* is not *vox dei*, but when
people feel the times are out of joint, then they are in fact
out of joint; there is no higher court to appeal to. The rise
of a populist temper is a sure sign that something has gone

wrong, and that reforms are very much in order. A populist upsurge always points to very real problems that ought to be on our political agenda. But populism itself usually misperceives these problems, and the solutions it proposes are, more often than not, illusory.

WHAT KIND OF TAX REBELLION?

It seems generally agreed that a major cause of the present populist discontent is taxation. But, typically, the populist temper seizes hold of this matter and twists it into a familiar paranoid shape; the tax issue, it proclaims, arises out of the manipulation of our tax laws by "vested interests" so that the rich are getting away scot-free while the common man bears the whole tax burden. The answer, obviously, is to soak the rich.

Now there is, as it happens, something to be said for soaking the rich. But that is not really the problem, nor is it really any kind of a solution. The average American, no matter what he may sometimes say or what is said in his name, is not rebelling against tax inequities. *He is rebelling against taxes, period.* He is rebelling against increased property and sales taxes. He is rebelling against the hidden tax that inflation represents. He is rebelling against all those itemized deductions from his paycheck, against the fact that his "take-home pay" diverges more and more from his formal salary, so that his hard-won wage increases seem to exist only on paper and never find their way into his pocket.

Since most social critics are members of the upper-middle class, for whom the income tax looms so large, it is easy to exaggerate the importance of the income tax for the American working man. True, as his wages increase he moves "progressively" up into higher tax brackets. But the actual impact of this process is minimal, since we are talking about relatively small spurts in income. The average American worker is *not* paying a greater proportion of his salary to Internal Revenue than he was ten years ago; as a result of the Kennedy and Nixon tax reforms, he is more likely to be paying less. He

is, however, witnessing a greater proportion of his salary
being preempted by inflation—itself the consequence of increased government spending on such things as welfare,
education, Medicare, and Medicaid. He also sees more of his
salary being funneled off into Social Security, supplemen-
tary private pensions, early retirement schemes, medical insurance, and so forth. Between 1965 and 1971, his weekly
earnings rose by 12 percent, but what we now call his "real
spendable earnings" did not increase at all. The American
worker finds this frustrating. He resents this whole process,
which bureaucratically insists on improving his longer-term
prospects at the expense of his shorter-term ones, on improving his general welfare at the expense of his specific well-
being. In short, he resents the present structure of the welfare state, and his "tax rebellion" is an expression of this
resentment. This intense dissatisfaction of the working class
and lower-middle class over the issue of "taxes" is not a
uniquely American phenomenon. The same resentment is
clearly visible in Britain, France, Germany, and Sweden—
nations where the question of tax inequities is barely raised
at all.

What is occurring is very interesting and very troubling:
the middle-class psychology which has created the welfare
state is on a collision course with a working-class psychology which, while not rejecting any of the benefits of the
welfare state, nevertheless feels victimized by it. This may be
shortsighted on the part of the working class—but, then, it is
in the nature of working-class people to be more shortsighted
(to have a shorter "time horizon") than middle-class people;
since their lives offer fewer gratifications, working-class people tend to want them more immediately. And there may well
be more than shortsightedness involved. After all, it is the
middle class that manages our welfare state, whereas our
working class is managed by it—and it is a lot more fun to
manage than be managed. Many workers who are angry at
those deductions from their paycheck would take pride in
making those deductions on a voluntary basis. They could
then find personal satisfaction in providing for their own
and their children's future. It is pleasing to fulfill such re-

sponsibilities in a "manly" way; it is apparently much less
pleasing to have a bureaucratic process do this *to* you and
for you.

How to get out of this impasse is not a subject we have
given much thought to. Indeed, we have for the most part
failed to realize just what kind of impasse we are in. Instead
we tend to permit ourselves to be caught up in the populist
current, and to believe that a populist reform—a more "progressive" tax system—will provide the answer to populist
discontent. Just how illusory such a notion is may be in-
ferred from the following report in the New York *Times*
for May 19, 1972:

For many New Jersey political leaders it didn't seem to make any
sense. Here was a Republican Governor urging a Legislature con-
trolled by Republicans to approve the most progressive, urban-
oriented, socially conscious tax-reform program ever proposed in
the state's history. Appearing before a joint legislative session in the
crowded Assembly chamber this afternoon, Gov. William T. Cahill
recommended a $2-billion tax program that included a graduated
state income tax and a statewide property tax of $1 on every $100
of true value.

He promised that the new taxes would cut local property taxes
in New Jersey by an average of 40 per cent and enable the state to
assume the entire financial responsibility of operating the public
schools. . . .

Stripped to its essentials, it is a controversial program that would
bear down hardest on the wealthy, predominantly Republican communities in the suburbs and offers sizable tax relief and new urban
aid to the predominantly Democratic poor people in the cities and
the working-class communities immediately surrounding them. . . .

It would follow, then, that the Governor should be able to count
heavily on the cities and the Democrats in his effort to reform what
he calls "an unjust, regressive tax system which places the greatest
burden on those least able to pay."

In reality, some of the most strident opposition to any reforms
will come from blue-collar neighborhoods who stand to benefit the
most from them.

For example, a number of legislators from the cities, such as
Anthony Imperiale of Newark, contend—probably rightly—that vir-
tually all their constituents are opposed to any kind of new taxes,
regardless of the higher benefits involved and regardless of any accompanying reduction in local taxes.

"I can't put my finger on it," Mr. Imperiale said today, but it was

apparent that the same sense of political, economic and social alienation that is encouraging thousands of working-class Democrats in
New Jersey to support Gov. George Wallace of Alabama would also
be a major factor in determining their opposition to any reforms.

One can fairly predict that many middle-class reformers
will find, to their surprise, that the populace is going to be
quick to bite the hand that aims to feed it. The populace
doesn't want to be fed; it wants more freedom to graze on its
own.

TAXING THE RICH

I am not suggesting that there are no inequities in our tax
system. On the contrary, there are many and their elimination or reformation is highly desirable. But one has to have
a clear idea of what this will accomplish. It will *not* have
any significant effect on the distribution of income in the
United States, and it will *not* have any significant effect on
the tax burden of the average American. It will *not* of itself
finance the prospective growth of existing social programs,
and it will most emphatically *not* finance any major new social programs (e.g., national health insurance, day-care centers, etc.). Its purpose will be primarily symbolic: to reassure the American people that the tax system is "fair."

Such a recognition of the limits of tax policy will depress
those who believe that the distribution of income is a major
problem for American society today. But is it, really? My
own guess is that, left-wing intellectuals and academics apart,
no one is terribly exercised by this issue. It is in the nature
of democratic politics that practically any discontent expresses itself in terms of a demand for greater "equality,"
when what is actually being demanded is fairness or efficiency—or even special privilege! I have suggested that
much of our working-class discontent is over the structure of
the welfare state: I would add that this discontent is exacer-
bated by the ways in which the welfare state is spending its
tax revenues—for ever-growing welfare rolls, for an educational system that seems to be falling apart, for a police force
that cannot cope with increased criminality, for low-income

housing that converts itself into instant slums, for Medicaid
to the poor which inflates medical costs for the nonpoor,
etc. It would not be an exaggeration to say that much of the
present discontent with taxation is provoked by the fact that
the welfare state, which these taxes support, is *too* committed
to equality—to expenditures that benefit primarily the minority who are poor.

The populist demand for "equality," back in the 1890s,
was in reality a protest against the emerging new shape of
American society, in which the large corporation was to be
a central institution. What the populists basically wanted,
and what in the end they got, was for government to take effective action to curb the economic power and political influence of the corporations. That end achieved, the populist
spirit gradually melted away. Today, populist dissent, as I see
it, is once again concerned with the emerging new shape of
American society. It is a society in which bureaucracies—
governmental, judicial, professional, educational, corporate
—make the crucial decisions which affect the common man's
life (e.g., busing his children away from their neighborhood
school, appropriating part of his salary to support people he
thinks unworthy of support, etc.). Most of these decisions involve specific costs to him, while promising only future benefits, some of which are vaguely "social." It is no wonder that
his anxiety becomes touched with paranoia, and that he
should smell foul conspiracy.

There is no conspiracy, but there is a problem. It is not a
problem of income distribution or of inequities of taxation.
The problem is the bureaucratization of American society
and the fact that this bureaucratization has failed to accomplish the only thing no bureaucracy dare fail at: the efficient
delivery on its promises. Populist dissent today is directed
against liberal politics—even when it votes for an "anti-
establishment" liberal politician. Liberals may find this incredible: How can the people possibly be against liberal
politics, when liberal politics so sincerely has the larger interests of the people at heart? So long as this question can
be asked so ingenuously, we shall not have got very far in
coping with the upsurge of populist dissent in the 1970s.

27

SOCIAL REFORM:

GAINS AND LOSSES

THE 1970s debate over the merits or demerits of the various programs inherited from the Great Society in the 1960s is an important one, but it is in danger of getting lost in a fog of swirling rhetoric. This is perhaps inevitable, but it is also too bad, for it is distracting us from learning the crucial lessons of the Great Society experience, lessons which raise some really interesting questions about social reform itself.

I am thinking of such questions as: How do we know whether or not a social reform has worked? What are the general characteristics of successful as against unsuccessful reforms? Are there any general principles of reform that can guide us toward success and steer us away from failure? After our experience of the past decade, such questions are certainly in order.

This does not mean they are easy to answer. Practically all social reforms "work" in that they do distribute some bene-

234 WHAT IS "SOCIAL JUSTICE"?

fits to the people whom they aim to help. Similarly, no social reform ever works out exactly as its proponents hoped; there are always unanticipated costs and unforeseen consequences. Still, one has to strike a balance. How is that to be done?

Our inclination these days—and this in itself is a "reform" of the 1960s—is to call in a social scientist and ask him to provide us with some kind of cost-benefit analysis. I myself used to believe this was a good idea, but I have been more recently persuaded that it is not. Today's social scientists, I have come to think, are not a solution but are themselves part of the problem. They are poor guides to social reform because, to the degree that they think economically, they tend to confuse the art of government with the pursuit of particular ideological objectives. It is extremely difficult for social scientists to do what I have previously described as thinking politically. Some do, of course; but they are likely to be regarded within their professions as old-fashioned and unsophisticated. And I should say that a major reason the social reforms of the '60s were so ill-conceived was that they were shaped so powerfully by the thinking of contemporary social scientists.

I can illustrate this point by reference to a social reform that was *not* adopted in the 1960s. Early in that decade, a small group of scholars—Daniel P. Moynihan being prominent among them—proposed that, in order to alleviate poverty in the United States, a system of children's allowances be instituted. This is a simple and feasible program, which has existed in Europe and Canada for decades now, and which is so taken for granted there that no one pays much attention to it anymore. The program, as proposed for this country, had obvious merit. It is a fact that one of the main reasons many families in the United States are poor is because their incomes are too low to support both parents and children—especially when, as is the case, poor families tend to be somewhat larger than average. The children's allowance simply gives every family a very modest sum (say $15 or $20 a month) for each child. To the poor family, this will mean a significant increase in annual income. For the most affluent family, especially if these allowances are classified as taxable income, it means a more or less marginal bonus. Everybody benefits, but the poor benefit far more than the rich. Moreover, the program creates no disincentives: the poor have as much reason as ever to strive to become less poor, since they lose practically nothing by doing so.

Despite the fact that the program seemed to be working well in other countries, the idea of children's allowances never got a favorable hearing in Washington or in reform circles. To some extent, this was because many middle-class liberals, worried about population growth, regarded it as "pro-natalist," though the evidence is overwhelming that, in countries that have such a program, people's decisions to have children are unaffected by the prospect of these modest allowances. More important was the fact that the program was bound to be expensive—costing anywhere from $10 billion to $20 billion a year, depending upon the scale of the allowances—and there was no such money in the budget. True, one could have begun the program with very small allowances, increasing them gradually over the years; but this would not have achieved the goal the reformers had their eyes set on, which was to abolish poverty *now*.

Above all, however, the idea of children's allowances did not commend itself to the reform-minded in Washington because it seemed so clearly "uneconomical" and "inequitable." What was the sense, it was asked, of having a universal program which gave money indifferently to everyone, to those who needed it and those who didn't? Why give children's allowances to the middle class and the affluent, who could take care of themselves? Why not give the money *only* to the poor? And so was born the "War on Poverty"— and, I would say, one of the great reform disasters of our age.

The trouble with giving money only to the poor is twofold. First of all, one has to decide who is poor. That decision, it turns out, is inherently arbitrary and controversial. The poor in our society, after all, are not an identifiable class— like the blind or disabled, for instance—set apart from other Americans. They are simply people with incomes below some official figure, and there is no possible consensus as to where the figure should be set. Does it make any sense to say

that a family of four with an income of $3,900 is poor and
is entitled to various benefits—welfare, Medicaid, housing—
while the family next door with an income of $4,200 is not
poor and is entitled to no such benefits? It makes no sense at
all, as both of those families quickly perceive. The "poor"
family feels demeaned at passing this peculiar test, the "nonpoor" family feels cheated at failing it. The upshot is political turmoil and general dissatisfaction. The War on Poverty
created divisiveness among the American people, whereas
the mark of a successful social reform, I would argue, is to
create greater comity among the people.

The second difficulty in giving money only to the poor is
that it quickly imprisons them in a "poverty trap." To the extent that they improve their situations and earn more money,
they disqualify themselves for all those benefits which the
various anti-poverty programs reserve for the poor. A huge
disincentive is officially established; it becomes positively
irrational for a poor family to try to move up a notch or
two along the income scale. Having been defined as poor,
they are encouraged to remain poor. Ironically, but pre-
dictably, the subsequent demoralization of those caught in
this "poverty trap" nullifies the supposed ameliorative effects
of their benefits. One can see this process only too clearly at
work in New York City, where welfare benefits—taken together with Medicaid, food stamps, etc.—bring all the poor
above the official poverty line. Statistically, we have abolished poverty in New York City. In actuality, poor people in
New York are not at all obviously better off than they were
ten years ago. They get more money, better housing, and
better medical care but suffer more crime, drug addiction,
juvenile delinquency, and all the other varieties of social
pathology which dependency creates.

MAKING MATTERS WORSE

In retrospect, the conception of social reform that developed
during the 1960s can be seen to have been warped by a misplaced sense of economic efficiency, reinforced by an egali-

tarian animus against any program which threatened to benefit the nonpoor. The result was a series of "selective" social programs that produced a succession of perverse consequences. Not only did these programs fail to achieve their goals; in many respects they made matters worse.

In contrast, if one looks at the kinds of social reforms which, in historical perspective, may fairly be judged to have been successful, one finds that they were all "universal." The outstanding such reform of this century was, of course, Social Security (and its subsequent corollary, Medicare). Back in the 19th century, the most successful social reform was the institution of free public education. No one was excluded from enjoying the fruits of these reforms, which nevertheless were of greater advantage to the poor than to the rich. Everyone benefited from them, since we are all young at some time, all old at another. Both reforms, once established, became noncontroversial. Both contributed to political and social stability by encouraging Americans to have a better opinion of their society—a "good" which the economist is at a loss to measure and which the ideologically oriented sociologist, interested in "social change," is likely to scorn.

To be sure, all such successful, "universal" reforms are extremely expensive. But this represents an insurmountable obstacle only if one insists that such reforms accomplish their ends immediately. Such insistence is itself a recent phenomenon, one of the feverish symptoms of the intemperate '60s. The public school system, at all levels, was the work of over a century; and Social Security was gradually phased into its current state over the course of the last 30 years. Had anyone demanded "public education *now*" or "Social Security *now*," he would have been making an unreasonable and self-defeating demand. Fortunately, very few reformers were then so peremptory, and government was able to institute these reforms in an orderly, gradual, and ultimately successful way.

The reforming spirit of the '60s—and of the '70s too—is less patient, more impassioned. It is bored with the prospect of gradual improvement, and sometimes seems to get a posi-

tive satisfaction out of setting American against American—
class against class, race against race, ethnic group against
ethnic group. This is why I think it fair to say that most of
the Great Society programs have failed. They have provoked
incessant turbulence within the body politic. A successful
reform has just the opposite effect.

One wonders what would happen if all the money spent on
Great Society programs had been used to institute, in however modest a way, just two universal reforms: (1) children's allowance, as already described, and (2) some form of
national health insurance? My own surmise is that the country would be in much better shape today. We would all—
including the poor among us—feel that we were making
progress, and making progress together, rather than at the
expense of one another.

Yes, such reforms are expensive and technically "wasteful," in that they distribute benefits to all, needy or not. But
to stress this aspect of the matter is to miss the point: social
reform is an inherently political activity, and is to be
judged by political, not economic or sociological, criteria.
When I say social reform is "political," I mean that its purpose is to sustain the polity, to encourage a sense of political
community, even of fraternity. To the degree that it succeeds
in achieving these ends, a successful social reform—however
liberal or radical its original impulse—is conservative in its
ultimate effects. Indeed, to take the liberal or radical
impulse, which is always with us, and slowly to translate
that impulse into enduring institutions which engender
larger loyalties is precisely what the art of government, properly understood, is all about.

28

THE POVERTY OF

REDISTRIBUTION

IS THERE a "problem" in the distribution of income in the United States today? We are frequently assured that there is, and are confronted with Census Bureau statistics to prove it. Those statistics, widely quoted, show that the top 20 percent of American families get 40 percent of the national income, while the lowest 20 percent of the population get only 5 percent. The statistics are accurate enough, but they are also wildly misleading.

One reason they are misleading is that they refer only to *cash* income. They omit in-kind transfers (e.g., Medicare, Medicaid, food stamps, subsidized housing, etc.), and it is precisely such in-kind transfers that have mushroomed during the past 15 years. Edgar K. Browning (*The Public Interest*, Spring 1976) has shown that, once such in-kind transfers are included, the lowest fifth gets almost 12 percent of the national income, the top fifth about 33 percent.

Moreover, even this revised picture grossly exaggerates the degree of income inequality. That is because the statistics are not corrected for age. Clearly, young people who have recently entered the labor force, and old people who have left it, will have significantly lower incomes than those in mid-career. Even in a strictly egalitarian society, where everyone's lifetime income is equal, a cross-cut statistical snapshot at any one moment will show substantial inequality.

The statistical problems involved in correcting the picture of income distribution for age are formidable, and there are no meaningful percentages to be quoted. But where statistical precision is lacking, common sense will take us at least part of the way. Let us assume that any revision which takes account of age has only modest effects—that perhaps it will show the top 20 percent of the population to receive 28 percent to 30 percent of the national income. Does this degree of inequality represent an "inequity"? Is it a "problem"?

Obviously, it is for those who believe in the ideal of absolute equality for all. But most Americans who express concern about inequality have no such extreme thoughts. Indeed, most of their interest in inequality arises from the very reasonable desire to eradicate, or at least alleviate, poverty. And this confusion between the issue of inequality and the issue of poverty is indeed a very serious problem.

The notion that income redistribution is the effective means to end poverty is age-old: one finds it expressed in the civil strife of the Greek city-states, the medieval peasant rebellions, and the socialist movements of the past 200 years. But if the modern science of economics has taught us anything, it is that the connection is usually spurious.

The redistribution impulse is most powerful today in those poor countries, the so-called less-developed countries, where it makes the least sense. In such countries, the alleviation of poverty is utterly dependent on economic growth. There never is enough money among the small number of wealthy citizens to make a significant dent in the poverty of the masses. When the rich are expropriated in such countries, everyone becomes equal in poverty—though the political authorities who do the expropriating usually end up being more equal than the rest.

Even in affluent, developed societies, where the poor are a minority, the alleviation of poverty is mainly dependent on economic growth. (The one instance where it makes sense to think of income redistribution as a cure for poverty involves the aged and infirm, that portion of the population who are not in the labor force because they are by nature dependent.) The experience of the United States over these past 15 years demonstrates how the idea of "abolishing poverty" through income redistribution turns out to be a will-o'-the-wisp.

POVERTY AND PATHOLOGY

Let us draw the poverty line at a fairly high level—at one half the median income. (This is the level preferred by most liberal reformers, as distinct from the official "subsistence" level fixed by government.) Well, in New York City, where our politicians are notoriously compassionate, we have achieved even that high level. A family of four on welfare receives in cash and kind, between $7,000 and $7,500 a year. (The median household income in the United States is about $12,500 annually.) *We have abolished poverty in New York City!*

So why hasn't anyone noticed?

The reason is that, for the non-aged and non-infirm, poverty turns out to be more than a simple shortage of money. Poverty as a human condition, as distinct from a statistical condition, is defined to a substantial degree by the ways in which one copes with poverty. A visitor to the Greek islands, or to an Italian village, is impressed first of all, not by the poverty of the people there—which is acute—but by their determination to make the best of things and their extraordinary ability to do so.

And what is true for the way one copes with poverty is also true for the way one goes about abolishing poverty. For the way in which poverty is abolished turns out to be more important than the statistical abolition itself. In New York,

we have tried to abolish poverty through a generous welfare
program, and have therewith rediscovered the truth of an
old adage: dependency tends to corrupt and absolute dependency corrupts absolutely. Our welfare population, statistically lifted out of poverty, has actually and simultaneously
sunk to various depths of social pathology. It is largely a
demoralized population, with higher rates of crime, juvenile
delinquency, drug addiction, teenage pregnancy, and alcoholism, than when the welfare checks were less generous.

The reason for this demoralization is obvious enough,
though scholars with a middle-class background have difficulty in perceiving it. Being a "breadwinner" is the major
source of self-respect for a man or woman working at a
tedious, low-paying job that offers few prospects for ad-
vancement. It is also the major source of such respect as he
(or she) receives from family, friends, and neighbors.
When welfare provides more generously for a family than a
breadwinner can, he becomes a superfluous human being.
Both self-respect and respect soon crumble, family ties un-
ravel, and a "culture of poverty" sets in that has more to do
with the welfare system than with poverty itself.

Meanwhile, there are many poor people (including, of
course, poor blacks) in this country who are too proud to go
on welfare, who prefer to work hard at low-paying jobs, earning less than if they had gone on welfare, whose spirits are
undestroyed, whose lives are less afflicted, and whose children are less likely to "get into trouble." It would be instructive to see a comparative study of those two groups of poor
people. But when the state of California tried to sponsor one,
liberal academe and the liberal media—committed to
reform-through-redistribution—denounced and killed the
idea.

WHATEVER HAPPENED TO . . .

So the evidence is clear that trying to abolish poverty
through income distribution does nothing of the sort. The
evidence is also clear that when poverty is abolished through

economic growth, something real and desirable has occurred. The history of the United States since 1940 testifies to the truth of this latter proposition. What happened to the "Okies" whom Steinbeck and others wrote so poignantly about? What happened to the poor whites who, in most American cities (and all American movies), lived on "the other side of the tracks"? And what is happening to Appalachia today, where a boom in coal mining is accomplishing what a dozen government programs failed to do?

But, ironically, efforts to redistribute income by governmental fiat have the precise effect of impairing economic efficiency and growth—and therefore of preserving poverty in the name of equality. All such schemes of income distribution imply higher rates of marginal taxation for the productive population, with a consequent diminution of work incentives and a shrinking of capital available for reinvestment. When this happens on a sufficiently large scale, the results become disastrous for everyone.

This is evidently the case in the United Kingdom today, where a massive redistribution has indeed taken place, and where the society as a whole is getting poorer with every passing year. Twenty years ago, there was no noteworthy "poverty problem" in Britain. As things are now going, however, there will surely be one tomorrow. Egalitarianism may be motivated by a sincere desire to abolish poverty, but it is one of the most efficient poverty-creating ideologies of our century.

29

REFORMING

THE WELFARE STATE

IT IS UNARGUABLE that the welfare state is in trouble. The results of recent Swedish and German elections, the disillusioning experiences of Britain and New York City, the rising tide of resentment in the United States and elsewhere against high taxes and intrusive government all serve to make this fact quite clear. What is not so clear is: (1) why the welfare state is in trouble, and (2) what should be done about it.

There are some, committed social democrats for the most part (in the United States called "liberals"), who sincerely believe that the welfare state is in trouble only because its critics have demagogically persuaded the people to have an erroneous opinion of it. Thus, Gunnar Myrdal reacted to the Swedish election results with disbelief and anger:

Why in hell should the protection of your life from economic disasters and from bad health, opening education for young people, pensions for old people, nursery care for children—why should that make you frustrated?

In this country, Senator Hubert Humphrey, John Kenneth Galbraith, George Meany, and others of that persuasion are possessed of that same bitter incredulity. They seem convinced that dissatisfaction with the welfare state is a fleeting, artificially induced sentiment, and that the people will shortly see through their own folly. I suspect that in their hearts they know they are wrong. But it is not a point of view that can be refuted in rational debate. Only time and political experience will, one hopes, instruct them. There is nothing like regular elections to nudge the ideologically intoxicated toward sobriety.

A more "sophisticated" explanation—popular among liberals and conservatives alike—also lays the blame for the crisis of the welfare state on the people, though in a very different way. This school of thought sees the crisis as arising from the fact that people insist on government expenditures for goods and services but then refuse to pay, in taxes, for what they receive. This makes for universal frustration. It also makes for inflation, as governments employ the printing press as a way out of this dilemma. But inflation very soon raises the specter of bankruptcy and economic chaos, which people don't want above all. So there is a vicious circle: we are all trapped in it; and all we can do is wriggle more or less gracefully and buy time.

There is certainly some truth to this argument. It fits what we generally know about human nature, and it does describe a reality in which specific interest groups will defend each and every government program while the sum of all interest groups—the people as a whole—demand that government cut back its expenditures. But one ought to be wary of accepting this explanation too readily. It is really an argument against democratic self-government. If people are indeed so inherently unreasonable, then a democratic politics must inevitably end up wrecking a democratic society and a free economy. Quite a few thinkers are gradually moving, explicitly or implicitly, towards such a conclusion, and this disturbs me.

It disturbs me not only because it is a counsel of despair, but because I take it to be a false counsel of despair. I happen to believe that, despite temporary irrationalities, the American people are fundamentally reasonable. Our democratic republic would not have lasted two centuries were this not the case, and I am not prepared to believe that the crisis of the welfare state is the final, inglorious chapter of that history.

This crisis, it seems to me, can be explained in a more limited, less apocalyptic way. The explanation lies in the fact that the welfare state of today has been constructed in such a heedless, often mindless, way that, like so many hasty reformations, it creates as many problems as it solves. And I see no reason why a reform of this reformation should not be acceptable to the American people.

I am talking about a reform of this reformation, *not* a counterreformation. Too many conservatives today, like the Catholic church of the 16th century, view the difficulties of the reformation we are living through as an opportunity to restore the *status quo ante.* They are wrong, as the Catholic church was wrong. There is no more chance today of returning to a society of "free enterprise" and enfeebled government than there was, in the 16th century, of returning to a Rome-centered Christendom. The world and the people in it have changed. One may regret this fact; nostalgia is always permissible. But the politics of nostalgia is always self-destructive.

The structural deficiencies of the welfare state, and the absurd economics that these embody, have been definitively described by the conservative commentator, M. Stanton Evans:

. . . . Between 1960 and 1971, the total level of expenditure on social welfare programs, broadly defined, increased from $50 billion in 1960, to $171 billion in 1971—about a $120 billion increase.

It so happens that, according to the Bureau of the Census, there are about 25 million poor people in the United States. . . . If we take those 25 million poor people and divide them into the $120 billion increase—*not* the whole thing, just the increase—we discover that if we had simply taken that money and given it to the poor people, we could have given each of them an annual stipend of

$4,800, which means an income for a family of four of $19,200. That is, we could have made every poor person a relatively rich person. But we didn't. . . .

What happened to the money? . . . It went to social workers and counselors and planners and social engineers and urban renewal experts and the assistant administrators to the administrative assistants.

Actually, that explanation is too crude, although not inaccurate. Most of the money was in fact distributed—but distributed in the form of benefits, to people who were not poor, and in some cases not even close to being poor. Congressional compassion is always tempered by political realism, and the congressional impulse is always to spread its compassion over the largest possible share of the electorate. That is why millions of middle-class children are now eating—or, more often, not bothering to eat—free lunches in schools.

Still, there can be no question that Mr. Evans has put his finger on the key question which the American people are directing to Washington. The question is: *Where has all the money gone?* The skyrocketing costs of the welfare state seem way out of line with its modest (if indubitable) benefits. And the reason these costs have skyrocketed is because the welfare state, over the past 25 years, lost its original self-definition and became something more ambitious, more inflated, and incredibly more expensive. It became the paternalistic state, addressing itself to every variety of "problem" and committed to "solving" them all—committed, that is, to making human life unproblematic.

The original conception of the welfare state had as its central idea the principle of "insurance." The state was to make it compulsory for citizens to insure themselves—and to help the less fortunate to insure themselves—against the three plagues of a dynamic, urbanized society: dependency in old age, serious illness, and unemployment. As a consequence of such social insurance, a "floor" would be provided, beneath which no one could suffer the misfortune of sinking.

And this kind of social insurance has worked reasonably well—so well that it has made the working class not the

instrument of revolution, but the solid anchor of an otherwise turbulent social order. (These days, if you want to find
a radical, go to the nearest college, not the nearest
factory.)

True, there are problems—above all, the problem of
demagogic politicians trying to stretch these programs beyond prudent economic limits. But such profligacy, inherent
in our political system as it surely is, also has inherent limitations. The connection between taxes paid and benefits received is reasonably clear; the threat of "bankrupting the
system" is so obvious even TV newscasters can perceive it,
and overly generous commitments can be held down, if not
easily scaled down.

PAYING THE BILLS

The wasted billions of today's welfare state are not to be
found in the older social insurance schemes, but rather in
the later efforts to "solve social problems," i.e., to take every
disagreeable condition and convert it into a "problem,"
maybe even a "deprivation." And here Mr. Evans has a point
in his reference to our urban experts, planners, and social
scientists generally. These are people who are convinced
that, if fully employed and given adequate budgets, they can
successfully practice the art of making everyone healthier,
wealthier, and happier. Congress has listened to them, and
has structured legislation according to their design; and we
are now paying the bills. It is these activities—in education,
urban revitalization, mental health, welfare, etc.—which
constitute an excrescence on the welfare state, properly understood. It is these programs, which do not work and
which involve vast intricate bureaucracies, that are bring-
ing the welfare state into disrepute.

It will not be easy to rid ourselves of these "Great Society"
barnacles on the original ideas of the welfare state. There are
vested interests attached to each program, and any move
against them will be denounced as a sin against "compassion." But when the money runs out, a sense of realism tends

to sink in—as one can observe even in New York City today. Most politicians may still regard it as unthinkable to cut back on such programs. But the electorate is obviously far readier to engage in such "thinking the unthinkable."

In the end, a reformation of the welfare state may permit us to hope to see—as any thoughtful person should wish to see—the welfare state removed from the center stage of democratic politics, so that we can devote our energies to more serious things. A nation whose politics revolves around such issues as day-care centers or school lunches or the "proper" cost of false teeth is a nation whose politics is squalid, mean-spirited, debasing. Young people growing up in such a society will find in it little to be respected, nothing to be revered. That indeed is what is happening to our young people today, and their elders are at last beginning to realize it.

30

OF DECADENCE AND

TENNIS FLANNELS

VARIOUS CRITICS have accused Henry Kissinger of harboring the un-American belief that the United States is a decadent nation, and of constructing his foreign policy around this belief. Mr. Kissinger has indignantly denied the accusation. At the risk of losing my patriotic credentials, I'd like to go on record as saying that what I take to be symptoms of decadence are clearly visible all around us.

The source of these symptoms is easy to locate. It is not poverty or the "urban crisis" or the "ecological crisis" or any other of those "crises" so much favored by our media. Rather, it is affluence—more specifically, our spiritual inability to cope with affluence. The bourgeois ethos, that compound of attitude, habit, and simple conviction which has provided the inner substance of "the American way of life," is being subverted by its own material achievements. For, as this ethos encourages us to "better our condition" (to use one of Adam Smith's favorite phrases), it simultaneously leaves us defenseless before the question: What do we do *after* we have bettered our condition?

The bourgeois ethos, itself a pretty sure guide to worldly success, has always assumed that our religious traditions would provide the answer to that non-bourgeois question. But it did not foresee that religion itself would become incorporated into our worldly efforts to "better our condition," and would redefine its task either as social reform or as providing us with a "healthy and happy life-style." That popular phrase, "life-style," is of crucial significance.

Those Americans who no longer need concern themselves with acquiring the necessities of a comfortable life now shop for the meaning of that life in a vast and variegated cultural supermarket. This is what the "pursuit of happiness" has sunk to: a ludicrous parody of capitalism, in which we consume in succession all possible brands of pie-in-the-sky.

It might be said that the phenomenon I am describing, though real enough, only affects a minority of Americans and is only of peripheral significance. A few years ago I would have said that myself, but I no longer believe it. The minority has grown so rapidly these past years, and its domination of our culture has become so complete, that the "silent majority" is gradually beginning to acquiesce in its sovereignty.

Take the following sentences from a recent issue of *Time*, concluding a conventional "success story" in its business section about that amazing chicken entrepreneur, Frank Perdue:

Down-to-earth though he may appear on television, Frank Perdue is no bumpkin. He wears Gucci loafers and drives a blue Mercedes, lives in a condominium in Ocean City, Md. (he and his wife recently separated) and plays a plucky game of tennis when he can.

This is Middle America? Where, oh where, are the bumpkins of yesteryear? If one is to believe that same issue of *Time*, with its cover story on "Sex and Tennis," they are all out on the tennis court with Mr. Perdue, playing a "plucky" and soul-shattering game of tennis.

I used to believe that it was the American male's passion for golf that neatly symbolized the spiritual vacancy which

accompanied material success. I would emphasize that word
"passion." Obviously, there is nothing wrong with golf per
se; it is a pleasant and harmless diversion. But when it becomes the focus of a fetishistic obsession—when a man's life
is divided into adult work and juvenile play, with nothing
left over—then we know that something has gone wrong
with the very conception of adulthood.

It is for this reason that, whenever I attend a conference
of corporate executives and watch so many of them escape—
yes, that is the term they use—to the golf course at the first
possible opportunity, I am reminded of those lines of
T. S. Eliot:

> In the land of lobelias and tennis flannels
> The Rabbit shall burrow and the thorn revisit,
> The nettle shall flourish on the gravel court,
> And the wind shall say:
> Their only monument the asphalt road
> And a thousand lost golf balls.*

If *Time* is to be believed, however, it is tennis balls, not
golf balls, that will be strewn over the desolate landscape. It
seems that one American in ten now plays tennis "seriously."
And how seriously! In and of itself, no doubt, tennis, like
golf, is a pleasant enough diversion. But according to *Time*,
tennis—especially in the form of mixed doubles—has now
become (1) a mating game (2) a divorcing game, (3) a
quasi-religious ritual, and (4) an active form of self-analysis
in which the players discover some terribly important truths
about themselves. There is Freudian tennis, Zen tennis,
women's lib tennis, yoga tennis, tennis for divorcees, mar-
riage-counseling tennis, etc., etc.

One wonders: what do the children think as they watch
their elders—and their parents, especially—scrambling so
desperately for shreds and tatters of meaning in which
to clothe their nakedness? That question pretty much answers itself. These children will decide that those adults have
nothing to teach them and are proper objects of pity rather

---

* Excerpted from "Choruses from the Rock" in T. S. Eliot, *The Complete Poems and Plays, 1909–1950.* Reprinted by permission of Harcourt
Brace Jovanovich.

than of respect. Indeed, they have already reached that conclusion, as anyone knows who has listened to the popular
songs of this past decade. Back in the 1950s, everyone was
worried about the tyranny of "Mom" and its supposedly
deleterious psychological consequences. Well, "Mom" is gone,
replaced by "Mrs. Robinson," flailing away on the tennis
court at the frustration of all her impossible dreams.

In the very same week that *Time* reported on all the amazing graces that Americans are pursuing on their tennis courts,
Newsweek had a cover story on "Getting Your Head Together." It was a report on "the consciousness revolution,"
solemnly described as just possibly "this century's version of
Colonial America's Great Awakening." (May God have mercy
on the author of those lines!) This "consciousness revolution," one is told, is "a religion without a creed, a catalyst
for new life-styles, a tournament of therapies." In short, millions of spiritually sick people are shopping around for a
patent medicine of the soul.

And, since demand creates supply, there are thousands of
hucksters—some by now successful entrepreneurs, others just
scraping along—who promote their specially prepared com-
pounds of theosophy, psychoanalysis, sexual liberation, and
amateur nihilism. Thus we are being offered, for whatever
price the market can bear, bioenergetics, guided fantasy,
primal scream, EST, lomi body work, nude marathon, and
every other variety of intellectual rubbish that the demi-
educated, when thrown back on their own resources, mistake
for spiritual nourishment.

None of this, of course, has anything whatsoever to do
with religion. Religion is not a kind of therapy, and while its
consolations are real, they don't necessarily make you "feel
good." All authentic religions provide authoritative information on how to *be* good, and take "true" happiness to be
a consequence of virtue, not vice versa. And I know of no
religion which subscribes to the two doctrines which, as
Newsweek points out, are common to all these modish cults:
the innate goodness of man and the inevitability of human
progress. It is acceptance of those two doctrines that permit
our bored middle-class "psychonauts" to navigate through

"inner space" with a sublime confidence that they will discover, and be reconciled to, their "authentic selves."

INFINITE EMPTINESS

But, as the history of 20th-century modernism in all the arts demonstrates, the pursuit of self suffers the same fate as the pursuit of happiness: he who is merely self-seeking shall find nothing but infinite emptiness.

It is true that, simultaneous with all these goings-on, there has been a marked upsurge in fundamentalist Christian activity. Both James Carter and Charles Colson have testified to its impact, and prayer breakfasts are becoming common events among businessmen (though not, so far as I can tell, among their secretaries). But with all due respect, I wonder how seriously the phenomenon is to be taken. At the grassroots level, in local communities, it seems to be more political than religious, deriving its fervor from an opposition to big government, pornography, and school busing. These are all excellent things to oppose—but they are not the stuff out of which true religious awakenings are made.

Similarly, as best I can determine, those prayer-breakfasts are regarded by the participants more as a kind of therapy for harassed selves than as a moment of selfless devotion. I'll be more persuaded of their significance when they are held, not at breakfast, but on a sunny Saturday or Sunday afternoon.

Still, it is interesting to note that even this simulacrum of genuine religiosity is regarded with the greatest of suspicion by our media and our educated classes. Mr. Carter's Christianity, unobtrusive though it is, apparently disturbs these people considerably. Whereas, if he were "into" transcendental meditation—which *Business Week* recommends for "executive stress"—they wouldn't give it another thought. Twenty-five years ago the situation would have been exactly reversed.

Call it what you will, I think I'll call it decadence.

EPILOGUE

"WHEN VIRTUE LOSES ALL HER LOVELINESS"—SOME REFLECTIONS ON CAPITALISM AND THE "FREE SOCIETY"

WHEN we lack the will to see things as they really are, there is nothing so mystifying as the obvious. This has been the case, I think, with the upsurge of radicalism since the 1960s that has been shaking much of Western society to its foundations. We have constructed the most ingenious sociological and psychological theories—as well as a few disingenuously naive ones —to explain this phenomenon. But there is in truth no mystery here. Our youthful rebels are anything but inarticulate; and though they utter a great deal of nonsense, the import of what they have been saying is clear enough. What they are saying is that they dislike—to put it mildly—the liberal, individualist, capitalist civilization that stands ready to receive them as citizens. They are rejecting this offer of citizenship and are declaring their desire to see some other kind of civilization replace it.

That most of them do not always put the matter as explicitly or as candidly as this is beside the point. Some of them do, of course; we try to dismiss them as "the lunatic fringe." But the mass of dissident young are not, after all, sufficiently educated to understand the implications of everything they say. Besides, it is so much easier for the less bold among them to insist that what they find outrageous are the defects and shortcomings of the present system. Such shortcomings undeniably exist and are easy polemical marks. And, at the other end, it is so much easier for the adult generations to accept such polemics as representing the sum and substance of their dissatisfaction. It is consoling to think that the turmoil among them is provoked by the extent to which our society falls short of realizing its ideals. But the plain truth is that it is these ideals themselves that are being rejected. Our young radicals are far less dismayed at America's failure to become what it ought to be than they are contemptuous of what it thinks it ought to be. For them, as for Oscar Wilde, it is not the average American who is disgusting; it is the ideal American.

This is why one can make so little impression on them with arguments about how much progress has been made in the past decades, or is being made today, toward racial equality, or abolishing poverty, or fighting pollution, or whatever it is that we conventionally take as a sign of "progress." The obstinacy with which they remain deaf to such "liberal" arguments is not all perverse or irrational, as some would like to think. It arises, rather, out of a perfectly sincere, if often inchoate, animus against the American system itself. This animus stands for a commitment—*to* what, remains to be seen, but *against* what is already only too evident.

CAPITALISM'S THREE PROMISES

Dissatisfaction with the liberal-capitalist ideal, as distinct from indignation at failures to realize this ideal, are coterminous with the history of capitalism itself. Indeed, the cultural history of the capitalist epoch is not much more than a record of the varying ways such dissatisfaction could be expressed—in poetry, in the novel, in the drama, in painting, and today even in the movies. Nor, again, is there any great mystery why, from the first stirrings of the romantic movement, poets and philosophers have never had much regard for the capitalist civilization in which they lived and worked. But to understand this fully, one must be able to step outside the "progressive" ideology which makes us assume that liberal capitalism is the "natural" state of man toward which humanity has always aspired. There is nothing more natural about capitalist civilization than about many others that have had, or will have, their day. Capitalism represents a sum of human choices about the good life and the good society. These choices inevitably have their associated costs, and after two hundred years the conviction seems to be spreading that the costs have got out of line.

What did capitalism promise? First of all, it promised continued improvement in the material conditions of all its citizens, a promise without precedent in human history. Second, it promised an equally unprecedented measure of individual freedom for all of these same citizens. And lastly, it held out the promise that, amidst this prosperity and liberty, the individual could satisfy his instinct for self-perfection—for leading a virtuous life that satisfied the demands of his spirit (or, as one used to say, his soul)—and that the free exercise of such individual virtue would aggregate into a just society.

Now, it is important to realize that, though these aims were in one sense more ambitious than any previously set forth by a political ideology, in another sense they were far more modest. Whereas, as Joseph Cropsey has pointed out,

Adam Smith defined "prudence" democratically as "the care of the health, of the fortune, of the rank of the individual," Aristotle had defined that term aristocratically, to mean "the quality of mind concerned with things just and noble and good for man." By this standard, all pre-capitalist systems had been, to one degree or another, Aristotelian: they were interested in creating a high and memorable civilization even if this were shared only by a tiny minority. In contrast, capitalism lowered its sights, but offered its shares in bourgeois civilization to the entire citizenry. Tocqueville, as usual, astutely caught this difference between the aristocratic civilizations of the past and the new liberal capitalism he saw emerging in the United States:

In aristocratic societies the class that gives the tone to opinion and has the guidance of affairs, being permanently and hereditarily placed above the multitude, naturally conceives a lofty idea of itself and man. It loves to invent for him noble pleasures, to carve out splendid objects for his ambition. Aristocracies often commit very tyrannical and inhuman actions, but they rarely entertain groveling thoughts. . . .

[In democracies, in contrast] there is little energy of character but customs are mild and laws humane. If there are few instances of exalted heroism or of virtues of the highest, brightest, and purest temper, men's habits are regular, violence is rare, and cruelty almost unknown. . . . Genius becomes rare, information more diffused. . . . There is less perfection, but more abundance, in all the productions of the arts.

It is because "high culture" inevitably has an aristocratic bias—it would not be "high" if it did not—that, from the beginnings of the capitalist era, it has always felt contempt for the bourgeois mode of existence. That mode of existence purposively depreciated the very issues that were its *raison d'être*. It did so by making them, as no society had ever dared or desired to do, matters of personal taste, according to the prescription of Adam Smith in his *Theory of Moral Sentiments*:

Though you despise that picture, or that poem, or even that system of philosophy, which I admire, there is little danger of our quarreling upon that account. Neither of us can reasonably be much interested about them. They ought all of them to be matters of great indifference to us both; so that, though our opinions may be opposite, our affections shall be very nearly the same.

In short, an amiable philistinism was inherent in bourgeois society, and this was bound to place its artists and intellectuals in an antagonistic posture toward it. This antagonism was irrepressible—the bourgeois world could not suppress it without violating its own liberal creed; the artists could not refrain from expressing their hostility without denying their most authentic selves. But the conflict could, and was, contained so long as capitalist civilization delivered on its three basic promises. It was only when the third promise, of a virtuous life and a just society, was subverted by the dynamics of capitalism itself, as it strove to fulfill the other two —affluence and liberty—that the bourgeois order came, in the minds of the young especially, to possess a questionable legitimacy.

FROM BOURGEOIS SOCIETY TO A "FREE SOCIETY"

I can think of no better way of indicating the distance that capitalism has traveled from its original ideological origins than by contrasting the most intelligent defender of capitalism today with his predecessors. I refer to Friedrich von Hayek, who has as fine and as powerful a mind as is to be found anywhere, and whose *Constitution of Liberty* is one of the most thoughtful works of the last decades. In that book, he offers the following argument against viewing capitalism as a system that incarnates any idea of justice:

Most people will object not to the bare fact of inequality but to the fact that the differences in reward do not correspond to any recognizable differences in the merit of those who receive them. The answer commonly given to this is that a free society on the whole achieves this kind of justice. This, however, is an indefensible contention if by justice is meant proportionality of reward to moral merit. Any attempt to found the case for freedom on this argument is very damaging to it, since it concedes that material rewards ought to be made to correspond to recognizable merit and then opposes the conclusion that most people will draw from this by an assertion which is untrue. The proper answer is that in a free society it is neither desirable nor practicable that material rewards should be made generally to correspond to what men recognize as merit and that it is an essential characteristic of a free society that an individual's position should not necessarily depend on the views that his fellows hold about the merit he has acquired. . . . A society in which the position of the individual was made to correspond to human ideas of moral merit would therefore be the exact opposite of a free society. It would be a society in which people were rewarded for duty performed instead of for success. . . . But if nobody's knowledge is sufficient to guide all human action, there is also no human being who is competent to reward all efforts according to merit.

This argument is admirable both for its utter candor and for its firm opposition to all those modern authoritarian ideologies, whether rationalist or irrationalist, which give a self-selected elite the right to shape men's lives and fix their destinies according to its preconceived notions of good and evil, merit and demerit. But it is interesting to note what Hayek is doing: he is opposing a *free* society to a *just* society —because, he says, while we know what freedom is, we have no generally accepted knowledge of what justice is. Elsewhere he writes:

Since they [i.e., differentials in wealth and income] are not the effect of anyone's design or intentions, it is meaningless to describe the manner in which the market distributed the good things of this world among particular people as just or unjust. . . . No test or criteria have been found or can be found by which such rules of "social justice" can be assessed. . . . They would have to be determined by the arbitrary will of the holders of power.

Now, it may be that this is the best possible defense that can be made of a free society. But if this is the case, one can fairly say that "capitalism" is (or was) one thing, and a "free society" another. For capitalism, during the first hundred years or so of its existence, did lay claim to being a just social order, in the meaning later given to that concept by Paul Elmer More: ". . . Such a distribution of power and privilege, and of property as the symbol and instrument of these, as at once will satisfy the distinctions of reason among the superior, and will not outrage the feelings of the inferior." As a matter of fact, capitalism at its apogee saw itself as the most just social order the world has ever witnessed, because it replaced all arbitrary (e.g., inherited) distributions of power, privilege, and property with a distribution that was directly and intimately linked to personal merit—this latter term being inclusive of both personal abilities and personal virtues.

Writing shortly before the Civil War, George Fitzhugh, the most gifted of Southern apologists for slavery, attacked the capitalist North in these terms:

In a free society none but the selfish virtues are in repute, because none other help a man in the race of competition. In such a society virtue loses all her loveliness, because of her selfish aims. Good men and bad men have the same end in view—self-promotion and self-elevation. . . .

At the time, this accusation was a half-truth. The North was not yet "a free society," in Hayek's sense or Fitzhugh's. It was still in good measure a bourgeois society in which the capitalist mode of existence involved moral self-discipline and had a visible aura of spiritual grace. It was a society in which "success" was indeed seen as having what Hayek has said it ought never to have: a firm connection with "duty performed." It was a society in which Theodore Parker could write of a leading merchant: "He had no uncommon culture of the understanding or the imagination, and of the higher reason still less. But in respect of the *greater faculties* —in respect of conscience, affection, the religious element— he was well born, well bred." In short, it was a society still permeated by the Puritan ethic, the Protestant ethic, the capitalist ethic—call it what you will. It was a society in which it was agreed that there was a strong correlation between certain personal virtues—frugality, industry, sobriety, reliability, piety—and the way in which power, privilege, and property were distributed. And this correlation was taken to be the sign of a just society, not merely of a free one. Samuel Smiles or Horatio Alger would have regarded Professor Hayek's writings as slanderous of his fellow Christians, blasphemous of God, and ultimately subversive of the social order. I am not sure about the first two of these accusations, but I am fairly certain of the validity of the last.

This is not the place to recount the history and eventual

degradation of the capitalist ethic in America.* Suffice it to
say that, with every passing decade, Fitzhugh's charge, that
"virtue loses all her loveliness, because of her selfish aims,"
became more valid. From having been a *capitalist, republican
community,* with shared values and a quite unambiguous
claim to the title of a just order, the United States became a
free, democratic society where the will to success and privilege was severed from its moral moorings.

THREE CURRENT APOLOGIA

But can men live in a free society if they have no reason to
believe it is also a just society? I do not think so. My reading
of history is that, in the same way as men cannot for long
tolerate a sense of spiritual meaninglessness in their individual lives, so they cannot for long accept a society in which
power, privilege, and property are not distributed according
to some morally meaningful criteria. Nor is equality itself
any more acceptable than inequality—neither is more "natural" than the other—if equality is merely a brute fact
rather than a consequence of an ideology or social philosophy. This explains what otherwise seems paradoxical: that
small inequalities in capitalist countries can become the
source of intense controversy while relatively larger inequalities in socialist or communist countries are blandly overlooked. Thus, those same young radicals who are infuriated
by trivial inequalities in the American economic system are
quite blind to grosser inequalities in the Cuban system. This
is usually taken as evidence of hypocrisy or self-deception. I
would say it shows, rather, that people's notions of equality or inequality have extraordinarily little to do with arithmetic and almost everything to do with political philosophy.

I believe that what holds for equality also holds for liberty. People feel free when they subscribe to a prevailing
social philosophy; they feel unfree when the prevailing social philosophy is unpersuasive; and the existence of con-

* See Daniel Bell's book, *The Cultural Contradictions of Capitalism,*
for a more detailed analysis of what happened and why.

stitutions or laws or judiciaries have precious little to do with these basic feelings. The average working men in nineteenth-century America had far fewer "rights" than his counterpart today; but he was far more likely to boast about his being a free man.

So I conclude, despite Professor Hayek's ingenious analysis, that men cannot accept the historical accidents of the marketplace—seen merely as accidents—as the basis for an enduring and legitimate entitlement to power, privilege, and property. And, in actual fact, Professor Hayek's rationale for modern capitalism is never used outside a small academic enclave; I even suspect it cannot be believed except by those whose minds have been shaped by overlong exposure to scholasticism. Instead, the arguments offered to justify the social structure of capitalism now fall into three main categories:

(1) *The Protestant Ethic.* This, however, is now reserved for the lower socioeconomic levels. It is still believed, and it is still reasonable to believe, that worldly success among the working class, lower-middle class, and even middle class has a definite connection with personal virtues such as diligence, rectitude, sobriety, honest ambition, etc., etc. And, so far as I can see, the connection is not only credible but demonstrable. It does seem that the traditional bourgeois virtues are efficacious among these classes; at least, it is rare to find successful men emerging from these classes who do not to a significant degree exemplify them. But no one seriously claims that these traditional virtues will open the corridors of corporate power to anyone, or that those who now occupy the executive suites are—or even aspire to be—models of bourgeois virtue.

(2) *The Darwinian Ethic.* This is to be found mainly among small businessmen who are fond of thinking that their "making it" is to be explained as "the survival of the fittest." They are frequently quite right, of course, in believing the metaphor appropriate to their condition and to the ways in which they achieved it. But it is preposterous to think that

the mass of men will ever accept as legitimate a social order formed in accordance with the laws of the jungle. Men may be animals, but they are political animals and, what comes to not such a different thing, moral animals too. The fact that for several decades after the Civil War, the Darwinian ethic, as popularized by Herbert Spencer, could be taken seriously by so many social theorists represents one of the most bizarre and sordid episodes in American intellectual history. It could not last, and did not.

(3) *The Technocratic Ethic*. This is the most prevalent justification of corporate capitalism today, and finds expression in an insistence on "performance." Those who occupy the seats of corporate power, and enjoy the prerogatives and privileges thereof, are said to acquire legitimacy by their superior ability to achieve superior "performance"—in economic growth, managerial efficiency, and technological innovation. In a sense, what is claimed is that these men are accomplishing social tasks, and fulfilling social responsibilities, in an especially efficacious way.

There are, however, two fatal flaws in this argument. First, if one defines "performance" in a strictly limited and measurable sense, then one is applying a test that any ruling class is bound, on fairly frequent occasions, to fail. Life has its ups and downs; so do history and economics; and those who can only claim legitimacy *via* performance are going to have to spend an awful lot of time and energy explaining why things are not going as well as they ought to. Such repeated, defensive apologies, in the end, will be hollow and unconvincing. Indeed, the very concept of "legitimacy," in its historical usages, is supposed to take account of and make allowances for all those rough passages a society will have to navigate. If the landed gentry of Britain during those centuries of its dominance, or the business class in the United States during the first century and a half of our national history, had insisted that it be judged by performance alone, it would have flunked out of history. So would every other ruling class that ever existed.

Secondly, if one tries to avoid this dilemma by giving the

term "performance" a broader and larger meaning, then one
inevitably finds oneself passing beyond the boundaries of
bourgeois propriety. It is one thing to say with Samuel John-
son that men honestly engaged in business are doing the least
mischief that men are capable of; it is quite another
thing to assert that they are doing the greatest good: this is
only too patently untrue. For the achievement of the greatest
good, more than successful performance in business is necessary. Witness how vulnerable our corporate managers are to
accusations that they are befouling our environment. What
these accusations really add up to is the statement that the
business system in the United States does not create a beautiful, refined, gracious, and tranquil civilization. To which
our corporate leaders are replying: "Oh, we can perform that
mission too—just give us time." But there is no good reason
to think they can accomplish this non-capitalist mission; nor
is there any reason to believe that they have any proper
entitlement even to try.

"PARTICIPATION" OR LEADERSHIP?

It is, I think, because of the decline of the bourgeois ethic,
and the consequent drainage of legitimacy out of the business
system, that the issue of "participation" has emerged with
such urgency during these past years. It is a common error
to take this word at its face value—to assume that, in our
organized and bureaucratized society, the average person is
more isolated, alienated, or powerless than ever before, and
that the proper remedy is to open new avenues of "participation." We are then perplexed when, the avenues having
been opened, we find so little traffic passing through. We give
college students the right to representation on all sorts of
committees, and then discover they never bother to come to
meetings. We create new popularly elected "community" organizations in the ghettos, and then discover that ghetto resi-
dents won't come out to vote. We decentralize New York
City's school system, only to discover that the populace is
singularly uninterested in local school board elections.

I doubt very much that the average American is actually more isolated or powerless today than in the past. The few serious studies that have been made on this subject indicate that we have highly romanticized notions of the past—of the degree to which ordinary people were ever involved in community activities—and highly apocalyptic notions of the present. If one takes membership in civic-minded organizations as a criterion, people are unquestionably more "involved" today than ever before in our history. Maybe that's not such a good criterion; but it is a revealing aspect of this whole problem that those who make large statements on this matter rarely give us any workable or testable criteria at all.

But I would not deny that more people, even if more specifically "involved" than ever before, also feel more "alienated" in a general way. And this, I would suggest, is because the institutions of our society have lost their vital connection with the values which are supposed to govern the private lives of our citizenry. They no longer exemplify these values; they no longer magnify them; they no longer reassuringly sustain them. When it is said that the institutions of our society have become appallingly "impersonal," I take this to mean that they have lost any shape that is congruent with the private moral codes which presumably govern individual life. (That presumption, of course, may be factually weak; but it is nonetheless efficacious so long as people hold it.) The "outside" of our social life has ceased being harmonious with the "inside"; the mode of distribution of power, privilege, and property, and hence the very principle of authority, no longer "makes sense" to the bewildered citizen. And when institutions cease to "make sense" in this way, all the familiar criteria of success or failure become utterly irrelevant.

As I see it, then, the demand for "participation" is best appreciated as a demand for authority—for leadership that holds the promise of reconciling the inner and outer worlds of the citizen. So far from its being a hopeful reawakening of the democratic spirit, it signifies a hunger for authority that leads toward some kind of plebiscitary democracy at best, and is in any case not easy to reconcile with liberal democracy as we traditionally have known it. I find it instructive that such old-fashioned populists as Hubert Humphrey and Edmund Muskie, whose notions of "participation" are both liberal and traditional, fail to catch the imagination of our dissidents in the way that Robert Kennedy did. The late Senator Kennedy was very much a leader: one can imagine Humphrey or Muskie participating in an old-fashioned town meeting; one can only envision Kennedy dominating a town rally. One can also envision those who "participated" in such a rally feeling that they had achieved a kind of "representation" previously denied them.

A CASE OF REGRESSION

For a system of liberal, representative government to work, free elections are not enough. The results of the political process and of the exercise of individual freedom—the distribution of power, privilege, and property—must also be seen as in some profound sense expressive of the values that govern the lives of individuals. An idea of self-government, if it is to be viable, must encompass both the private and the public sectors. If it does not—if the principles that organize public life seem to have little relation to those that shape private lives—you have "alienation," and anomie, and a melting away of established principles of authority.

Milton Friedman, arguing in favor of Hayek's extreme libertarian position, has written that the free man "recognizes no national purpose except as it is the consensus of the purposes for which the citizens severally strive." If he is using the term "consensus" seriously, then he must be assuming that there is a strong homogeneity of values among the citizenry, and that these values give a certain corresponding shape to the various institutions of society, political and economic. Were that the case, then it is indeed true that a "national purpose" arises automatically and organically out of the social order itself. Something like this did happen when liberal capitalism was in its prime, vigorous and self-confident. But is that our condition today? I think not, just as I think Mr. Friedman doesn't really mean "consensus" but rather the mere aggregation of selfish aims. In such a blind and accidental arithmetic, the sum floats free from the addenda, and its legitimacy is infinitely questionable.

The inner spiritual chaos of the times, so powerfully created by the dynamics of capitalism itself, is such as to make nihilism an easy temptation. A "free society" in Hayek's sense gives birth in massive numbers to "free spirits," emptied of moral substance but still driven by primordial moral aspirations. Such people are capable of the most irrational actions. Indeed, it is my impression that, under the strain of modern life, whole classes of our population—and the educated classes most of all—are entering what can only be called, in the strictly clinical sense, a phase of infantile regression. With every passing year, public discourse becomes sillier and more petulant, while human emotions become, apparently, more ungovernable. Some of our most intelligent university professors are now loudly saying things that, had they been uttered by one of their students twenty years ago, would have called forth gentle and urbane reproof.

THE REFORMING SPIRIT AND THE CONSERVATIVE IDEAL

And yet, if the situation of liberal capitalism today seems so precarious, it is likely nevertheless to survive for a long while, if only because the modern era has failed to come up with any plausible alternatives. Socialism, communism, and fascism have all turned out to be either utopian illusions or sordid frauds. So we shall have time, though not an endless amount of it, for we have already wasted a great deal. We are today in a situation not very different from that described by Herbert Croly in *The Promise of American Life* (1912):

The substance of our national Promise has consisted . . . of an improving popular economic condition, guaranteed by democratic political institutions, and resulting in moral and social amelioration. These manifold benefits were to be obtained merely by liberating the enlightened self-enterprise of the American people. . . . The fulfillment of the American Promise was considered inevitable because it was based upon a combination of self-interest and the natural goodness of human nature. On the other hand, if the fulfillment of our national Promise can no longer be considered inevitable, if it must be considered as equivalent to a conscious national purpose instead of an inexorable national destiny, the implication necessarily is that the trust reposed in individual self-interest has been in some measure betrayed. No pre-established harmony can then exist between the free and abundant satisfaction of private needs and the accomplishment of a morally and socially desirable result.

Croly is not much read these days. He was a liberal reformer with essentially conservative goals. So was Matthew Arnold, fifty years earlier, and he isn't much read these days, either. Neither of them can pass into the conventional anthologies of liberal or conservative thought. I think this is a sad commentary on the ideological barrenness of the liberal and conservative creeds. I also think it is a great pity. For if our private and public worlds are ever again, in our lifetimes, to have a congenial relationship—if virtue is to regain her lost loveliness—then some such combination of the reforming spirit with the conservative ideal seems to me to be what is most desperately wanted.

I use the word "conservative" advisedly. Though the discontents of our civilization express themselves in the rhetoric of "liberation" and "equality," one can detect beneath the surface an acute yearning for order and stability—but a legitimate order, of course, and a legitimized stability. In this connection, I find the increasing skepticism as to the benefits of economic growth and technological innovation most suggestive. Such skepticism has been characteristic of conservative critics of liberal capitalism since the beginning of the nineteenth century. One finds it in Coleridge, Carlyle, and Newman—in all those who found it impossible to acquiesce in a "progressive" notion of human history or social evolution. Our dissidents today may think they are exceedingly progressive; but no one who puts greater emphasis on "the quality of life" than on "mere" material enrichment can properly be placed in that category. For the idea of progress in the modern era has always signified that the quality of life would inevitably be improved by material enrichment. To doubt this is to doubt the political metaphysics of modernity and to start the long trek back to pre-modern political philosophy—Plato, Aristotle, Thomas Aquinas, Hooker, Calvin, etc. It seems to me that this trip is quite necessary. Perhaps there we shall discover some of those elements that are most desperately needed by the spiritually impoverished civilization that we have constructed on what once seemed to be sturdy bourgeois foundations.

INDEX

Wealth of Nations (Smith), 3
Weidenbaum, Murray, 52
West Germany: economic growth
  in, 105; elections in, 244; income
  distribution in, 185; taxation in,
  229

Whyte, William H., 155
Wilde, Oscar, 256
Wilson, Harold, 137

Yugoslavia, mixed economy of, 186